Discourse and
Performance of
International Teaching Assistants

Discourse and Performance of International Teaching Assistants

·

Carolyn G. Madden
Cynthia L. Myers
Editors

·

TEACHERS OF ENGLISH TO SPEAKERS OF OTHER LANGUAGES, INC.

Typeset in Times Roman and Optima by
World Composition Services, Inc., Sterling, Virginia
and printed by
Pantagraph Printing, Bloomington, Illinois USA

Helen Kornblum *Director of Communications and Marketing*
Ellen Garshick *Copy Editor*
Cover design by Ann Kammerer

Teachers of English to Speakers of Other Languages, Inc.
1600 Cameron Street, Suite 300
Alexandria, VA 22314 USA
Tel 703-836-0774 • Fax 703-836-7864

ISBN 0-939791-52-8
Library of Congress Catalog No. 93-061813

Contents

■

Introduction

∎

In the past decade one of the most challenging areas of concern to emerge in the field of applied linguistics has been the teaching and training of international teaching assistants (ITAs). Literature about ITAs has included articles in *TESOL Quarterly*, an early survey of ITA issues (Bailey, Pialorski, & Zukowski/Faust, 1984), and a special issue of *English for Specific Purposes* (Young, 1989). Concern about the instruction of ITAs parallels a move in higher education to bring more attention to the needs of all teaching assistants (TAs), native and nonnative alike, and to the role of ITAs in undergraduate education (Smith, Byrd, Nelson, Barrett, & Constantinides, 1993). These concerns have formed the focus of three national conferences and the following volumes of conference proceedings: *Institutional Responsibilities and Responses in the Employment and Education of Teaching Assistants* (Chism & Warner, 1987), *Preparing the Professoriate of Tomorrow to Teach* (Nyquist, Abbott, Wulff, & Sprague, 1991), and *The TA Experience: Preparing for Multiple Roles* (Lewis, 1993). These collections cover a wide range of issues related to program development, administration, and TA training.

This book, however, is the first ITA volume devoted entirely to language and teaching research. It focuses on issues related to the language needs of ITAs in their varying roles in the university setting and places these issues in the broader context of applied linguistics and English for specific purposes (ESP). Our intention is to align the concerns and research in the language development and performance of ITAs with ongoing empirical investigations of the discourse of both native and nonnative speakers.

In the 1990 volume of the *Annual Review of Applied Linguistics*, devoted entirely to discourse analysis, William Grabe stated:

> The broad implications to be drawn from [the] relationship between discourse analysis and applied linguistics is that discourse analysis constitutes a, if not the, crucial research foundation for applied linguistics.
>
> Over the past ten years, discourse analysis itself has evolved to the point at which it is emerging as a discipline in its own right, rather than being viewed primarily as a set of disparate research techniques and approaches. (p. vii)

While acknowledging the diversity of discourse theory and methods, Grabe recognized the "near-universal emphasis on the social and political focus underlying language use" (p. viii), and Kress stated in the same volume that "all forms of discourse analysis . . . share an interest in the understanding of extended text socially or at least contextually situated and in producing accounts of texts that draw on features of the context . . ." (p. 84). Nowhere is this emphasis more evident than in the training and development of ITAs in the social and political context of the undergraduate classroom, laboratory, and office hour. As interest in discourse analysis continues to grow, the publication of a volume devoted to the discourse needs, development, and performance of ITAs is relevant.

The research in this book draws on a rich and varied background that includes interaction and discourse analysis, and incorporates methodology from ethnography. Insights that underlie this work come from researchers like Sinclair and Coulthard (1975), who characterized the classroom discourse of students and teachers, and from studies of specific features of communication in the university classroom, such as the effect of different types of professors' questions in stimulating discussion (Andrews, 1980) or the process of student questioning in a lecture environment (McKenna, 1987). Researchers have also examined the structuring of semantic coherence in several contexts: in native-speaking professors' lectures (Strodt-Lopez, 1987, 1991), in nonnative TAs' presentations (Tyler, Jefferies, & Davies, 1988), and in TAs' responses to student questions (Robinson, 1993). Also relevant to ITA discourse work is the body of research that specifically examines nonnative speakers as students in their language classrooms (cf. Long, 1983; Doughty & Pica, 1986; Pica, 1989; Yule & Macdonald, 1990) and as students in certain ESP environments like the undergraduate physics lab (Jacobson, 1986). (See Chaudron, 1988, for an in-depth survey of classroom-based research.)

In conjunction with the efforts of other researchers to bring coherence to the understanding of language in use, we also intend to demonstrate the uniqueness of problems related to classroom discourse and to the training of international students unfamiliar with the pedagogical and cultural mores of the U.S. classroom. Although ITAs are, in essence, second language learners, their needs are simultaneously *more* and *less* complex than those of the majority of university-bound or enrolled international students. As Hoekje and Williams suggest in chapter 1, most ITA courses and programs emphasize "success in the required role rather than the development of language skills in general" (p. 14). In other words, ITAs need to know expedient and effective language, not necessarily to develop accurate and/or grammatically sophisticated language. Shaw and Garate (1984) have pointed out that most training programs assume that "trainees arrive with a good command of the grammatical, lexical and semantic system of the language . . . a general competence in the language" (p. 22). Time and experience, however, have shown that programs indeed need to take into account the lack of homogeneity in language skills, cultural awareness, and pedagogical experience in providing an effective methodology for ITAs.

In responding to these diverse needs, ITA programs continue to develop and use innovative approaches that meet the contextualized needs of ITAs. For example, Smith, Meyers, and Burkhalter (1992) and Anderson-Hsieh (1990) have demonstrated ways to use field-specific materials in ITA courses. Stevens (1989) suggested having native student "tutors" provide immediate modeling and feedback to ITAs on pronunciation as well as on cultural issues. Davies, Tyler, and Koran (1989) and Schneider and Stevens (1991) have emphasized the importance of frequent interaction and monitoring between ITAs and native-speaking undergraduates. Axelson and Madden (1990) have highlighted the need for a negotiating component of ITA input in response to the language, behavior, and style of the classroom.

In addition to these practical pedagogical issues, others have pointed out the importance of contextualizing the ITA curriculum, taking into account the varied environments and disciplines in which TAs teach (Byrd & Constantinides, 1988; Young, 1989c). Johns and Dudley-Evans (1991) have noted the importance, in many ESP contexts, of defining students' needs and identifying "the actual language difficulties that they face on a day-to-day basis in classes in their disciplines or in their professional lives" (p. 304). Certainly a knowledge of the discourse that is appropriate in different academic disciplines as well as in different settings is of utmost importance in helping ITAs develop the skills they need to teach successfully. Studies that describe native-speaking professors show that typical academic discourse may differ between such subject areas as engineering (Shaw, 1985) and mathematics (Byrd & Constantinides, 1992). Also important are differences between teaching environments. Research on the particular needs and performance of nonnative-speaking TAs in diverse academic settings has included work on TAs teaching in the math recitation (Rounds, 1986, 1987a), the lab (Myers & Plakans, 1991; Tanner, 1991), and across the environments of the office hour, the recitation, and the lab (Madden & Axelson, 1990; Myers, Axelson, & Madden, 1991). These concerns are further developed by several writers in this volume.

Discourse and Performance of International Teaching Assistants is divided into three main parts: Frameworks, Discourse, and Interaction and Performance.

The four chapters in part I sketch generally how ITA training fits into the theoretical framework of second language learning and teaching.

They bring coherence to the diversity of specific skills and behaviors of ITAs and to the development, instruction, and evaluation of ITA education.

Hoekje and Williams (chapter 1) place the learning and teaching of ITAs in a sociolinguistic framework. They argue that their framework provides an appropriate basis for understanding "emerging models of ITA competence and . . . ITA language use" (p. 11). Using the communicative competence model of Hymes, Savignon, and Canale and Swain, the authors outline four major elements of the model: grammatical, sociolinguistic, discourse, and strategic competence. They further analyze how each element relates to the linguistic, pedagogical, and cultural challenges of ITAs in a university context.

Chapters 2 and 3 glance backward and forward at issues of theory, pedagogy, and curriculum. Shaw (chapter 2) adds to the theoretical understanding of the issues and concerns related to syllabus and curriculum in ITA education. He emphasizes differences across disciplines and suggests that, in addition to focusing on the specific-purpose language of ITAs, an appropriate model for ITA education must incorporate the specific discourse structures of those disciplines and the discourse events particular to the college classroom. Smith (chapter 3) enhances the practical understanding and appreciation of ways programs can support ITAs in taking charge of their own development as users of the English language for the specific purpose of teaching in a university setting. Her typology of issues and activities supports renewed and relevant curriculum development that will make ITA education more effective and sustain the professional development of ITA educators.

In the fourth chapter in part I, Briggs relates current theories of communicative language development and use to the design and features of instruments to assess the performance of ITAs. She examines the salient features of acceptable and not-so-acceptable discourse of ITAs in screening situations and discusses the patterns with reference to current research on the pedagogical discourse observed across the teaching roles of ITAs.

Part II, Discourse, contributes insights into the ways ITAs use language in different academic environments. The chapters look at ITAs in context and are informed by an understanding of the complexity of the variables found in ITAs' teaching environments. A recurring theme is that in many cases ITAs' abilities to interact with their students—often one-on-one—is a complex and important feature of TA discourse.

In chapter 5, Myers examines the teaching laboratory, describing features of lab discourse that may challenge ITAs: the informality of students' questions caused by the students' perception of shared context and the problem-solving features of their language, among others. Myers also classifies the kinds of questions that ITAs use and characterizes the most successful ITAs, who take advantage of their role as teacher to ask frequent questions about both the content of the course and student progress in the experiment. She closes the chapter with suggestions for helping ITAs develop their abilities to interact effectively with their students in the lab.

Rounds (chapter 6) investigates student questions as a basis for devising pedagogical materials that will help develop ITAs' communicative competence and encourage them to teach interactively. She compares data from mathematics classes taught by TAs with data on student questions in a phonetics lecture taught by a professor (McKenna, 1987). Some teaching situations, she finds, elicit infrequent questions from students, and most student questions in these settings are requests for more information or for repetitions. She notes that ITAs may need to learn to handle digressions or challenge questions and must learn to manage classroom discourse in order to handle the flow of questions.

Tyler (chapter 7) describes a useful role-playing methodology in which ITAs practice resolving conflicts with a NS student. She notes the difficulty of dealing with these situations; they are "emotionally charged and involve a complex, conflicting set of goals for the participants" (p. 116). The method encourages ITAs to analyze both their own communicative goals and the intentions of the student in the discourse, helping ITAs to become aware of the effect of the choices they make in handling the conflict. Because the ITAs are given immediate feedback and allowed to replay their roles, they can practice the strategies needed in each situation. In addition, the series of role plays presents ITAs with roles of gradually increasing difficulty: The conflict situations are first introduced in a nonthreatening format, and subsequent situations become more emotionally charged. The chapter provides a practical method of helping ITAs gain facility with complex one-on-one interactions.

McChesney (chapter 8) analyzes the discourse of the office hour, illustrating differences between professors and TAs as well as typical functions of TA interaction. Students visit professors and TAs for different reasons: In her data, students primarily saw their TAs for advice about studying and test taking, including help with homework problems; they were more likely to visit professors for advice about such matters as course assignments or their major. The typical functions of TA discourse in office hours include directing students' learning, encouraging and reinforcing their attempts to solve problems, correcting students' mistakes, reminding students of connections between their homework problems and the text or lecture, and giving study advice. McChesney notes that TAs are fairly direct in correcting students' errors and that the most effective TAs use questions to help direct students in solving problems.

In chapter 9, Axelson and Madden compare the language demands of ITAs across three teaching contexts: the classroom, the lab, and the office hour. The authors analyze both native and nonnative discourse in video- and audiotaped interactions in these contexts and examine the similar patterns of discourse and differences across contexts in terms of language skills, strategies, and demands. They organize the diversity of the discourse demands on ITAs and suggest discourse-based tasks that serve as effective teaching tools.

Part III, Interaction and Performance, includes contributions from varied research perspectives: Yule, from research into features of nonnative speaker interaction; Davies and Tyler, from work in pragmatics; and Douglas and Selinker, from discourse domain theory. All three studies use ITAs as subjects, deal with different aspects of ITA interaction, and provide insights that can inform ITA program design. These chapters demonstrate the usefulness and diversity of ITA research, both to those involved in the practical training of ITAs and to those interested in other areas of applied linguistics.

Yule (chapter 10) emphasizes the importance of interactive activities in giving ITAs negotiated and immediate feedback that leads to improved performance. Practice only on a transactional skill like lecturing, Yule points out, may not encourage ITAs to develop a clear awareness of their listeners. He shows the importance of helping to "sensitize ITAs to different types of resolutions for communication difficulties," as well as increasing their awareness of "outcomes that are communicatively successful" (p. 198). Additionally, Yule's research illustrates how ITAs' perceptions of their role as dominant or subordinate affect their ability to cope with difficulties in communicating during an interaction. His chapter provides both a clear justification for including two-way interactive activities in ITA classes and recommendations for designing such activities, including suggestions about pairing students of varying proficiency levels.

Davies and Tyler (chapter 11), like Yule, note the importance and complexity of interaction, and their research methodology also offers a direct pedagogical application. They describe a technique in which ITAs receive immediate, contextualized feedback from their native-speaking student interlocutor or their course instructor. This feedback allows the ITAs to focus on features of discourse that might remain unclear in a normal setting. Davies and Tyler's research suggests that balanced and nonthreatening feedback favorably affects the ITAs' language development. They emphasize helping to develop ITAs' awareness of subtle cues in their listener's responses and helping ITAs to understand the complex pragmatic features of interaction with a student. The chapter describes the research methodology in such a way that it can be directly used in ITA development courses.

In the final chapter in part III, Douglas and Selinker present research that highlights some of the complexities of interaction faced by a nonnative-speaking TA. They examine TA discourse as it relates to interlanguage and genre by comparing data from a native- and a nonnative-speaking TA performing in two domains (talking about work and about their lives) and in two genres (an informal interview and a lecture). Their research suggests that nonnative-speaking TAs may not be able to shift appropriately from one genre to another and may, for example, apply the discourse features of a lecture to the informal setting of a one-on-one discussion. This finding illustrates a particularly problematic area for nonnative-speaking TAs who work in labs and office hours, situations in which the subject matter signals a formal style but the expectations of the student and the context demand an informal discourse style.

All three chapters in part III relate the broader issues of applied linguistics to the particular issue of ITA training and development. This book thereby forms a link between the practical and the theoretical as well as between research designed to answer specific questions about ITAs and research in discourse analysis. It constructs new frameworks for ITA issues, suggests specific pedagogical techniques for the classroom, and helps to fit ITA research into the related areas of research in communicative competence, English for specific purposes, and applied linguistics.

I
.
Frameworks

1

Communicative Competence as a Theoretical Framework for ITA Education

Barbara Hoekje
Drexel University

Jessica Williams
University of Illinois at Chicago

The "international teaching assistant (ITA) problem" is by now well known to TESOL professionals in higher education. Conferences, studies (see, for example, Bailey, Pialorsi, & Zukowski/Faust, 1984; Young, 1989b), textbooks (Byrd, Constantinides, & Pennington, 1989; Pica, Barnes, & Finger, 1990; Smith, Meyers, & Burkhalter, 1992), and three preconference TESOL symposia have explored the topic. In this chapter we unify these findings within a framework from which to pursue further research and pedagogical innovation.

We take the position that in the case of ITAs, language skills cannot be separated from the context in which they are practiced, that is, in the teaching assistant (TA) role. This role encompasses a wide variety of behaviors and skills, and implies a unique set of authority relationships with students that are permutations of the roles played by faculty (McKeachie, 1978; Hoekje & Tanner, 1987). Thus ITA curriculum and assessment are best set within a theoretical model of language use that takes into account social relationships, language appropriateness, and context. Sociolinguistic models of language use, such as those of communicative competence proposed by Hymes (1972a), and more specifically in their more pedagogical applications, those put forth by Savignon (1983), Canale and Swain (1980), and Canale (1983), are an appropriate basis for the emerging models of ITA competence and can form a useful framework for examining ITA language use. Such a framework can provide trainers with a central organizing principle and a basis on which to set goals, design curriculum, and evaluate results.

We are not the first to consider communicative competence as an appropriate goal for ITAs; in fact, ITA research is increasingly being carried out within this or compatible perspectives, as demonstrated, for example, in the preconference TESOL ITA colloquia in the work of such researchers as Rounds (1990), Tyler (1990), and Myers (1991). Our purpose is to propose communicative competence as a general, theoretical framework for ITA instruction and to demonstrate the advantage of this framework as an organizing principle for ITA curriculum and evaluation.

In the following sections we discuss the overall construct of communicative competence and examine in more detail the individual components of linguistic, sociolinguistic, discourse, and strategic competence in terms of how they have been defined and how they apply to ITAs. We also review a number of studies of ITAs in light of this model and give examples from our own observations of ITAs in the classroom.

Communicative Competence as a Goal for ITAs

The framework we use here is explicitly within Hymes' conception of the term *communicative competence*. That is, it includes the notion that language behavior can be viewed in terms of its appropriateness as well as its correctness (Hymes, 1972a). In addition, of particular importance to ITAs is that communicative competence includes the ability to use as well as know language. Hymes is not alone in pointing out this crucial difference; Widdowson (1978) stresses that in language teaching linguistic skills and communicative abilities must not be seen as equivalent. Savignon (1983) rejects any practical distinction between competence and performance, stating that the only way of determining the level of a speaker's communicative competence is through performance. We stress this notion of ability to use the language for ITAs because frequently they display a thorough knowledge of content material and even of the rules of language yet are unable to communicate effectively because they have little ability to convey their knowledge. Any framework for determining the communicative competence of ITAs must minimally include the presentation of information in comprehensible form, a familiarity with the speech situation and the roles of participants, and the development of styles of speech and interaction.

ITAs participate in speech events that are clearly quite complex, and in many areas they may fall short of their communicative goals. Curriculum development must therefore begin with an integrated framework for ITA communicative competence. Canale and Swain (1980) and Canale (1983) have proposed a theoretical basis for communicative language teaching that may be usefully applied to the preparation of ITAs. They state that a theory of communicative competence is one in which there is a synthesis of knowledge of basic grammatical principles, knowledge of how language is used in social contexts to perform communicative functions, and knowledge of how utterances and communicative functions can be combined according to the principles of discourse. (Canale & Swain, 1980, p. 20)

They stress that the success of communication must be judged by behavioral outcomes. Thus, although the "ITA problem" is often perceived as a problem of effectiveness in English oral proficiency, we maintain that for ITAs the aim is effective language usage *while performing the role of TA*. This most general aim subsumes more specific objectives that address language ability, cultural awareness, and teaching skill.

What, then, are the elements of communicative success for the ITA? To begin, we again turn to Canale and Swain's model, as modified by Canale (1983), which states that communicative competence consists minimally of grammatical, sociolinguistic, discourse, and strategic competencies. Neither we nor Canale and Swain suggest that these are the only sorts of competencies necessary to be communicatively successful in any given context. Clearly, in the case of ITAs, for instance, knowledge of the discipline is crucial. In addition, an ITA's ability to gauge the knowledge and learning styles of his or her students may be as important as communication skills. Finally, the desire to teach well, and basic personality variables such as confidence before a group, also affect the ability to communicative effectively. Without these basic prerequisites, even an ITA with considerable competence in the areas outlined below may be unsuccessful in the classroom.

Grammatical Competence

In the Canale and Swain (1980) framework, grammatical competence refers to knowledge of the rules of morphology, syntax, sentence-grammar semantics, lexical items, and phonology: "how to determine and express accurately the literal meaning of utterances" (p. 30). Promoting grammatical competence is one of the goals of ITA training; however, it has proved a particularly problematic area to address.

One reason is that ITA programs are usually multilevel, with a wide variety of learners in the same class. As second language acquisition theory proposes, learners construct learner varieties of the target language with some inherent systematicity; the process of acquisition represents the movement from one variety to another (Klein, 1986). Thus a reasonable goal for developing grammatical competence in a second language would be to facilitate the transition between varieties in the direction of the target through the ordered presentation of material appropriate to the learner's current variety (Rutherford, 1988). But with learners at widely varying levels, such facilitation within the classroom is not easily practicable and therefore is perhaps an unrealistic goal. Moreover, reinforcement of input and opportunities to use English outside the classroom are often lacking (Ard, 1987).

Perhaps most important is that the time for training is short whereas improving grammatical accuracy can be a time-consuming, long-range process. ITA courses typically range from an average of 1 to 8 weeks preterm, one to two terms (several hours per week) concurrent with the academic program, or both (Barnes, Finger, Hoekje, & Ruffin, 1989). During this relatively short time, ITA programs are required to prepare students, who are often new to the United States and may have a low level of language skills, to handle a demanding teaching role successfully. In light of the time constraints, and keeping in mind the needs of the undergraduate population to whom ITA educators are ultimately responsible, the most effective means for an ITA to improve communication may be through pragmatic rather than linguistic means. For example, students who mispronounce terms can become more intelligible more quickly by learning to recognize problematic terms and write them on the board than by changing their pronunciation.

A third area of concern in teaching grammatical accuracy has been the efficacy of traditional approaches. A case in point is pronunciation. Although pronunciation is often the most overtly identified problem associated with ITAs, in many cases the ITA curriculum addresses it only peripherally. Stevens (1988, 1989) has discussed this issue, proposing that pronunciation may have been demoted in the ITA curriculum because trainers were frustrated in dealing with pronunciation problems according to more traditional methods. This is not to deny that pronunciation still plays a major role in many programs. One approach has been to focus on the pronunciation of vocabulary in field-specific contexts, with change in these contexts gradually applied to more general contexts (Lane, 1989; Byrd, Constantinides, & Pennington, 1989; Anderson-Hsieh, 1990). Once again, the emphasis is on success in the required role rather than the development of language skills in general.

Vocabulary is an issue that has begun to attract attention among ITA educators. Whereas early ITA programs focused on technical vocabulary, more recently the focus has shifted to what has been called "subtechnical" vocabulary. Both Myers and Douglas (1991) and Smith et al. (1992) have stressed that it is items such as *bulb*, *squeeze*, and *barrel* that are particularly problematic for ITAs to control and comprehend.

Finally, linguistic and nonlinguistic factors have been confounded in the perception of ITAs' linguistic abilities, which has further confused the role of grammatical accuracy per se in ITA speech. In Brown's study (1988), in which college students viewed videotapes of nonnative-speaking teachers, the perceived country of origin of the speaker affected the students' judgments of his or her language competence. In an earlier study, Orth (1982) had also demonstrated that students' attitudes toward the course and their expected grade affected their perceptions of the ITAs' pronunciation.

With greater experience over the years, ITA educators have increasingly come to see a basic competence in English as necessary before ITA education can be effective. Bailey (1982) originally formulated this competence as a "threshold" level of a Foreign Service Institute (FSI) rating of 2, below which ITAs were perceived as significantly poorer performers than those scoring 2 or above. Some programs have instituted minimum Speaking Proficiency in English Assessment Kit (SPEAK) scores for participation in the training program activities (Barnes et al., 1989). The relationship of these overall scores in speaking proficiency to particular grammatical competencies has varied but has generally correlated more highly with pronunciation and fluency than with grammar subsections (Clark & Swinton, 1980).

Sociolinguistic Competence

In the original Canale and Swain (1980) model, sociolinguistic competence included knowledge of both the rules for sociocultural language usage and the rules for producing coherent discourse. Canale's (1983) revised model included only sociocultural rules of use. This area refers to the appropriateness with which speakers produce and understand language within a particular social context. In the case of ITAs, the issue is how fully they understand and can respond according to the norms of interaction and interpretation (Hymes, 1972a) in the classroom.

Researchers recognized early on that cultural differences in the classroom were a primary basis for ITA failure (Landa & Perry, 1984). ITAs may have difficulty adjusting to the teaching setting. Although some may have held teaching positions in their own countries (Berns, 1989), the classroom setting to which they are accustomed tends to be quite different from those they confront as TAs in the United States. In place of large, impersonal lectures, they find themselves in front of small, more intimate classes in which personal interaction is not only possible but expected. ITAs may nevertheless seek to transform the new setting into one that is more familiar to them, leading their undergraduates to perceive them as impersonal "mechanical problem-solvers" (Bailey, 1984, p. 113). As these problems were acknowledged, a culture component soon became standard fare in ITA training programs (Turitz, 1984); this component often included readings about the U.S. university and the goals of U.S. education, and involved the use of undergraduates as informants and ethnographic-style observations of classroom behavior (Pialorsi, 1984). The basis for this curricular emphasis has been that understanding the cultural assumptions behind the U.S. educational system and the differences between this system and the ITA's own would help the ITA-student communication process (Byrd et al., 1989).

Overt attitudinal differences stemming from culturally different educational values have proved difficult to measure, however. Stevens (1989) developed an instrument for this purpose but found that ITAs showed few differences from U.S. undergraduates in their *overt* attitudes toward the underlying values of U.S. education, even in the case of ITAs from very different cultures. Although these differences may be hard to measure by questionnaire, differences between educational systems and cultures clearly affect virtually all aspects of the organization of language behavior in the classroom, including the appropriate role relationships between students and TAs. A TA who has never taught must learn a new role of authority relative to students; one who has had teaching experience before coming to the United States must relearn the role relationships in the U.S. context, a task that some ITAs find even more difficult than beginning teaching (Landa & Perry, 1984). The understanding and appropriate handling of roles in teaching is more difficult because of the many roles that instructors play in the educational process (McKeachie, 1978) and the permutations on those roles that are expected of TAs. The easy phrasing of a NS chemistry TA's "Shall we roll, folks?" as a way to signal the beginning of class reveals the delicate balance of informality and authority expected of TAs in the U.S. classroom (Hoekje & Tanner, 1987).

Unfortunately, providing the ITA with experience in a role of authority is particularly difficult in the ITA course, given that the ITA is a peer relative to the other students and a student relative to the instructor. Excerpt 1[1] illustrates the problems that may occur when the TA in a training program takes on a pretend-role that differs from social reality. In this example, a physics ITA was assigned to present an elementary concept to his "class"—actually his fellow ITAs.

[1] **TA:** I want to ask a question about can you tell what's the difference speed and velocity?
(General laughter followed by silence)
   TA: Yes, all of you are graduate students. It's too easy.

This student was attempting to take on the role of the teacher but was prevented from doing so because the "class" had not taken on its role appropriately. Clearly, practicing language items and functions is ineffective when isolated from an appropriate context. It is becoming more apparent that ITAs need to go beyond role playing for authentic practice in their new roles. Increasingly, ITA programs are inviting undergraduates to participate. Although their perspective is not necessarily unbiased, as noted above, the feedback ITAs receive in a mock lesson in front of undergraduates is far more valuable than the same exercise in front of their fellow ITAs. One of the problems with including undergraduates in ITA training is, of course, cost. In programs with restricted budgets, it may be more cost effective to use actual classes. If ITAs are permitted to teach and take an ITA preparation course concurrently, then real class material may be used, either for real-time or delayed analysis. If ITAs are required to complete a preparation course before taking on teaching responsibilities, it may be necessary to begin with more receptive activities, such as observation and analysis of other classes, taught by both NS TAs and experienced ITAs.

Bailey (1985) has discussed the social differences between the training-testing program and a classroom of students. A number of researchers who have examined ITA effectiveness have concluded that few ITAs are able to employ a range of speech styles, including especially the use of humor that may contribute to classroom effectiveness (Bailey, 1984; Orth, 1982; Davis, 1984). Bailey's typology of ITAs suggested that, according to undergraduate evaluations, the most successful ITAs were ones who commanded a range of speech styles, engaged in considerable interaction with students, and used humor in their presentations. In contrast to the NS TA's genial class opener discussed above, we observed an ITA who had charmed his fellow training program participants with his lucid and entertaining presentations in the training program yet in the actual physics lab was unable to find the appropriate tone in gathering students together to begin, simply announcing, "We start!"

In another example of formally correct language that failed because of sociolinguistic inappropriateness, Tanner (personal communication) described an ITA circulating around the students in the chemistry lab. She approached each student work group, using the phrase, "What are you doing?" This phrase had an accusatory tone that startled and alarmed the students but was unintended in the situation, as she was merely trying to elicit information about what part of the procedure the students were currently working on.[2] Rounds (1987a) pointed out that a native speaker's greater use of inclusive pronouns when addressing students in the science laboratory—for example, "OK, here *we* go. Now *we're* making progress"—contributes to a shared sense of participation that nonnative speakers are less likely to achieve. This may stem from differences in how the two groups conceptualize the role of the TA.

Receptive skills are equally important for ITA effectiveness, and it is often difficult for ITAs to know how to interpret the language and behavior that is addressed to them or that they observe, especially when the language is couched in an unfamiliar register. Differences in register may surface in a variety of ways, including word choice and idiomatic usage. Myers and Douglas (1991) observed that students' use of vocabulary items of relatively low lexical content, such as *stuff*, *thing*, and *a bunch*, in asking questions rather than specific technical names is often particularly troublesome to ITAs. Myers (this volume) has described the informal register of students' speech in the science laboratory. After talking to their lab partners, students may turn to their TAs without changing register, using slang and idioms that confound ITAs and prevent them from participating in the conversation. She cites a student in a zoology lab who asked his ITA, "Ya get a needle for the hydra? to poke that dude?" The ITA was unable to respond effectively and therefore was left out of subsequent similar interactions.

In another instance that shows the importance of being familiar with norms of interaction in the classroom, Shaw and Bailey (1990) described the subtle negotiating of norms between instructors and students in the first few weeks of a course that establishes patterns of classroom behavior, such as the initiation and recognition of student questions. Without access to the cultural norms of the U.S. classroom, ITAs are unable to participate in this process effectively, neither communicating their own expectations nor reading their students' behavior accurately. Most ITA programs go through the obvious points that eating in class and tardiness are not necessarily signs of disrespect. Often, however, misinterpretation can be more subtle and disturbing. As part of an ITA training program, one participant taped one of his office hours. When a student responded to his explanation with silence, followed by some words of comprehension, the ITA interpreted the encounter as successful. Later discussion with the undergraduate revealed that she had simply said, "Yeah, OK, fine," in order to leave the ITA's office gracefully. In fact, having understood almost nothing of the explanation, she abandoned any attempt to pursue her questions, left frustrated, and sought an explanation from one of her classmates. ITAs may also interpret a dwindling number of students attending their sections as evidence of U.S. students' lack of seriousness in their studies rather than of a teaching problem.

More recently, there has been a growing realization that norms of interaction and interpretation in the classroom differ according to academic discipline. Byrd and Constantinides (1988) have pointed out that different disciplines prefer different teaching styles and have warned ESL professionals not to assume that the teaching style they have used in ESL classes is appropriate in the disciplines of their ITA students. Rounds (1987a) has described the language of the mathematics classroom in terms of its particular routines and lesson organization. The nature of the classroom, TA assignment, and lesson also affects the organization of talk. Tanner (1991b) investigated the relationship between student and TA questions in a chemistry laboratory and the particular functions of that setting. In such cases, the ESL staff of ITA programs may want to cooperate with faculty and experienced TAs in the disciplines in an effort to provide effective field-specific instruction. This can be accomplished in many ways. Faculty members from relevant departments may be included at any stage: They can collect materials, evaluate and analyze mock teaching, or serve as models for the ITAs to observe and analyze but not necessarily imitate. Some institutions have begun to involve other faculty and native-speaking TAs in a mentoring system (Hawkins, personal communication). In the first term the ITAs team teach with an experienced TA and teach classes of their own only in the second term; even then the mentor continues to observe them.

ESL faculty must also become more knowledgeable about field-specific requirements. At one institution, a belated visit to the chemistry department revealed that the faculty explicitly did not want TAs giving presentations in the laboratory. They complained that their new TAs were always trying to give lectures when instead they should have been circulating through the lab, answering individual questions. Because much of the ITA preparation course had focused on presenting information, departmental needs and ITA training were clearly operating at cross purposes in this case. In short, we are just beginning to understand what is involved in an adequate sociolinguistic competence for TAs. The information provided in the typical culture component to date is useful, but it is only a very small part of the picture.

Discourse Competence

Grammatical and sociolinguistic competence, though important, do not give a complete picture of ITA communicative competence. It is equally important to know how to integrate other components to produce and interpret cohesive and coherent discourse. Canale (1983) has referred to this component as discourse competence, encompassing both productive and interpretive abilities.

Cohesion refers to the ways in which utterances are connected so as to produce unified oral or written text. Evidence shows that ITAs often fail to produce texts that attain the level of cohesion necessary for easy interpretation. In the following excerpt, the speaker, an L1 Mandarin ITA, consistently overuses and overgeneralizes the connectors *and* and *so* at the end of an introduction to the law of the conservation of energy, often making the relationships among propositions difficult to interpret. Of a group of 22 ESL professionals who listened to this presentation, 16 identified the use of these connectors as a source of confusion.

[2] . . . a few days ago I met an American friend and he's a very pious person and he tell us—he told me—he recommend me study the Bible and the first thing he told was that God create every-

thing . . . so I think it disobey the energy conservation law because according this law energy cannot be create and cannot be destroy so that is a contradiction and a very interesting problem.

Coherence is the other important element of discourse competence, according to Canale. Two areas of coherence, continuity and progression, are essential aspects of ITA discourse. Continuity may be indicated by repetition and rephrasing; progression, by a variety of discourse markers that identify the parts of an explanation and the relationship among the parts. Adequate marking of this kind has been shown to be an important element of comprehensibility (Chaudron & Richards, 1986). Recently ITA courses have begun to use materials that stress the importance of discourse marking by having ITAs analyze transcriptions of presentational discourse (Wennerstrom, 1991a).

Discourse competence has been investigated in the context of ITA production in a number of studies. The results of these studies have yet to be fully incorporated into ITA curricula but are indicators of crucial elements of ITA effectiveness. Rounds (1987a) has noted in particular that in comparison to NS TAs, ITAs frequently fail to adequately elaborate the key points of their presentations. They often do not name important steps, mark junctures explicitly, or make cohesive links between ideas. Tyler (1988) maintained that unsuccessful ITAs consistently fail to orient their listeners adequately to the relative importance of ideas and how they are linked to one another. According to Tyler, they misuse various cues on the lexical, syntactic, and prosodic levels on which NS listeners depend in order to interpret discourse. Taken together, these misuses can seriously reduce comprehensibility. Williams (1989) found that two different sets of raters, ESL professionals and undergraduate students, unequivocally rated ITA presentations in which discourse moves were more overtly and explicitly marked as more comprehensible than presentations with fewer and less explicit discourse markers. The difference in the level of syntactic and morphological errors between the two productions, however, was insignificant, suggesting a relatively greater role for discourse marking than for grammatical accuracy in comprehensibility. It is not at all clear, however, that ITAs normally attend to these sorts of discourse markers, or to much of anything else, in the lectures they attend as students. Ard (1987), for example, noted that ITAs attend almost not at all to these lectures, relying instead on written information to learn content material. Both the role of discourse markers in increasing comprehensibility, and the ITAs' possible lack of awareness of them, indicate that this may be a productive area for consciousness raising (Rutherford, 1987). Beyond a certain threshold level of grammatical competence, which we have yet to establish, discourse competence should perhaps be the focus of instruction.

Our knowledge of discourse competence is far from comprehensive. For example, some rules for making an effective oral presentation can be taught, such as including an introduction and conclusion, using repetitions and clear framing statements, and so on. However, many more features have yet to be described, such as appropriate encoding of topic and information focus, consistent tracking of referents, and other elements of cohesion in text, which are features nonnative speakers often omit. At the more global level, strategies for organizing information may differ from the expected style: Tyler (1991) found a significant difference between the organizational strategies of a Korean TA, who relied on a general-to-specific strategy in presenting information, and a U.S. TA, who used a specific-to-general strategy.

Even less understood is the area of receptive discourse competence. Evidently, ITAs often experience difficulties in interpreting questions directed at them, even if they understand the individual words contained in them. In the following explanation of a chemistry experiment, the ITA may have understood the lexical items contained in the undergraduate's question—at least he is able to repeat them—yet he fails to interpret the meaning of the question.

[3] **TA:** Any question?
    S: Do we have to calculate the gas that's left in the rubber tubing?
    TA: In the rubber tubing?
    S: Yeah, do we have to include it?
    TA: Pardon me?
    S: Do we have to calculate what's left or is that given?
    TA: I don't understand.

Myers (this volume) documents how the lack of shared context between TAs and students in the science laboratory may cause comprehension problems that do not typically occur in more traditional classrooms, where a shared context for interpretation of questions is more available; as Myers points out, lab discourse tends to be "disconnected, interrupted, and unpredictable." As the TA circulates from group to group, students may ask questions without providing sufficient orientation for the TA to interpret the question correctly. In the question, "Where d'ya see these brown things at—is it the brown things?", a student was trying to identify the hydra among the contents of the jar. The TA responded by identifying other brown things, namely the hydra's prey. The resulting miscommunication was caused by the student's and the TA's incorrect assumptions about shared context. In such cases, the ITA may search for his or her lack of comprehension or guess at what the student means. In either case, the likely end result is a breakdown in communication.

Although coherence and cohesion are the focus of Canale's discourse competence component, other important areas of discourse need to be explored in ITA program development. For example, the difference between written and oral discourse has been well documented (Danielewicz, 1984; Biber, 1988; Tannen, 1982). ITAs who rely on prepared notes in teaching often present information orally in a style that is more appropriate for written texts. The role of planning in the presentation of information may also be important. The results of Williams (1989) indicate that planned presentations, though syntactically more complex, are more comprehensible than relatively unplanned presentations.

Other important areas of discourse competence involve the differences in competence that may be tied to specific discourse domains. Most ITAs are well prepared in their disciplines but still have difficulties transmitting their knowledge. Myers (1991) and Tanner (1991b) discuss the discourse-specific functions of questions in the science laboratory, where the TA must attend to students' performance of the lab procedure as well as their knowledge and understanding of the theory. Tanner's study demonstrates that, contrary to most other classrooms studied, the laboratory makes greater use of referential rather than display questions, relating question function to both the TA's role and the purposes of the chemistry laboratory.

A number of studies of second language production have indicated that topic may have a significant impact on accuracy, amount of production, and comprehensibility (Selinker & Douglas, 1985; Eisenstein & Starbuck, 1989; Woken & Swales, 1989; Zuengler, 1989b; Gass & Varonis, 1984). These differences may be positive or negative and have been variously attributed to expertise, perceived expertise, and emotional investment. However, Smith (1989b), in an effort to apply some of these findings to ITA issues, devised a field-specific version of the SPEAK. Her results yielded no significant differences in language proficiency across topics for the ITAs as a group, although individual differences did emerge. Smith focused on domain-specific competence in terms of language ability, as measured by the SPEAK. This is an area for further investigation. Possibly, ITAs are relatively successful when speaking in their area of expertise but less so in the interpersonal interaction that is so important to successful teaching.

The studies named above have addressed differences in comprehensibility and accuracy across discourse domains in terms of linguistic form. Expertise clearly extends beyond linguistic message form and affects the ways in which content is selected, organized, and presented in the classroom. As noted, there is growing acceptance of the fact that this expertise may be discipline specific (Rounds, 1987a; Byrd & Constantinides, 1988; Tanner, 1991b). For example, the inclusion of subject-specialist informants (SSIs) (Selinker & Douglas, 1989b) can reveal content-based problems with message form. During an ITA preparation course, a chemistry SSI who attended a simulated problem-solving session suggested that the new ITAs' most serious potential communication problem lay in their lack of knowledge of how the undergraduate students expected the chemistry problems to be written. U.S. undergraduates are taught to carry their units (e.g., gm/mole) all the way through the problem-solving sequence, then rationalize them and cancel where possible. Chinese students approach problems in the opposite way: All rationalization and cancellation of units occurs before the problem is solved. Thus the ITAs were presenting the problems in a form that was extremely confusing to the undergraduates. This confusion cannot be due to a language problem, but message form and thus communication are affected in crucial ways. Furthermore, the issue of approach never would have occurred to the ESL specialist in charge of the course. Most ESL instructors do not have the background to provide this kind of information and training. Domain-specific competence is clearly an area that needs to be investigated further in ITA training and may be important to the fields of second language acquisition in general and language for specific purposes (LSP) as well (see Selinker & Douglas, 1989b).

Strategic Competence

Strategic competence is described by Canale as the mastery of verbal and nonverbal strategies that can be used either to compensate for deficiencies in other components of competence or to increase communicative effectiveness in general. Because ITAs, almost without exception, demonstrate gaps in the first three areas of communicative competence, this component may prove to be a crucial one. It may be possible to teach ITAs to use their knowledge and abilities in one area of competence in order to make up for knowledge or abilities that are weaker in other areas; in other words, they may learn to use compensatory strategies to increase their effectiveness as teachers.

On the nonverbal level, strategic competence could include the knowledge of the advantages and disadvantages of particular speech settings or participant structures in which communication occurs. Tyler (1990) reported an escalating argument held in a lab between an ITA and a student dissatisfied with his grade. The discussion between the two took place in the presence of other students and in the face of time pressure on the TA to supervise the lab and on the student to begin doing the lab. As time went on, difficulty in communication and the mounting time pressure made each speaker increasingly frantic and more rigid in his position and increasingly unable to understand the other. As Tyler pointed out, the decision to move the discussion to an office-hour setting where the two could talk more privately and leisurely would probably have been the single best strategy for a more positive outcome between the two.

On the verbal level, the notion of compensatory strategies is somewhat alien to language teaching programs, where targetlike competence is usually the stated or unstated goal. Because many ITA courses are housed within ESL programs that tend to use NS proficiency as the target for their students, it is not surprising that programs have often adopted similar goals somewhat automatically. However, the goal of most ITA programs is to improve communication skills in the teaching context so as to better serve the undergraduate population, not necessarily to foster the second language acquisition of the ITAs. Although these two goals certainly overlap, they are not identical and should not be confused. Typically, the approach taken to second language education is developmental; learners are guided through a series of stages of acquisition of language rules and functions, with the eventual aim of approaching a NS standard. Although most ITA program developers and instructors know that this process needs to go beyond linguistic competence, the assumptions underlying the goal of a NS target have not been explicitly challenged. Various needs analyses and other studies (Bailey et al., 1984; Rounds, 1987a; Williams, Barnes, & Finger, 1987; Gillespie, 1988) include the collection of baseline data from NSs, suggesting that these studies share the underlying assumption that ITAs should strive to emulate (effective) NS TAs in their linguistic, interactional, and presentation skills. Because using a NS model as target is standard procedure in second language acquisition research and, to an even greater extent, in LSP, it is reasonable that such an assumption be made in designing an ITA curriculum. However, a real sense of urgency underlies the establishment of ITA preparation programs, as they play such an important role in higher education. It is perhaps appropriate, therefore, to reexamine this assumption of NS competence as the target.

First, NS-like behavior may not be attainable, especially in the short time usually allotted to ITA education. Second, and perhaps more important, the language production, in terms of pronunciation, grammaticality, lexis, and so on, of effective ITAs does not always approach NS status; rather, they may be successful as a result of compensatory strategies they use. Bailey (1984) reported that one of the TAs who was rated highest in her study was, in fact, an international TA. His English proficiency was quite good but far from perfect. He was able to overcome his language problems because his interpersonal and pedagogical skills were exceptional. Bailey goes on to suggest, however, that compensatory strategies may be ineffective below a certain threshold level of language proficiency.

Training in the use of compensatory strategies may be more effective than language instruction that uses NS behavior as a target. Williams (1989) found that the increased use of discourse markers and elaboration of key concepts led to significantly higher comprehensibility ratings by undergraduate students and ESL specialists. The use of these markers was found to be far more significant for ITAs than for NS TAs, for whom discourse marking and elaboration appeared to be relatively unimportant. This disparity was presumably a result of the NS TAs' high level of competence in other areas as well as the ITAs' lack thereof. Nonlinguistic strategies, such as the extended use of written material on handouts or overhead transparencies, may help to ameliorate communication difficulties. Although linguistic competence may not improve, teaching may become more effective. Many of these strategies are essentially avoidance rather than achievement strategies (Faerch & Kasper, 1983), in that they do not usually expand linguistic resources. Because the goal of ITA programs may be to improve communicative performance over linguistic competence, instructional strategies may be at odds with the goals of general ESL programs.

Improvement of strategic competence is increasingly a part of ITA education. According to Davies (1991b), when ITAs have the opportunity to role play interactions with students and then view their performance on videotape, receiving feedback on their communication strategies and other pragmatic aspects of performance, the ITAs' "strategic" performance, as well as accuracy, improved. Strategic and other compensatory skills become particularly important in preparation courses aimed at ITAs of widely differing linguistic competence, a situation typical particularly of smaller institutions with limited resources (Boyd, 1989b). Whereas it may be possible to maintain NS target models for some of the more proficient students, the less proficient students, too, must learn how to carry out the tasks that will be demanded of them. The development of strategic competence may be an effective focus of instruction especially for this population.

Conclusion

We have suggested the theoretical model of communicative competence as a basis for examining the growing field of ITA education. We propose that the goal of ITA education is to prepare the student to effectively take on the role of TA, with all that role entails (teaching, managing the classroom, advising, etc.). The specifics may vary from institution to institution and from department to department, but if the objective of ITA education is seen as helping the ITA to manage a new role successfully rather than to teach the ITA a new set of linguistic or behavioral skills, the ITA preparation curriculum may become truly contextualized. Hymes' notion of communicative competence is as applicable now to ITAs as it was when it was first proposed almost 25 years ago: Language is used within a social context. The ITA classroom is a social context, and there is little point in teaching language items without situating them within this context.

The ITA curriculum has developed from perceived needs of ITAs in language, pedagogy, and culture. At the same time, researchers have continued to add information about ITA communication, discourse genres, and the U.S. classroom. The use of the communicative competence framework as an organizing principle for ITA education provides a principled basis for evaluating and using this research, assessing language use, and integrating this new information into the ITA curriculum.

Notes

1. All examples come from observations of ITAs by the authors at the University of Illinois at Chicago, the University of Pennsylvania, and Drexel University.

2. Whether ITA preparation programs should try to modify ITAs' personal styles is an ethical question that we do not address here. Stevens (1988) has suggested that ITAs be encouraged to take on different temporary roles rather than attempt to change long-term behavior. Clearly, however, a disparity is expected, and actual speech styles may have an important effect on the success of ITAs.

■ 2 ■

Discourse Competence in a Framework for ITA Training

Peter A. Shaw
Monterey Institute of International Studies

■

The purpose of this chapter is to revisit a general model for the training of international teaching assistants (ITAs) that was developed at the University of Southern California in the late 1970s and summarised in the National Association of Foreign Student Advisers (NAFSA) collection on ITA training programmes (Shaw & Garate, 1984). I argue that the validity and relevance of that model can only be maintained by incorporating considerations of discourse. Two specific instances are examined: one of discourse structure, the other a discourse event.

The chapter is organised as follows. The first section reviews the model in its 1984 form. I then introduce considerations of discourse structure; this is followed by a discussion of discourse events. The final section presents a revised version of the model.

A Note on Discourse

I use the term *discourse* here to refer to the totality of communicative behaviour, verbal and nonverbal, that occurs within a given situation. *Discourse analysis* (see Sinclair & Coulthard, 1975) is the level of analysis between (though with frequent overlaps) grammar, on the one hand, and nonlinguistic organisation, on the other. In the present case, the latter identifies, for example, courses, which may consist of lectures, discussion groups, laboratory sessions, and so forth. The kind of discourse analysis pioneered by Sinclair and Coulthard is then applied to a data sample gathered, say, from 10:02 to 10:54 a.m. on a given Thursday, representing a complete class session of a discussion section conducted by a TA. They would label this rank of the analysis a *lesson*, which is broken down into *transactions*, which in turn consist of *exchanges*, themselves analysed into various *moves*, which are composed of *acts*. At this point, discourse gives way to grammar, which characterises the phonetic, morphological, lexical, and syntactic nature of the data.

Thus by discourse structure I mean either the hierarchical system itself or an element of a hierarchical system that is larger in temporal and linguistic scope than a single utterance, but not larger than the unit of nonlinguistic organisation (here, the class or lecture); that consistently occurs within larger elements and co-occurs with fellow elements with related but different purposes; that has predictable linguistic and nonlinguistic markers; and that recognisably and regularly fulfills one or more communication functions. By discourse event, I mean an utterance or series of utterances that constitute one or more moves but normally no more than one exchange, and that may be explicated not only through interpretation of the linguistic behaviour of the participants but also through the locus of the move or moves within the larger discourse structures.

The 1984 Model

The proposed training model was based on the concepts in Shaw and Garate (1984), shown in Figure 1. My additions to the model, indicated by italics and dashed lines, are discussed in the final section of the chapter.

ITA Training Is a Form of ESP

Given the time constraints inherent in most training programmes, and assuming an adequate level of general competence in English, the model approached ITA training as an exemplar of specific purpose instruction. The language components would thus focus on the language of the discipline to be taught, together with the language of undergraduate pedagogy. In addition, the model holds as a fundamental tenet that an English for specific purposes (ESP) course must be constructed around a central core of activity in which the nonnative trainee actually performs tasks central to the specific purpose, either in a real or simulated context. In other words, in ITA training courses, ITAs must teach.

In hindsight, the model failed to express an awareness that the specific purpose language will have crucial discourse dimensions. A physics lecture, for example, will have particular discourse structures not necessarily found in mathematics or economics classes. The registers associated with different disciplines do not differ solely in terms of technical and subtechnical lexis and a predilection for certain syntactic structures.

Precourse

Course

Postcourse

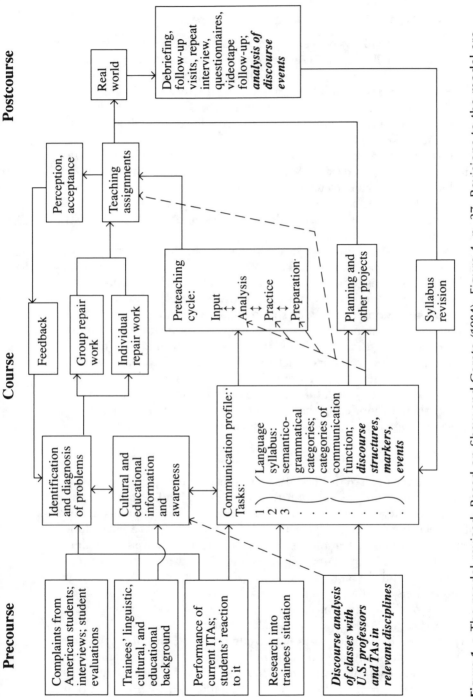

Figure 1 ▪ The model revised. Based on Shaw and Garate (1984), Figure 4, p. 37. Revisions to the model are indicated by italics and dashed lines.

Linguistic Versus Communicative Competence

The model distinguishes between the expression of propositional content (equated with Wilkins' [1977] semanticogrammatical or notional categories) and the realisation of the functional uses of language (his categories of communicative function). Training would therefore ensure, for example, that a physics TA could successfully express notions of quantity in English, on the one hand, and could provide recognisably accurate definitions of key concepts, on the other.

Although functions such as definition may be realised in a single sentence, we recognised (Shaw & Garate, 1984, p. 25) that other functions develop over lengthier stretches of language—presenting a classification or a hypothesis, for example. When an ITA is involved in a breakdown of communication, we suggested, the whole design of the discourse may be at fault.

What kinds of "discourse designs" are involved, however, was not discussed in the original model. The TESOL profession of the late 1970s and early 1980s was somewhat preoccupied with language functions and the possibility of notional syllabi. Although the realisation existed that there was no tidy one-to-one correspondence between language functions and sentences, it was not yet clear to me (as it was to others; see Coulthard, 1977) that functions, although a very significant concept, were not serviceable as a unit of discourse analysis. The functional syllabus for ITA training (with units covering definitions, classification, descriptions of process, explanation, etc.), then claimed as sharp and contemporary, is now clearly not founded in the relevant discourse realities found in the classroom language of the various disciplines.

Cross-Cultural Communication

A fundamental tenet of the model is that ITAs will be engaged in communication across cultures, with all the complexities and pitfalls that involves. The international TA on the one hand and U.S. students on the other will bring different expectations to the situation. These will include background and preparation in subject matter (with U.S. students falling short of the TA's expectations in, for example, math skills), classroom procedures (students, for instance, expecting to interrupt the instructor with questions and the TA anticipating only respectful silent listening), and levels of clarity and simplicity (the students perhaps wanting the TA to make clear what the professor has left cloudy or incomplete, and the TA expecting basic material to be already mastered and often proving incapable of providing the fundamentally clear remedial explanations).

Any ITA training programme must address this lack of fit. This means a dual approach: to trainees' expectations (through exposition and discussion of relevant aspects of the target culture) and to trainees' capabilities (through discussion and practice of planning, management, materials preparation, evaluation, and so on). Both aspects will arise in the cycle of activities built around the trainees' actual teaching, where all components of their communication strategies are treated.

To this approach must be added the following point: An important part of the expectations brought by the students will be that the discourse of an engineering lecture or a discussion section in economics will be organised in a particular manner. Students also expect classroom discourse procedures (such as the appropriate placement of student questions in the discourse structure) to be established (see Shaw & Bailey, 1990, for the detailed case) through a covert negotiation between instructor and students during the early weeks of a course.

Needs Analysis

The model drew from the work of Munby (1978) and Mackay and Bosquet (1982) in emphasising the value of gathering detailed information before undertaking any course development: hence the preprogramme stage, which involves a variety of devices, including informal conversations with key personnel (faculty supervisors, native students known to have complained about an ITA, graduate advisors, experienced ITAs), class visits, questionnaires, and analysis of student evaluation data. When sufficient information has been gathered, then goals may be set and detailed course development may begin.

The original model failed to emphasise that a vital aspect of the preprogramme stage was the collection and analysis of language data from relevant classrooms: finding out how native-speaking professors and TAs lecture, answer questions, lead discussions, and in general conduct communication about chemistry or marketing.

Once the programme has a set of objectives, a syllabus, an instructional format, and materials, it is trialed. The postprogramme stage then permits a post hoc assessment, including long-range feedback as ITAs go to work in classrooms and reflect on their own performance as well as undergo evaluation by their students. These data often provoke changes in subsequent versions of the training course.

Three Steps to Successful Communication

Work in cross-cultural situations reported by Gumperz, Jupp, and Roberts (1979) suggested three stages to successful communication: perception, acceptance, and repair. All three stages are necessary; none is sufficient by itself; and none is easy to accomplish. They may be characterised as follows.

Perception means a statement from the trainee to the effect that

> I can see that communication involving me and this group of students has not been entirely successful.

Aggregations of this experience in repeated trials leads to the general perception:

> My attempts at communication with native-speaking students in classrooms are not always successful.

Acceptance means a statement from the trainee to the effect that

> A breakdown in communication has occurred between the students and myself. I accept that fact and I further accept that a deficiency or deficiencies in my communication skills contributed significantly to the breakdown.

Repeated instances of such insights leads to a general acceptance:

> Unless I improve my communication skills, communication breakdowns will continue to occur in my classes.

Repair involves five elements:

1. relevant information about the background, nature, expectations, and skill levels of U.S. students and about the educational system that has produced them
2. relevant information about the general culture of the area (for example, southern California) and the subculture (for example, athletics, fraternities and sororities, grading practices) of the university
3. remedial language work (for example, in pronunciation, stress and intonation, lexical choice, sentence structure, and nonverbal behaviour)
4. remedial pedagogy (for example, selecting examples, handling questions, structuring a presentation from parts to whole or whole to parts)
5. integrated remediation of language and pedagogy (for example, having trainees write their lesson plan on the blackboard and leave it there throughout the class session as a way of overtly structuring the lesson and easing language problems with transitions or cross-reference).

The chief mechanism posited in the model for achieving these three steps is the series of short teaching assignments, each videotaped for detailed review. Although a few ITAs experience perception and acceptance (and even occasionally attempt repair) during the teaching, using feedback from the audience as a guide, most depend on the structured feedback from the audience immediately following the minilesson or, more commonly, on working with a trainer in reviewing the videotape and analysing instances of miscommunication. Some trainees never achieve the first step, never seeing that understanding on both sides is less than complete. Others have the perception that there are problems but eschew acceptance, choosing to blame the inadequate background or slow thought processes of the students. The model predicts that such trainees will make little progress in their teaching, often taking the first opportunity to leave direct instruction in favour of grading papers or assisting in research.

In the model, repair work is conducted at the individual and group levels. On the individual level, the instructor reviews the videotape of a teaching session privately with the trainee. They scrutinize the behaviour of students during the lesson for feedback clues and sift the spontaneous feedback provided by the students immediately after the lesson for pointers. The trainer, exploiting the relative comfort of the one-on-one situation, then tries to elicit suggestions for kinds of repair from the TAs themselves, amplifying and adding to their ideas. On the group level, the trainer reviews the feedback given to the group as a whole and develops activities and strategies that will benefit most if not all the trainees.

The Course Model

The course model, based directly on the precourse activities described above, consists of three principal areas: the identification and diagnosis of problems, the necessary cultural and educational information and awareness, and the communication profile. Of course, the problems of individual TAs cannot be accurately predicted from their background; their teaching performance is heavily influenced by their personality and their interaction with the new environment. For this reason, the content of the problem identification and diagnosis stage is not well defined at the outset and is constantly reassessed during the course.

The second component, however, has a more constant nature. The films, materials, and activities that convey the cultural and educational information need only be updated from one course to the next as the institution changes. The communication profile is also relatively stable, although it will be modified on the basis of postcourse activities, principally follow-up studies of ITAs at work.

From the data in these three categories, two course components are constructed: the planning and materials preparation projects and the preteaching cycle. The former include writing behavioural objectives, planning lessons, and preparing materials. The latter involves a teaching assignment based on a language function identified in the precourse research: for example, *define a significant concept in your field*. The cycle begins with a demonstration of the assignment, followed by discussion and rehearsal of the linguistic and pedagogic realisations. Trainees then select their own topic, plan, rehearse, and give their lesson. This then leads into the feedback and repair loop discussed above.

A weakness of the preteaching cycle in the original model was the exclusive use of language functions (definition, process, explanation) as the basis for the teaching assignments. Although these might serve for one or two introductory units, the assignments should be based on observed discourse realities and correspond, for example, to the transaction rank of analysis (see below).

Discourse Structures

The requirements of the ITA training programme (plus the need to provide a more relevant curriculum for international engineering students enrolled in ESL classes) led to a detailed study of the language of engineering professors (Shaw, 1983). Below I summarise some findings in terms of discourse structure, followed by comparable data from a subsequent study of business classes.

Engineering Lecture Discourse

I now return to the issue of levels of analysis briefly addressed in the opening section. Following the work of Sinclair and Coulthard (1975), Montgomery (1976) offered the following configuration of levels for analysing lecture discourse:

■ lecture
■ transaction
■ sequence
■ member.

A transaction is defined by the presence of a unifying topic and by focusing members at its boundaries: a prospective member at the outset, making some statement about what is to follow, and a retrospective member, providing closure. A sequence is also a topical unit, on a smaller scale than a transaction. It is partly defined on phonological grounds, its onset being marked by relatively high key, and its termination, by declination to a relatively low key. Montgomery suggested that all material within such an intonation contour is semantically related. Informally, then, sequences are groupings of informing members within a transaction. A member (the term is from Winter, 1977) is defined as a free clause or a free clause with any subordinate clauses bound to it.

The central unit of discourse in these classes discussed here is the *problem-solving transaction*, with the following proposed internal structure:

Prospective Focusing Member
- Sequence 1: Posal
- Sequence 2: Solution
- Sequence 3: Evaluation
- Retrospective Focusing Member

Let us consider this in terms of the following excerpt from an aerospace engineering class. The lecture was essentially organised around the review of a recent midterm examination.

[1] so to continue ( ) THEN the second part was to compute the velocity er to fly at (3.1) v infinity (4.1) at pr min that's what velocity do I fly at to be at maximum power well (2.5) v star is v infinity over v at l over d max and we know that at minimum power that's five point seven six it ( ) right so (1.7) v infinity at minimum power zero point seven six times let me now put the number here ( )d (2.5) l over d max which we have computed and that gives one oh five point eight (5.7) feet per second (1.6) ok (6.2) so that's part two

This excerpt is recognisable as a transaction because of its topical unity and because it is bounded by focusing members: The material in line 1 indicates the onset of a new transaction, the solving of a new problem. The phrase *the second part* (line 1) labels the problem, identifying it for the audience. Lines 1–3 then specify the details of the problem; the phonological criterion of declination indicates that a sequence ends with the words *minimum power*.

Further data support this analysis. The word *well* is a boundary marker, its purpose being to indicate the beginning of a new sequence and to label the nature of this sequence as a solution (*well* is a typical marker at the beginning of a response, particularly in the speech of higher- to lower-status participants—as heard in many of President Ronald Reagan's responses to press conference questions, for example). The final indicator of a new sequence is nonverbal: The professor moves from the table, where he has been reading the examination sheet, to the blackboard, the work site where problems are solved.

On the declination criterion, the solution sequence is maintained until line 8. There is a pause, the professor moves back to the table, utters *ok* with a rising intonation (constituting, as I claim below, an abbreviated evaluation sequence), pauses for more than 6 seconds as he moves from the blackboard back to the table, bounding the evaluation sequence as he gives students time to respond to the *ok?*, and closes the transaction with the retrospective focusing member *so that's part two.*

A more complex example of a problem-solving transaction is found in this extract from a mechanical engineering class:

[2] okay let's do the homework (8.2) first one was six eighteen on page two seventy six (3.4) a load l is hoisted by the pulley and cable combination shown if the system starts from rest and the upper cable is ( ) at a velocity v equals four meters per second ( ) a constant acceleration when the load is six meters above its starting position calculate the acceleration of the load and find its velocity at this instant (5.6) well have the ceiling here and er (2.0) a pulley to another pulley to another pulley and then the load (1.8) if this moves a distance ds (1.8) then this moves a distance d s over two (2.3) and if this moves a distance d s over two then this moves a distance d s over four (1.2) okay (3.4) and therefore this moves a distance d s over eight (3.2) so the load moves a distance d s over eight when (1.9) this cable here moves a distance d s (3.0) in other words ds for the load is equal to one eighth of ds (2.9) or if I divide by dt (3.0) I have ds dt which is the velocity (3.7) is equal to one eighth of ds dt which we are told is four so this is half a meter per second (2.6) now v v squared is equal to two a s (2.7) so that the acceleration is equal to er v squared which is one fourth divided by two times s which is six meters and therefore this is one over forty eight (2.3) or its point of two oh eight meters per second per second (7.2) any questions (4.8) all right (2.6) the next one I

Again, prospective foci (general: *ok . . . let's do the homework,* and specific: *first one was*) lead into the problem sequence, which names and specifies the task to be addressed. This sequence is clearly delineated from what follows: the pause (of 5.6 seconds), the declination, with relatively low tone reached on *at this instant,* the marker *well,* and the move to the blackboard. The solution sequence, bounded initially by the 5.6 second pause and launched with the marker *well,* displays declination from the relatively high tone on *have the ceiling here* to its relatively low destination on *per second per second* (line 21). Within this sequence, a typical succession of members proceeds step-by-step to assemble the knowledge necessary for solving the problem. These members are related by a repertoire of cohesive devices: *and, then, if . . . then, so, therefore, or,* and *in other words.* Observe that there is a slight break in this process in line 11, with a significant pause on either side of *okay*. This is a regular feature of extended solutions and represents, I suspect, not only a literal pausing for breath but also the professor's recognition that there is an audience to consider.

As in Excerpt 1, there is a highly truncated evaluation sequence in which students are invited to comment on or question the solution. Such cases would make it difficult to make the argument for such a sequence and to properly characterise it. However, in other cases, professors themselves comment on the solution:

[3] I didn't see anyone that really made a big mistake on that topic in any event the fact that this number was seven hundred and seventy three pounds roughly given the fact that you had that if you had a number which was very far from that you should be concerned this—two weights are not very much different ok generally speaking people did very well in that problem (6.7) in problem two

These evaluative comments are particularly common when the problem is worked on the blackboard as a model, perhaps of a type not previously encountered. Here is another example, with the very end of the solution sequence, followed by the evaluation. .

[4] and I'm left with one half of m r squared (4.3) ok (3.0) if all of the mass were concentrated at the radius and not distributed throughout then the answer would have been m r squared the moment of inertia would've turned out to be m r squared cos its all concentrated on the rim and you wouldn't be doing any integration (1.0) in this case er it's distributed throughout the mass so you get one half m r squared for the moment of inertia of this cylinder (3.9) any questions (5.0) all right let's go on to the next one

Here the professor's evaluation precedes the opportunity offered to the students for a turn at talk, which is again the final element in the transaction before the focusing begins for the next one.

Thus I propose that an engineering lecture consists of a series of transactions. These transactions begin with a prospective focusing member, followed by three sequences: posal, solution, and evaluation; they are closed by a retrospective focusing member. A posal sequence consists of naming and then specifying the problem. In complex cases, certain presuppositions or complications implicit in the problem also need to be discussed. Here are two examples, the first from electrical engineering, the second from environmental engineering:

[5] now just to emphasise re-emphasise that then I tackle another
problem and say well what happens if I interchange these two
(2.7) now if I interchange the components (1.5) if I interchange
the components am I going to change the voltage drop across any
of them
S: =( )
=if (1.0) we interchange (1.3) since they're in series (3.3) ok so
now er supposing I do that now

[6] and you have to think about this a little bit suppose we had um
(3.8) let's say five moles of phosphate in the water a-n-d (4.7) ten
moles of nitrate (3.6) ok moles is a complicated term let's say
we had a er five atoms of phosphate in the water in proportion
there were ten atoms of er molecules of nitrate (2.0) ok which
would be the scarcest nutrient

Some key linguistic features of posal sequences can be seen here:
lexical markers such as *problem, supposing, suppose,* and *let's say*; verbs such
as *take, consider,* and *assume*; and the rhetorical question in Excerpt 5,
line 2, which is apparently mistaken for a genuine question by a student,
who attempts a response only to be ruthlessly overridden.

A solution sequence, as shown, consists of a series of members linked
together by cohesive devices, of which the most common are *and, but,
so,* and *if . . . then.* A closer look (not elaborated here) suggests a repeated
pattern within solution sequences: a three-part structure corresponding
very closely to that of the transactions in which they are enclosed. Consider the following:

[7]   so that er
  [P] if I differentiate this now
  [R] omega x dot which is b and that's equal to er two b theta dot
      but theta dot is omega
  [D] and so I get put a minus sign sine theta

A solution sequence proceeds by carrying forward some product
from the previous step (here indicated by *this* in line 2) and then proposing ([P]) some further manipulation; the reaction ([R]) member (or members) then expresses the manipulation itself, and the determination ([D])
conveys the outcome. This product then becomes the input for the following step, until the final step, when the outcome is the solution to the
whole problem.

Solution sequences may be complicated by sheer length, causing
professors to pause at appropriate points and divide the sequence, at
least informally, into segments. In addition, at any time the professor

may interpose evaluative comments or asides. These are particularly common in the working of sample problems that will serve as models for future problems to be solved by students:

[8] I can now write this equation (2.4) in this form (3.3) h is equal to i times i x x omega x minus i x y omega y minus i x z er y no x z omega z plus j times minus i er y x omega x plus i y y omega y minus i z y omega y plus i z z omega z (4.6) now we have a very complicated type of thing so this is what we bump into in three dimensions because omega dot r is not necessarily zero (1.0) also to be noted although I write i y x i y x is equal to i x y because this is certainly commutative so er we do that for convenience and memorise how to write it er by interchanging it we can now write

The solution sequence is thus interrupted at line 4, with *now* functioning as a signal for an explanatory aside or side sequence, and is resumed in line 9.

Writing about lecture discourse is frustrating because only a handful of data fragments can be exhibited for the reader's inspection. I therefore only claim to have illustrated the suggestion that the unmarked discourse form of engineering lectures is a series of problem-solving transactions with the internal structure described here. I explore the implications of this for the ITA training model in the final section.

Lecture Discourse in Business and Management

Whereas the dominant form of engineering discourse might thus be characterised as the problem-solving type, a second paradigm was apparent in the data: a concept-based or topic-based type, the appearance of which could be predicted from either the branch of engineering (common in environmental engineering, for example) or the type of course (found in introductory courses or courses for nonmajors). Rather than solving a series of problems, this type of lecture introduces and treats a sequence of related ideas or concepts. A subsequent study of lectures in various areas of business and management (still in progress; an early report was presented in Conrad, 1987) identified this type as the dominant form, with problem-solving as a minor feature, occurring in certain subject areas (accounting, for example) or in consolidation sessions when problems are worked as a means of illustrating or detailing a particular concept.

According to the data thus far, concept-based lectures are clearly more complex than problem-based ones both in their discourse structure and in the extent to which one exemplar varies from another. A detailed presentation is not possible here, but Figure 2 gives some idea of the possibilities. A concept-based lecture consists of one or more topics, each of which may optionally be broken down into two or more subtopics. Subtopics consist of one or more transactions, which, as before, are composed of sequences (orientation, definition, formal account, and so on). As Figure 2 shows, however, the complexity arises in part from the repeated occurrence of the different sequences at each of the levels. Thus, even though a particular topic might occupy a whole lecture, at the conclusion of the various subtopics it will still exhibit an interaction-evaluation sequence and a recapitulation sequence, plus a closing retrospective focusing member.

Space does not permit the adequate illustration of any of these concepts. However, a typical transaction, this one from a marketing lecture, gives some indication:

[9] *Prospective Focusing Member:*
the other type is where you have an administered system
Definition:
that just means that the manufacturer and the manufacturer's advertising for the pull through feature of the marketing channel is so strong that they can administer what happens in the retail store
Formal Account:
they can sorta say we're gonna need ye know 20 foot
Informal Account:
of shelf space or how ever many ever like Procter and Gamble with several hundred feet of shelf space cause they're gonna demand to get an they re gonna service it they're gonna keep enough but there's gonna be high volume flow through so that they can sort of push or or lean on the uh managers of the supermarkets to go along with whatever it is they're trying to accomplish
Interaction-Evaluation:
ok (2.0)
Recapitulation:
that's why its administered because they have a lot of uh a- influence in the decisions that go on in the retail store even though they haven't got the investment in it
Retrospective Focus:
(4.1) [Professor scans notes, moves overhead projector slide]
Prospective Focus (Next Transaction):
the next level is this contractual system level

The transaction thus opens with the prospective focusing member and orientation together clarifying the new direction of the discourse, namely a discussion of *administered systems*; the orientation includes the notion of

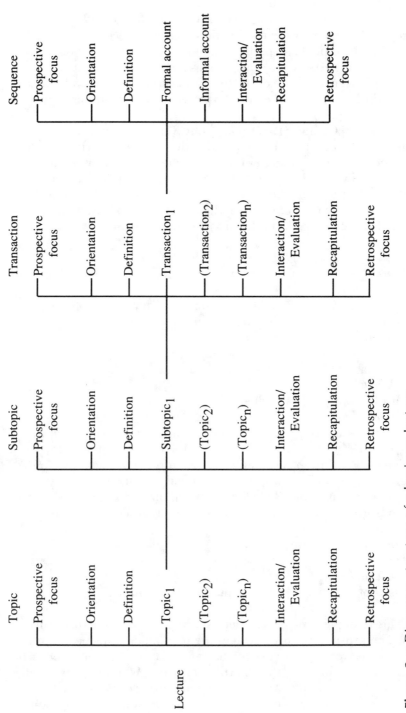

Figure 2 ▪ Discourse structure of a business lecture.

contrast with the previous transaction through the word *other*. The new concept is then defined and the definition restated in less technical terms in the formal account. A specific example is presented in the informal account and, there being no evaluation as such and no student questions, the definition is recapitulated, and the transaction concludes with a pause, during which the professor exhibits typical transaction-closing nonverbal behaviour.

In fact, as Conrad (1987) points out, very few transactions in the business lecture corpus fully demonstrate the complete structure posited. As in the engineering data, evaluation sequences are commonly truncated or totally elided, especially in the absence of student comment or questions. The formal account is also frequently omitted, as seen here in a transaction from a subtopic on the objectives of banks, itself part of a topic that defines banks in the macroeconomic sense.

[10] *Prospective Focusing Member:*
now
Orientation:
you don't like to think of it this way but banks are profit making corporations so certainly paramount in any (2.4) discussion of what banks are up to
Prospective Focus (reprise):
profitability has to be the number one item on the list
Definition:
banks have to be profitable
Informal Account:
if they're not this low return lower than average return will cause resources to flow to other sectors of the economy and no corporation can afford to constantly have resources flowing away from it it limits its ability to acquire new capital it limits the ability to grow basically impossible kind of situation you've got essentially to be earning a return at least equal to other alternatives in society
Retrospective Focusing Member:
ok
Recapitulation:
so profitability has to be the number one concern

This example contains further aspects of variation across transactions. The prospective focus bridges the orientation sequence, with the common marker *now* serving to indicate that the first of a series of transactions (in this case, the objectives of banks) is coming and *number one concern* emphasising that fact. The definition is clearly not a definition as such but a plain statement of the main idea of the transaction (I assume that these economics students were expected to know what *profit* and *profitability* mean), leading from the orientation to the informal account, which explains why profitability is necessary to banks. The purpose of this brief outline of business lecture transactions has been to further illustrate the notion of discourse structure in college classes and to show a type of structure very different from that proposed for the engineering data in. I will sketch some implications in the conclusion.

A Discourse Event

I now present an analysis of the repeated utterances of *Any questions?* by engineering professors and try to show how, assuming the analysis to be correct, its implications can be applied to ITA training.

First, students in the engineering classes studied (15 classes from 7 different subdisciplines—aerospace, chemical, electrical, and so on) have very few turns (226 during 2,250 minutes of instruction), and those turns are usually brief (averaging 5.88 words per turn). The notion of turn is not applicable to the great majority of professors' speech (consisting of extended monologue), but a comparison in terms of number of words uttered shows a ratio of teacher talk to student talk of 215 to 1. Of the 226 turns, 84 were requests, broken down as follows: 7 for a turn at talk, 37 for clarification, 14 for repetition, and 26 for information. All the requests took the form of a question, yet only 15 were in immediate response to the invitation: *Any questions?* Professors uttered this phrase 412 times in the data. Further, in interviews, 13 of the 15 professors stated that it was "of considerable importance" or "of the greatest importance" that students ask questions in class. Professors rated asking questions as one of the most significant means of learning, ranked only behind individual problem solving and group problem solving under a TA's guidance (and ahead of students listening to the professors' monologues!).

How can one account for the fact that professors think it important for students to ask questions and apparently give them many opportunities by asking *Any questions?* on average once every 5 or 6 minutes, yet that students ask very few? An adequate explanation must begin with an outline of how social structures are assembled in educational settings. A suitable starting point is the work of Mehan (1979a), who presented an account of elementary school interaction based on the three-part sequence *initiation-reply-evaluation*: A correct reply must eventually co-occur with an elicit and an accept with a reply. If this does not happen immediately, Mehan showed, the initiator (generally the teacher) must work at it, thus developing extended sequences incorporating prompts, repeated initiations, simplifying initiations, and so on. Both teachers and pupils employ a variety of improvisational strategies, centering particularly on cases in which the latter talk out of turn. During the school year, in fact, students become increasingly successful at taking the floor: Instead of indiscriminately interrupting an ongoing sequence, they were able to recognise what Mehan called the "seams" in the teacher-controlled discourse. Pupils also took advantage of moments when the teacher was "away" (Goffman's term)—writing at the blackboard, for example—to get into the lesson. As the pupils became more skilled at selecting the appropriate slot to insert talk, teachers' sanctions of misplaced intrusions by pupils diminished. Competence in the classroom thus demands both the possession of relevant information and the means to express it, a combination of academic knowledge and interactional skills. The engineering data contain evidence that students often lack either form or content in their interactions and that, although students may detect implicit rules for classroom interactions, they apparently find them either difficult to interpret or difficult to follow.

The task of the questioner in the lecture situation may be formulated as follows:

1. bid for a turn
2. teacher-select or self-select
3. orient backward move
4. indicate difficulty or misunderstanding.

The third step is of particular interest. A student asking a question because of incomplete understanding must indicate the location of the misunderstanding before its nature can be explained. This is particularly important when the question concerns the solving of a problem: The professor may have gone through many steps, and the questioner must take him back to the point of confusion and then ask his question. The necessity for this lies in the wider organisation of the discourse. The professor conducts the problem-solving process so as to make it extremely difficult for the students to intervene and ask questions. After nominating the problem to be solved (posal sequence), the professor moves to the blackboard and works there (solution sequence). Much of the talk is directed over the shoulder, and eye contact is minimal. Although there are pauses in the flow of talk, they almost all occur during blackboard work: sketching a diagram or writing numbers and symbols. As a result of these circumstances, students' attempts at questioning are nearly always unsuccessful when launched during the solution sequence; I frequently observed hands raised, held for a while, and then lowered. Finally, the professor leaves the blackboard having completed the solution sequence, returns to a more accessible location such as the table, and entertains questions.

Here is an example:

[11] **S:** question
 P: yes
 S: erm isn't it true that you actually never have to go through
 that step because er that m the bisector of thater
 P: you mean this bisector
 S: no this one on the other side
 P: this one
 S: yes that should be equal to the half of the er er side of the tri-
 angle because this is a right angled triangle
 P: er half of this
 S: no no half of the bisector of the side half of er ( )
 P: half of this
 S: right

Here the student successfully bids for a turn but encounters some difficulty in establishing the location of her inquiry. When she does so and
articulates the question (roughly, *Can the problem also be solved in this way?*),
it is still not clear that the professor understands it:

[12] **P:** . . . all right that's another way (2.0) but you should always
 come out with the same answer but er what you're saying is
 that this is equal to that
 S: right so that's the equal magnitude of this of er g
 P: in other words you claim that when I bisect this side er that I
 get an equilateral I get an isosceles triangle and why would
 that be
 S: because if you continue that bisector by its own length its =
 the
 P: = here
 S: no no the other
 P: here
 S: yes and then er draw two parallel lines
 P: you mean like this
 S: you get the isosceles tri=angle
 P: =all right another way of doing it (1.0) ok another way of do-
 ing it

Clearly, the students' lack of access to the blackboard makes asking questions even more difficult. In this case, the professor goes to considerable
lengths to make sense of the question. This is normally not the case. A
much more typical case is the following:

[13] **S:** how do you know it's a triangle
   P: what triangle
   S: a b er (2.8) er

Unable to appropriately locate his question, the student gives up. In other cases, the question never gets off the ground at all.

[14] **S:** what's the I don't understand ( )
   P: yes
   S: I just-it's-ni I ( ) problem
   P: you don't speak very clearly do you
   S: no I talk to myself

In addition to these problems, students' questions were often acknowledged in peremptory fashion:

[15] **S:** why did you use w there
   P: I talked about that already

In other cases, in sessions devoted to reviews of midterm examination questions, professors uniformly assumed students' questions to be devoted to soliciting extra points rather than to seeking better understanding.

   To review, students' attempts to ask questions are often incoherent and seem to indicate lack of confidence and expertise. To successfully take a turn and, say, ask a question, the student must be able to:

■ successfully enter the discourse
■ successfully locate that part of the preceding discourse to which the question or comment is relevant
■ successfully express the nature of the misunderstanding
■ convince the professor that the question is asked with appropriate motives
■ be prepared to reformulate or restate part of the turn that the professor does not successfully comprehend.

   Does the difficulty and complexity of this task fully account for the very low rate of response to *Any questions?* I think not. A further issue is the placement of the utterance in the discourse structure. In the discussion of the engineering extracts I postulated a transaction structure based on a linear occurrence of three types of sequence: posal, solution, and evaluation. Although the professor extends evaluative comments to a minority of the exemplars of the latter, most consist of either *ok* (rising intonation) or *Any questions?* I continue to assume that, however abbreviated, these are indeed evaluation sequences.

In discourse terms, then, the meaning of *Any questions?* is an invitation to the students to evaluate the preceding text: in other words, something like, *I have nothing to add in evaluative terms, do you?* Silence would then be a positive evaluation, meaning, *Your solution is perfectly clear.* A question is then a negative evaluation, suggesting a flaw in the professor's exposition.

This analysis corresponds with the findings of a longitudinal ethnography I conducted over the course of a semester as a quasi participant-observer in a mechanical engineering class. (Handicapped by lack of knowledge, my participation was extremely limited; however, my true identity was known only to the professor. To the other students, I was merely a rather inept and ignorant colleague.) Just as Mehan might predict, I witnessed an unspoken process, a covert negotiation, whereby the professor established the discourse rules of the class. He ignored questions or bids for a turn occurring during posal or solution sequences, causing such attempts to cease almost completely after the third week of the semester. Questions asked in the evaluation sequence slot received a response, but often of such a cold, even hostile nature that they became infrequent. Instead of putting their difficulties to the professor, I discovered, students sought help elsewhere: from each other outside class or from the TA.

In summary, then, I interpret the data as follows: By their behaviour, professors limit students' questions to one discourse seam, namely the evaluation sequence. Students ask very few questions, in part because of the difficulties inherent in appropriately formulating one and in part because of the discouraging nature of the response. To an outsider the events surrounding the use of the phrase *Any questions?* might seem like a cruel double bind (*I want you to ask questions and now is the time, but when you do the response may well be a putdown*), but an analysis in discourse terms indicates that the adjacency pair

    Professor: Any questions?
    Class: [silence]

is, particularly for the professor— the controller of the discourse—an entirely appropriate way to conclude a transaction. Once the students come to terms with this and seek to resolve their difficulties and consolidate their learning by other means, the discourse pattern proceeds without interruption.

These facts, and the accompanying speculation, are included here because I believe they carry important implications for the training of ITAs. If native speakers bring to college classes their discourse expertise accumulated from a dozen years in the U.S. educational system and are thus able to quickly and readily detect the professor's covert negotiations, and if they are prepared to quietly deal away their potentially most powerful learning tool—asking real questions and getting serious answers—then ITAs must experience the consequences as they face these same students under apparently identical circumstances.

The Model Revised

General Implications

From studying discourse structures and discourse events, I have become convinced that significant, useful information can be derived and shared with ITAs during training or orientation sessions. This information has implications at various levels. Most generally, I believe it can serve as a useful, perhaps the most useful, means of showing ITAs systematically the realities of communication in U.S. college classrooms. Second, a direct relationship exists between discourse structure and planning lessons. Third, and more specifically, knowledge of typical discourse markers can help instructors as they guide students through the material. Finally, an awareness of discourse events as they reflect the covert negotiation of classroom norms can help ITAs avoid problems and, in fact, by helping them see the need for an *overt* discussion of procedures, can make ITAs effective teachers. By taking responsibility for the form of classroom events, or perhaps by sharing that responsibility with their students, ITAs improve their own classes and can empower students to be more effective in their encounters with other instructors. I have always felt that ITA training could and should be the thin edge of the pedagogic wedge in this regard, with native-speaking TAs and, subsequently, professors being trained to make use of insights from discourse analysis.

I emphasise the restricted nature of these insights. Particularly when supported by classroom observations, the analysis of discourse samples carries a strong ethnographic flavour, which is, as Clifford Geertz has often pointed out, ineluctably local knowledge. Hence the revised model (Figure 1; revisions in italics) is intended to suggest that all ITA training include such analysis as part of the precourse component and, further, that the preteaching cycle include discourse considerations in the analysis of demonstration lessons. Eventually, perhaps, a sufficient number of studies of particular genres of lectures or workshops or seminars will result in widely held generalisations that will be of use to all ITA programmes. In the meantime, in the cause of face validity and fresh relevance, ITAs should be confronted in their training with samples of discourse from the classrooms in which they themselves will go to work.

Discourse Structure

The clearest applications of information about discourse structure in target situations are in setting teaching tasks and in training for lesson planning. Thus ITAs in engineering, whose instruction will include going over problems, can practice—initially as separate tasks—posing the problem, giving the solution, and evaluating the solution. As the training course progresses, these elements can be blended together into a full-length transaction. Similarly, ITAs in business subjects can practice different elements of concept-based transactions.

As the different sequences are stitched together during training, ITAs can also consider the various markers that label the transitions between sequences, first identifying them from demonstrations and videotapes and then practicing in their own teaching. As ITAs develop their repertoire in this regard, I see no problem with offering them fuller, more formal versions so that they can be appropriately explicit (and I take it as a basic maxim here that when nonnative speakers are involved in such discourse situations, more overt and explicit verbal behaviour will help avoid breakdowns in communication):

- Let me present a solution to this problem. [As opposed to *Well* or *Okay*]
- Let me point out why this solution is important.
- Let me restate that definition in a different way.
- Here is an example of that.

In my experience ITAs' early efforts will sound rather stilted and overformal, but such formulae or learned chunks will facilitate the management of the discourse and mark its shape so that the listeners are clearly informed of the speaker's progress through the various transactions that constitute the lecture or discussion.

In addition to this verbal training, various pedagogic devices can ensure that the ITAs' communication is effective. Figure 3 shows a blackboard with two vertical lines drawn about one quarter of the length in from either end. The left-hand space is used for the outline of the day's class and is not erased; rather, as each transaction is completed, the ITA checks it off. Remaining deficiencies in the marking of discourse may thus be offset by this constantly visible outline. This visibility not only proves beneficial to the listener but forces the ITA to pay conscious attention to the shape of the lesson. The right-hand space is for new or unfamiliar words, also left for the duration of the class so that the ITA can accompany further use of the word by a gesture toward the written form. In this case the written form compensates for deficiencies in the

Class outline	Diagrams & calculations	Vocabulary

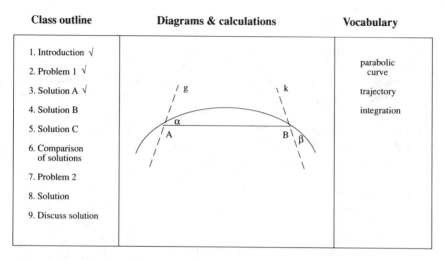

1. Introduction √		parabolic curve
2. Problem 1 √		
3. Solution A √		trajectory
4. Solution B		integration
5. Solution C		
6. Comparison of solutions		
7. Problem 2		
8. Solution		
9. Discuss solution		

Figure 3 ▪ Blackboard organization.

pronunciation by ITAs of such key vocabulary. The central space is used for diagrams and calculations and may be erased and used again.

Discourse Events

The control of ITAs over discourse events is twice weakened from that enjoyed by native-speaking professors: by depreciated status and possibly by lesser linguistic and communicative competence. I suggest that a process of overt negotiation and discussion may redress both weaknesses. Collis and Dalton (1990) suggest that the continuum of classroom leadership styles may be characterised by the following three points. At one end, teacher ownership and control:

- ■ Do as I say.
- ■ I'll decide.

in the middle, shared ownership and control:

- ■ Do as we agree.
- ■ Let's decide together.

and at the other end, student ownership and control:

- ■ Do as you want.
- ■ You decide. (p. 19)

Both ends are dangerous for ITAs—perhaps equally so, with attempts at total control failing as badly as experiments with letting students take charge. If they can be trained, however, to properly engage their classes in negotiated, shared control, ITAs can avoid many subsequent procedural problems. Thus the course begins with open discussion about rules of procedure and behaviour. Suppose, for example, that engineering students indicate a desire to ask questions during a solution sequence. The TA may indicate:

> I agree. It is important for you to ask questions at the time the difficulty arises. However, remember that I will often be at the blackboard drawing and writing. So I suggest that you do not raise your hand but call out "Question." I may sometimes ask you to wait briefly until the end of that particular step but usually I will tell you to go ahead with your question. What do you think? Can we do this without causing chaos?

In return for this share of decision making, students are asked to take responsibility for their own learning and classroom behaviour. Incidentally, in some cases this negotiation may—and should—be extended to content as well as procedure, but that is not my focus here.

In this manner, problems such as the double-bind nature of *Any questions?* can be avoided and ITAs do not struggle with a power-seeking, covert negotiation that they do not understand (or, often, even recognise) and in which they cannot play any functional role. The experience will be a different one for U.S. students, but perhaps a refreshing one that leads not only to effective learning but also to a more conscious realisation of the choices they enjoy as university students. Both instructor and learners are thus empowered by the process.

The Model Revised

Figure 1 incorporates the important and powerful role of discourse that I have come to appreciate from working with different kinds of university classroom data. Indeed, the effects may be even more pervasive than the new boxes and arrows on the diagram suggest. Familiarity with the target discourse will affect the feedback given by trainers, the modeling of presentations, the formal language instruction, and the projects. Lesson planning is enhanced by knowledge of discourse structures; appropriate use of markers guides the listeners through a lecture; thinking about discourse events in advance enables appropriate procedures to be established. Eventually, ITAs will become models to be emulated rather than problems to be retrained or hidden away grading papers; all TAs will be armed with insights from discourse analysis; and eventually professors will, too.

■ 3 ■

Enhancing Curricula for ITA Development

Jan Smith
University of Minnesota

■

Over the past decade, nearly every major university in the United States has established a program for the instruction of international teaching assistants (ITAs). ITA development programs are becoming crucial components of the university teaching mission and as such are ongoing items in university budgets. As graduate schools depend more than ever on international students and graduate students depend more on teaching assistantships, ITA programs will remain an integral part of U.S. university campuses.

ITA educators have worked to establish themselves in the academic community. Two publications document the increasing sophistication of ITA programs (Bailey, Pialorsi, & Zukowski-Faust, 1984; Young, 1989c), and the collected papers from three national conferences on the education and employment of graduate teaching assistants (TAs) highlight the ideas and accomplishments of ITA developers (Chism & Warner, 1987; Nyquist, Abbott, Wulff, & Sprague, 1991; Lewis, 1993). Three textbooks specifically devoted to ITA development have been published (Byrd, Constantinides, & Pennington, 1989; Pica, Barnes, & Finger, 1990; Smith, Meyers, & Burkhalter, 1992), and two sets of videotapes and accompanying materials are now available to aid in the instruction of ITAs (Douglas & Myers, 1990; Wennerstrom, 1991b). These publications demonstrate the commitment on the part of ITA developers to legitimizing their efforts in the eyes of fellow academicians through sound methodology and serious scholarship.

The pioneers of ITA development have been entrepreneurs who rose to a challenge and created programs to fit the needs of each particular campus. The initial success of the programs may leave the impression that no further challenges remain to hold the attention of those who created them, but this is not the case. New effort is needed to refine, enhance, and in some cases totally redesign the programs developed to date so that they continue to operate efficiently and effectively.

In his article on curriculum renewal for ITA development programs,

Young (1990) described three phases in the life of an ITA program: "(a) an initial design phase; (b) a phase of ongoing curriculum reform; and, in the case of some programs, (c) an effort at radical renewal of the existing curriculum" (p. 59). In an effort to identify the changes that have occurred in ITA programs during the first phase of their existence, Young compared early ITA programs as described in Bailey, Pialorsi, and Zukowski-Faust (1984) with the more recently developed programs described in the *English for Specific Purposes* volume that he edited (Young, 1989). In this chapter I extend Young's work into the future to the reform and renewal phases of ITA program development. In doing so, I draw on ideas developed during 10 years of work in ITA development and summarize my beliefs about curricular development for the next generation of ITA programs.

Initially, most ITA development programs have focused on the development of a testing component along with instructional components in spoken language, intercultural communication, and teaching skills. The testing component generally includes a screening instrument and may involve some type of exit criteria. The spoken language component most often concentrates on making the ITA's rhythm, stress, and intonation patterns more intelligible, correcting the pronunciation of key vocabulary from the ITA's field, and encouraging improvements in grammatical accuracy. The intercultural component usually seeks to aid ITAs in becoming aware of U.S. students' expectations of their TAs. The teaching component typically encourages ITAs to teach with organization, clarity, and a sufficient level of redundancy and with the goal of promoting their students' learning even if the ITAs continue to have a foreign accent.

Having successfully created these components, the staff members of an ITA program can focus their time and energy on additional areas that ITA educators have identified as important to continued curriculum development. These areas include

■ the ITA affective domain
■ the incorporation of English for specific purposes (ESP) methodology to direct ITAs in departmentally based needs assessment and to create field- and classroom-specific materials for ITAs to use in practicing the spoken language
■ practice in listening comprehension and interactive skills for the U.S. university classroom
■ attention to the interface between teaching and testing and the need to incorporate performance testing into programmatic exit requirements
■ an examination of the relative benefits of preservice versus inservice ITA programs and the value of postprogram observation and follow-up

- staff training for instructors new to ITA development
- an extension of ITA development programs to meet the needs of nonnative English-speaking university faculty, graduate research assistants, undergraduates entering the job market, and nonnative English-speaking professionals in medical, technical, and business settings.

ITA Affective Domain

Crucial to the willingness of ITAs to participate in and benefit from ITA programs are their attitudes, values, and beliefs about using English to teach at the university level in the United States. Programs that encourage ITAs to take charge of their own development as teachers and as users of English can assist ITAs in examining their assumptions about their teaching roles. By encouraging ITAs to participate in a process of guided introspection and authentic self-development, ITA educators can empower ITAs to make their own choices and to be responsible for them. ITAs can thus prepare to confront a wide variety of instructional situations as independent decision makers who are aware of the consequences of their actions.

Prescriptive approaches to ITA development may force ITAs into adopting behaviors imposed from outside rather than from within. ITAs do not own change that occurs primarily in response to the demands of an ITA development program, and they may easily discontinue the behaviors when the pressure is off. On the other hand, ITAs who are invested in self-development are more likely to be open to permanent change in their teaching. For example, ITAs who see the improved learning that results from incorporating interactive questions into classroom presentations are more likely to continue to interact with students than are ITAs who include interactive questions in their teaching in order to pass the performance test. ITA educators have the opportunity to demonstrate by their own actions that experience teaches more than prescription and that facilitation results in more lasting change than expertise. By promoting self-knowledge and introspection on the part of ITAs and by providing resources that encourage ITAs to continually set goals by which they can assess themselves, the ITA educator can have an important impact on the ITA's development as a teacher and participant in U.S. academic culture (cf. Stenson, Smith, & Perry, 1983).

One way that ITA programs can foster introspective attitudes and a commitment to ongoing self-development is by teaching ITAs effective ways of giving feedback to each other in microteaching situations. Peer feedback is an important skill for ITAs to learn; ITAs who can constructively criticize their peers have made the first step toward effectively monitoring their own teaching performance. Constructive and supportive peer feedback is not part of many of the cultures from which ITAs typically come, but it can be taught. By playing the role of undergraduates for one another in microteaching sessions, ITAs can begin to empathize with their students and look at teaching from the learner's point of view. By identifying the techniques used by their peers that encourage them to try their best, ITAs can sort out which of their own techniques may be most effective with their students. By becoming aware of what types of feedback are most useful for them, ITAs can learn to convey feedback to others in a manner that will promote change. For this to happen, ITA instructors may need to help build group trust and willingness to communicate. They may also need to model appropriate types of feedback, facilitate initial attempts at peer feedback, and continually support individual ITAs and the microteaching group as a whole. ITAs who master the techniques of constructive peer feedback have begun to develop introspective attitudes about their teaching that will help them deal with new situations, take appropriate risks, evaluate their successes, and review and reduce their failures. When ITAs can constructively critique themselves and others, they have begun to strive for excellence in teaching and can be expected to continue the process once they have left the ITA development program.

ITAs who have come to value self-development will also benefit from a self-assessment in which ITA instructors include ITAs in decisions about their own education as teachers. One way is to give consistent and continual feedback about the progress they are making toward goals set by the program or by the ITAs themselves. Such feedback is best given in one-on-one tutorial situations where the ITA and the ITA instructor have developed a sense of trust and cooperation. Another way is for instructors to show a willingness to negotiate with ITAs regarding what they will work on during the program. ITAs who participate in decisions about their instruction have begun to take charge of their own development as teachers and are more likely to continue to assess their teaching performance. ITAs who graduate from programs that include ITAs in the process of their own instruction are more likely to employ what they have learned from the program throughout their teaching careers.

English for Specific Purposes

To instruct ITAs in the language, culture, and pedagogy of the U.S. university classroom is to teach ESP. Thus ITA developers would do well to use the many tools created for ESP needs assessment, such as classroom observation, interviews, and the examination of textbooks, syllabi, and other course materials. Needs must be assessed on two levels: (a) the language of teaching and learning in the U.S. university-level classroom and (b) the specific language, discourse, methodology, and culture of individual academic fields. The basic assumption of the needs assessment is that practicing general language skills alone is not sufficient for learning to use English effectively in the university-level field-specific classroom (cf. Smith, 1992). Field-specific practice in the language of university-level teaching is the most effective way for ITAs to prepare for teaching in their discipline.

Ard (1987) pointed out that the asymmetric nature of teacher-student discourse, among other factors, contributes to the lack of attention that ITAs as students pay to the language of teaching. The student's goal in the classroom is to acquire knowledge of the subject matter, not to note the teacher's language and behavior. In making the transition to the role of teacher, ITAs have difficulty adjusting not only to the language required of teachers, but also that required for a specific teaching context. The language skills required for teaching in a laboratory are very different from those required in a recitation, an office hour, or a lecture (cf. Myers, this volume). In addition, many ITAs are only exposed to professorial classroom language and may not be aware of the more informal language used by many native-speaking TAs.

Rounds (1987a) provided an excellent example of techniques for researching the field-specific discourse of the mathematics classroom. Such research is essential to characterize more fully the field-specific use of vocabulary, grammatical structure, discourse, and rhetorical patterns. Anderson-Hsieh (1990) emphasized the need to effectively use what is known about field-specific language by encouraging practice within the individual ITA's academic field. Smith, Meyers, and Burkhalter (1992) listed field-specific terms, visuals, problems, questions, topics, and passages that can be integrated into the practice of rhetorical tasks. An even more effective method is to ask ITAs themselves to use available entry-level texts in their field for practice with glossaries, indexes, visuals, study questions, problem sets, and passages for reading aloud.

Programs may also ask ITAs to assess their own needs in the teaching roles they are about to assume. Such departmentally based needs assessments can challenge ITAs to examine their values and beliefs about university-level teaching in the United States. By interviewing fellow TAs, professors, and undergraduate students about the expectations placed on TAs within their academic departments, ITAs can gain access to and interact with the individuals who can best help them perform their roles effectively. In addition, they may begin to question their preconceptions of what students and colleagues will expect of them. ITA programs may also want to consider employing experienced TAs from certain academic departments to orient ITAs to the culture of the departments in which they will work. It is only through this hands-on experience that ITAs will begin to internalize important information and form new beliefs about the TA role. Merely conveying information to them about their new environment is not sufficient; personal interaction with students and colleagues is necessary for ITAs to begin to understand the complexities of their new role in the U.S. university classroom.

Classroom Interaction and Listening Comprehension Skills

Effective classroom presentation is only one of several modes required of ITAs. Others include leading discussions, fielding questions, motivating group activities, and one-on-one coaching during office hours. ITAs who are instructed only in presenting information in a lecture format may be unfamiliar with many important English language skills they need to teach in situations requiring interaction with students. These skills may include the ability to (a) understand and respond to the casual English of U.S. undergraduates, (b) ask real rather than rhetorical questions at an appropriate level, (c) provide sufficient time for students to answer, (d) comment constructively in response to wrong answers and give positive feedback to correct answers, (e) assist students in working through answers to problems rather than giving them the answers, (f) encourage students to discuss issues and work together on problems in large and small groups, and (g) use compensation strategies to remedy miscommunications and misunderstandings in the classroom.

Byrd and Constantinides (1988) caution that ITA instructors must take care not to challenge the accepted teaching methodology of a particular academic field. However, those who educate native English-speaking TAs appear to be challenging what was previously accepted as appropriate teaching methodology across the university curriculum. Numerous articles in a recent volume from a conference on the training and employment of graduate teaching assistants (Nyquist, Abbott, Wulff, & Sprague, 1991) have stressed the importance of classroom interaction for effective learning, lamented the current lack of dialogue in university classrooms, and called for improved techniques to promote interaction.

Classroom interaction can be defined as the use of questioning strategies and other techniques to encourage students to hold a dialogue with the instructor and with each other about the subject matter of the class. Interaction should be a part of every university classroom, recitation, lab, and discussion section, and it is the role of the TA to promote this interaction. ITA programs can have an important effect on classroom interaction by encouraging ITAs to use questions to motivate and involve students and to repeatedly check whether students understand the materials presented and discussed. ITA programs may also want to promote interactive classroom techniques as a way to compensate for a lack of oral communication skills. ITAs who use interaction to develop a good sense of their students are more likely to communicate effectively in the classroom.

For ITAs to become proficient in promoting interaction, they must understand the role of discussion in internalizing information, the reluctance of undergraduates to take the risk of contributing in class, the importance of asking specific rather than overly broad questions at an appropriate level of thinking, and the multitude of techniques available to encourage ongoing classroom discussion. ITA programs that intend to encourage ITAs to become proficient in classroom interaction need to instruct them in interactive classroom techniques, offer multiple ways to practice such techniques, and require a demonstration of interactive teaching in the testing process for exit from the program.

To lead classroom discussions or to work with students in small groups or one-on-one, ITAs need to understand what their students are saying to them. Many ITAs are unprepared to understand the reduced speech, colloquial expressions, and slang of undergraduate speech because of their lack of exposure to everyday U.S. English. ITA programs can address the needs of such ITAs through individualized practice in the language laboratory, English-speaking conversation partners who are acquiring the ITAs' native language, or conversation groups organized by the program. The program might also refer ITAs to course work in intensive English programs. Whatever the method, ITA programs must promote ITA understanding and use of colloquial English both inside and outside the classroom.

Testing

ITA developers must examine the interface between testing and teaching in ITA programs. Testing and teaching should be separate activities that reinforce each other. Tests may be used to determine which ITAs need to undergo instruction, how well ITAs have learned what they were taught, or which ITAs need additional instruction before entering the classroom or support as they continue in the classroom.

Most ITA programs have a testing component designed to determine whether ITAs need instruction. Programs must also develop testing components to determine whether ITAs have acquired the skills they need to be ready to teach. Such tests document the program's recommendations for individual ITAs in a manner that more subjective recommendations by instructors cannot. Independent testing measures reinforce instructors' recommendations and can also counteract the natural bias that comes from wishing one's students well.

Many ITA programs have developed teaching performance tests as screening and/or exit devices. These tests have many advantages over tests that only measure spoken English skills (Plakans & Abraham, 1990), although some experts remain unsure of their value (Byrd, 1987). Performance tests at various universities rate ITA language and teaching skills in a real or simulated classroom and one-on-one situations using a variety of techniques (Hinofotis, Bailey, & Stern, 1981; Carrell, Sarwark, & Plakans, 1987; Abraham, Anderson-Hsieh, Douglas, Myers, & Plakans, 1988; Gallego, Goodwin, & Turner, 1991; Hoekje & Linnell, 1991; Simon, 1991; Smith, Meyers, & Burkhalter, 1992). Each test was developed with the resources and needs of a particular campus in mind, but ITA programs may profit from comparing existing tests for the purposes of refining or redeveloping them. The eventual standardization of procedures, descriptors, and scoring across campuses would be of great use in communicating about individual ITA performance and in developing a common standard of what constitutes an acceptable level of skill in language, teaching, and cultural awareness.

Teaching activities should prepare ITAs for the postprogram testing process by giving them an opportunity to practice what they are being asked to learn before they are tested on it. Instructors should provide extensive practice of vocabulary items, rhetorical tasks, and interactive techniques before asking ITAs to demonstrate their newly acquired skills on videotape. Although microteaching sessions may be very similar to the teaching performance test, they should not be seen as testing situations but as opportunities for individual feedback. Videotape should be used carefully so as to encourage rather than threaten ITAs by making sure that evaluation measures give supportive as well as critical feedback. Throughout the program ITAs should be advised of the criteria that will be used to evaluate them, and at the close of the program they should have access to individual documentation of their progress. By making the teaching process more supportive and the testing process more transparent, ITA programs can advocate for the growth and self-esteem of individual ITAs.

Program Models

ITA programs can be categorized as preservice or inservice programs. Preservice programs include intensive programs of more than a week with several hours of instruction per day, orientation programs of a week or less, and quarter- or semesterlong courses before teaching. Inservice programs provide instruction or consultation during a teaching assignment in the form of pronunciation work, microteaching, cultural orientation, and/or limited or extensive in-class observation. Either program model must allow sufficient time for each ITA to develop skills that are good enough for successful classroom performance. Most ITAs need work in pronunciation and/or classroom communication skills, and al-most all would benefit from cultural orientation. Providing opportunities for those most in need of such skills to receive sufficient instruction is crucial. Some ITAs may need instruction beyond the limits of the initial program in pronunciation or teaching skills. Most ITAs would also bene-fit from observation and follow-up during their initial quarter or semester of teaching. This observation can be extensive, with regular consultations between the ITA and the observer, or brief, with limited observation and consultation.

Postprogram observation and follow-up of ITA program graduates can also provide evidence of the program's success in developing effective classroom communication skills in ITAs (cf. Hendel et al., 1993). Sarwark (1991) has suggested that individual departments may wish to request in-class follow-up of ITAs as a group to determine their effectiveness. Follow-up procedures can be important to ITA programs seeking to demonstrate their success in improving the classroom communication skills of ITAs to university administrators, parents, and state legislators.

Staff Training

The current generation of ITA educators created new programs by consolidating existing university resources and working with colleagues across the nation to extend a shared knowledge base into new domains. These individuals were selected by their universities to investigate options for ITA testing and instruction and to implement programs appropriate for their particular campuses. The process of networking with colleagues at conferences, institutes, and symposia was an ideal training experience for those who would direct and instruct in the emerging programs. Through this process it became evident that ITA education differs sig-nificantly from the teaching of ESL or the education of native English-speaking university-level teachers. In particular, ITA education empha-sizes the instruction of ITAs as peers within the university context, while acknowledging important cultural differences related to teaching and learning in the university-level classroom. ITA education also focuses on a level of proficiency in the teaching of oral skills not normally attended to in intensive ESL programs.

Many ITA programs are currently faced with the phenomenon of a new generation of ITA instructors who were not present for the original establishment of the programs in which they work. These individuals may have been trained within the fields of ESL, intercultural communication, second language education, or communication disorders. Despite their excellent qualifications for the position of ITA instructor, their profes-sional education may not have prepared them to assume the attitudes, internalize the methodology, and utilize the techniques of the ITA program in which they are to teach. Hence, newly hired ITA instructors need to be trained. Without training, they may not fully comprehend that the ITAs in their classes, as fellow teachers at the university, are colleagues who know a great deal about their fields but lack English skills and information about their role in the U.S. classroom. New ITA instructors may also be unaware of the specific situations ITAs will confront in the classrooms of different university departments. To further ensure that instructors continue to carry out the ITA program's objectives, the program must pay significant attention to their ongoing professional development. Ideally, this should include regular staff meetings, inservice workshops, and attendance at regional and national conferences frequented by experienced ITA developers.

Future Directions

The ITA program is an excellent way to introduce advanced training in English language communication skills to a broader professional audience. Many university ITA programs now include services for nonnative English-speaking faculty, research assistants and graduate students who are not ITAs, undergraduates entering the job market, and professionals holding positions in medicine, science, technology, and business. The groundwork laid by the ITA development program may allow many English language centers to begin to offer ESP courses in such areas as accent reduction in a professional context, dissertation writing, business writing, telephone skills, and the language of networking and teamwork to many others in need of such services. The University of Michigan's English Language Institute (Morley, 1992) serves as an excellent example of language courses for ITAs offered side by side with a series of courses designed to support graduate students' speaking and writing skills throughout the university. As the need grows for sophisticated communication skills among the many nonnative speakers working in U.S. business, industry, and health care services, such courses are now in high demand by professionals outside the university community. The development of additional advanced proficiency-level course work to serve nonnative English-speaking professionals is an excellent way to further integrate ITA development into the mainstream of the university.

In this chapter I challenge existing ITA programs to evaluate themselves in order to determine whether aspects of their curricula would benefit from refinement or dramatic change. The evaluation may be conducted through a formal review process, outside consultants, an examination of the skill level of ITAs who have participated in the program, or extensive soul-searching by administrators and instructors. The dynamic and inspiring growth of ITA programs over the past decade can serve as the model for a continuing effort to create even more effective program curricula.

Acknowledgments

This chapter is a revision of a paper presented at the Third National Conference on the Training and Employment of Teaching Assistants, Austin, TX, November 1991, and the 26th Annual TESOL Convention, Vancouver, BC, April 1992. My thanks to Karin Smith, Colleen Meyers, and Mark Landa of the Minnesota English Center, who offered excellent feedback on earlier versions of this chapter.

▪ 4 ▪

Using Performance Assessment Methods to Screen ITAs

Sarah L. Briggs
University of Michigan

▪

Many U.S. universities have found that determining whether a nonnative speaker of English has an adequate command of English for the duties of a teaching assistant (TA) requires a special assessment of spoken language abilities. Consequently, several universities have implemented some kind of oral language testing for this purpose. Some universities have recognized further that, to demonstrate their communicative abilities in spoken English, prospective international teaching assistants (ITAs) need to be observed in language use situations similar to those they meet in their roles as TAs. Thus oral testing procedures often include some kind of teaching simulation.[1]

> In performance tests, language knowledge must be demonstrated in the context of tasks and situations which represent or simulate those for which examinees are preparing to use their second language. Such tests are expected to predict how successfully the examinee will be able to communicate using the second language in certain target situations. (Wesche, 1985, p. 1)

Wesche (1987) has suggested that performance tests for second language proficiency testing are only appropriate when the language use situation is identifiable and homogeneous; when the important aspects of language use, namely discourse types, subject matter, and tasks, can be recreated; when scoring criteria reflect the same judgments made in real life; when testing productive skills can be individualized; and when test development allows for systematic attention to test reliability and validity.

In this chapter I focus on the assessment of ITAs via performance tests. I also discuss the evaluation of communication, research on instructor effectiveness, and studies of ITAs at work that are relevant to developing and operationalizing procedures that allow prospective ITAs to demonstrate their communicative abilities.

Constructing a Performance Test

No uniform consensus has emerged on how to determine whether a candidate possesses communicative abilities sufficient to perform the duties of a TA. The complexity of testing ITAs may be attributed, at least in part, to the realization that using language on the job involves the same factors acknowledged as necessary in ITA training courses, namely language, teaching, and cultural competencies. (See, for example, Rice, 1984; Fisher, 1985; Landa, 1988; Constantinides, 1989.) Bailey (1985), in a critical analysis of an oral test she helped develop in the late 1970s, noted that variables other than strictly linguistic ones were significant in how undergraduates rated their TAs. Bailey suggested that those evaluating ITAs keep in mind the reality of a college classroom when designing a performance test for ITAs and choosing the participants, setting, and tasks in the test. She cautioned, however, that a second language performance test that deals with actual language use may in fact assess teaching ability, a skill not necessarily assessed in U.S. TAs. In this regard, Brown, Fishman, and Jones (1989) have expressed concerns that legislated screening of ITAs may have discriminatory implications.

Hoekje and Williams (1992), however, have argued that successful education and assessment of TAs should not take a narrow view of language. They have suggested that emerging models of communicative ability may help resolve the theoretical and practical dilemma of what to include in the ITA curriculum and assessment measures. The theoretical explication of communicative competence set forth by Canale and Swain (1980) has provided a framework for analyzing communication and has widened the scope of the assessment of second language proficiency. In addition to grammatical competence, their conceptualization of communicative competence includes sociolinguistic competence, understanding the social context in which language is used; discourse competence, understanding how utterances form a text; and strategic competence, making the best use of how a language works to negotiate meaning. Canale (1983), in a discussion of how this framework may apply to language teaching and testing, distinguished between communicative competence (viewed as knowledge) and actual communication (viewed as skills).

Bachman (1990) used the term *communicative language ability* to expand a theoretical framework that encompasses both knowledge, or competence, and the capacity of using competence:

> Communicative language ability consists of language compe-
> tence, strategic competence, and psychophysiological mechanisms.
> Language competence includes organizational competence, which
> consists of grammatical and textual competence, and pragmatic com-
> petence, which consists of illocutionary and sociolinguistic compe-
> tence. Strategic competence is seen as the capacity that relates lan-
> guage competence, knowledge of the language, to the language
> user's knowledge structures and the features of the context in which
> communication is taking place. Strategic competence performs as-
> sessment, planning, and execution functions in determining the most
> effective means of achieving a communicative goal. Psychophysiolog-
> ical mechanisms involved in language use characterize the channel
> (auditory, visual) and mode (receptive, productive) in which compe-
> tence is implemented. (pp. 107–108)

Bachman makes a distinction between competence as construct or trait
and test method, which, he posits, can also affect test performance.
Aspects of test method include the testing environment, the way a test
is organized, the specification of procedures and tasks, and facets of the
input and responses, which include authenticity of language use. He
observed that there are two approaches to a persistent problem in language testing: the relationship between the language use required by
test tasks and that required by everyday communicative use of language.
One approach is to design tests that mirror "real-life" language use, and
the other, to attempt to identify the critical features of actual nontest
communicative language use.

What Language Features Should the Tests Cover?

An appeal of performance tests is that testers are encouraged to design
instruments that attempt to mirror or simulate real-life language use.
However, to do this one must know what real-life language use is like
for TAs and recognize, as Bachman and other testing specialists have
noted, that aspects of the test method will affect test performance. Where
evaluators conduct the performance tests, who the participants in the
simulations are, what the tasks are, and how the tasks are described will
affect the authenticity of the language use in the performance tests.
Practical constraints make mirroring the context of the target language
use complex, however, so evaluators must be cautious in generalizing
about what a particular student can or cannot do. Bachman also warned
about making inferences about language ability from performance tests.
For example, a particular ITA may demonstrate that he can coherently
talk through a blackboard diagram of fiber optics transmission, but one

should not assume that the ITA has complete knowledge of the vocabulary of his field, nor can one generalize that he can understand a query from a student on what to do to bring up a lab grade. Consequently, researchers need to monitor whether performance tests have predictive validity, that is, whether the test results correlate well with actual communicative ability demonstrated on the job.

To have predictive validity, tests should sample language similar to that used on the job and test performance should be evaluated according to the same communication factors that are important in instructional encounters with undergraduates. Special attention must be given to the method of evaluation, that is, the tasks prospective ITAs are asked to do and the way their performance of the tasks is rated.

Seminal research on one way to rate ITA test performance was conducted at a large university in California in the late 1970s. Hinofotis, Bailey, and Stern (1981) developed an oral communications rating instrument based on a checklist used in an oral communications skills class. The instrument was piloted as a tool for rating the videotaped performance of prospective ITAs in a teaching simulation. In the task, which was intended to simulate an office-hour situation, the prospective ITA explained a discipline-specific vocabulary term to a mock student played by a communications course instructor, who interacted with the TA and asked questions about the term to get about a 5-minute sample of the TA's language. Through research on the rating instrument, performance behaviors were organized into three main categories: language proficiency, delivery, and communication of information. Each main category contains four subcategories:

Language proficiency
- vocabulary
- grammar
- pronunciation
- flow of speech

Delivery
- eye contact
- other nonverbal aspects
- confidence in manner
- presence

Communication of information
- development of explanation
- use of supporting evidence
- clarity of expression
- ability to relate to student

Pilot raters were asked to determine a numerical rating ranging from 1 (poor) to 9 (excellent) for each of the above categories. They were also asked to rate their overall impression and to decide whether the subject's English was good enough for a TA who would lecture, lead a discussion, or conduct a lab section. In their research on the instrument, the subcategories of grammar, enthusiasm (which they later termed *presence*), and development of explanation seemed to be the principal factors contributing to ratings in the three main categories. They found high interrater reliability for the instrument but large variance in the way raters reacted to the videotaped performances of the nonnative speakers. Hinofotis and Bailey (1981), in using the instrument with undergraduates, found that average ratings were higher than those of the ESL professionals. Both groups ranked pronunciation as the most important factor in the overall rating, but undergraduates ranked the ability to relate subcategory as more important than the ESL teachers did. Bailey (1985) reported that the ESL raters generally rated TAs judged acceptable for TA assignment 7 or higher on the 9-point scale, and those not acceptable, 4 or lower.

Basically, then, rating behavior in performance tests consists of two main aspects: the features to rate (such as language proficiency, delivery, and communication of information) and the gate-keeping purpose of ITA tests. The former is improved when evaluators consider features that are important in communicative language use. The latter refers to judgments about whether a particular individual has demonstrated adequate communicative ability for a particular TA job.

For their instrument, Hinofotis et al. selected certain features of communication that have been used to evaluate communication in an ESL oral communications skills class. Bailey (1985) observed that the three main categories of the instrument seem to parallel three components of communicative competence—linguistic, strategic, and sociolinguistic competence. Her ethnographic research on TAs suggested a high affective influence on TA instructor ratings, and she posited that strategic and sociolinguistic competence may be more important variables than linguistic competence.

I infer from this that the features rated on performance tests are important and that some are more important than others in predicting sustained competence in on-the-job interactions. Faerch, Haastrup, and Phillipson (1984) have been interested in how native speakers react to and assess a second language user's communicative competence. In their model the components of communicative competence include phonology-orthography, grammar, lexis, pragmatics-discourse, communication strategies, and fluency, which are operationalized as performance. They concluded that communicative competence is never independent of social competence, as the expression of speech act modality assumes an ability to identify relevant social roles and their corresponding status. In a tolerance study of learner's English, Faerch et al. (1984) found that all kinds of errors may impair comprehensibility but that discourse errors (i.e., errors involving conjunctions, pronoun references) were more likely to lead to misunderstanding or low comprehensibility. They also found that extensive hesitation related to comprehensibility, that fluency appeared more important than correctness, and that a high density of errors of any type was distracting.

Evaluating Native Speaker Communication

Several clinical models for evaluating the communication of native speakers based on current linguistic theories have emerged in the discipline of speech communication. Simon and Holway (1985) described what they termed a clinician's model of expressive communicative competence. A comprehensive approach developed by Simon includes an assessment of both competent and incompetent features in a functional-pragmatic approach that includes form, function, and style. *Form* is viewed as including syntax and semantics; *function* includes topic maintenance, appropriateness of speech acts, supporting opinions, variation in code, social and cognitive language use, contextual adaptation of language, tactfulness, and the ability to modify and clarify; *style* includes consideration of the listener's information needs, coherent planning of content, ready access to words, fluency in expression, intelligible speech, comfortable speech rate, and volume adaptations to context.

Another approach to clinical discourse analysis was set forth by Damico (1985), who used Grice's speech maxims to categorize language behaviors. He has demonstrated that aspects of ineffective communication can be grouped in ways that may bring to light new patterns in speech performance. *Quantity of discourse* includes insufficient information, nonspecific vocabulary, information redundancy, and need for repetition. *Quality* includes message inaccuracy. *Relation* is poor topic maintenance, inappropriate responses, failure to ask relevant questions, situational inappropriateness, and inappropriate speech style. *Manner* is linguistic nonfluency, revisions, delays before responding, failure to structure discourse, turn-taking difficulty, gaze inefficiency, and inappropriate intonational contours.

Although such models of language evaluation have been developed to diagnose communicative disabilities in native speakers, they offer evidence of the range of performance aspects that may also affect judgments of nonnative speaker performance. ITA evaluators need to continue developing instruments to rate ITAs and to reexamine what the tests assess.

Evaluating College Teaching

Research on effective college teaching has identified several communicative behaviors that correlate with effective teaching. Based on an analysis of observed teaching behaviors of 48 college instructors, Murray (1985) examined several behaviors, which he then categorized through factor analysis. Several behaviors correlated significantly with students' ratings on teacher effectiveness:

Enthusiasm
- speaks expressively or emphatically*
- moves about when lecturing*
- gestures with hands and arms*
- shows facial expression*
- uses humor*
- reads lecture verbatim from notes**

Clarity
- uses concrete examples of concepts
- gives multiple examples of concepts*
- points out practical applications
- stresses important points*
- repeats difficult ideas

Interaction
- addresses students by name*
- encourages student comments*
- talks with students after class
- praises students for good ideas*
- asks questions of class*

Task orientation
- advises students regarding exam
- provides sample exam questions
- proceeds at rapid pace
- digresses from theme of lecture
- states course objectives

Rapport
- friendly, easy to talk with*
- shows concern for student progress*
- offers to help students with problems
- tolerant of others viewpoints

Organization
- puts outline of lecture on board
- uses headings and subheadings
- gives preliminary overview of lecture
- signals transition to new topic*
- explains how each topic fits it

All behaviors marked with an asterisk correlated significantly positively with teaching ratings; the one marked with a double asterisk correlated negatively with the ratings. It is noteworthy that many of the significant observable behaviors reflect how the instructor is using language in the classroom. Overlap is also present in the categories identified by Hinofotis et al. as performance categories on their rating instrument. For example, a subcategory *presence* (called *enthusiasm* on an early version of the instrument) is found on the ITA rating instrument, and Murray identified a whole category called *enthusiasm*. All the behaviors in this category were identified as significantly correlated with effective teaching. Language may not be separable from teaching in examining language use for instructional tasks.

Some elements on the list of effective college teaching behaviors might be added to an instrument for rating ITA performance—for example, the behaviors in the category *interaction*. Evaluators must be explicit about all language behaviors that may influence judgments of overall performance.

Models for Evaluating ITAs

The rating criteria for the Test of Spoken English (TSE)–Speaking Proficiency in English Assessment Kit (SPEAK)[2] and the Hinofotis et al. communications rating instrument have influenced the development of other rating instruments for ITAs. The Taped Evaluation of Assistants' Classroom Handling (TEACH), created at Iowa State University in 1985 and discussed in Plakans and Abraham (1990), uses the TSE-SPEAK scale of 0 to 3 to score each performance on 4 categories and 14 subcategories:

Overall language comprehensibility
- pronunciation
- grammar
- fluency

Cultural ability
- familiarity with cultural code
- appropriate nonverbal behavior
- appropriate register

Listening and question-handling ability
■ basic listening ability
■ question handling and responding

Lecturing and teaching ability
■ development of explanation
■ clarity of expression
■ use of supporting evidence
■ eye contact
■ use of chalkboard
■ teacher presence

In addition to the performance categories, raters give their overall impression of the ITA and make recommendations about the type of teaching assignment the TA can take on.

In the TEACH, a teaching simulation, the prospective ITA explains a topic to an audience of three students, two raters, and a test proctor while a technician videotapes the procedure. The raters are ESL or speech instructors. Abraham and Plakans (1988) reported that their use of a teaching simulation combined with a general measure of speaking ability has resulted in fewer complaints to university departments about the speaking ability of those who passed the screening. In addition, nonnative-speaking TAs received above-average ratings from their undergraduate students, though ratings of acceptable classroom performance were lower than those of native-speaking TAs.

Smith, Meyers, and Burkhalter (1992) have developed a rating instrument for ITA tests given at the end of a training course for ITAs. ITAs are asked to present 5 minutes of field-specific instructional information and then to answer questions from a panel of instructors. The panel is composed of ITA instructors, representatives of the graduate student's department, university administrators, and undergraduate students. The authors acknowledged inspiration from the TEACH and have adopted SPEAK-type criteria and scales for rating performance. The rating instrument is similar to the TEACH; one noteworthy difference is that language performance behaviors (pronunciation, grammar, fluency, comprehensibility) are rated twice, once in relation to presentations and again in relation to interactive language use:

Presentation language skills
■ pronunciation
■ grammar
■ fluency
■ comprehensibility

Teaching skills
- organization of presentation
- clarity of presentation
- relevance of content
- use of blackboard and visuals
- manner of speaking
- nonverbal communication
- audience awareness
- interaction
- teacher presence
- aural comprehension
- method of handling questions
- clarity of response to questions

Interactive skills
- pronunciation
- grammar
- fluency
- comprehensibility

Evaluator's overall impression

Rating instruments reflect the variations in tasks ITAs are asked to do in the test situation. Importantly, TAs demonstrate different language skills in different tasks. The features included in the Smith et al. rating instrument suggest that raters can observe, for example, different pronunciation when an ITA is presenting than when he or she is answering questions.

Also relevant here is that systematic investigation of the range of duties assumed by TAs has revealed that native speakers may need to enhance their communication skills to perform effectively. Gray and Buerkel-Rothfuss (1991) reported that the TAs they have surveyed particularly want training in interaction-based activities such as giving and accepting criticism, handling upset students, and saying "no" to students. Even U.S. TAs seem to recognize that aspects of teaching other than presentation skills enhance their effectiveness as TAs.

If ITA performance tests actually reflect real-life language use, then it seems logical to incorporate interactive language use in tests. Prospective ITAs should have an opportunity to demonstrate their language use in varied tasks that reveal the range of their abilities.

The training and testing of ITAs has provided a unique opportunity in higher education in the United States: to follow nonnative speakers into a language use situation and observe their effectiveness. At best, a symbiotic relationship can exist between the education and the evaluation of ITAs. Researchers can probably learn most from carefully observing those who examine the communicative effectiveness, and ineffectiveness at times, of ITAs who have assumed TA positions on U.S. campuses. (See, for example, Axelson & Madden, this volume; Bailey, 1982; Shaw & Bailey, 1990; Gillette, 1982; Gillespie, 1988; Katchen, 1990; Langham, 1989; Myers & Plakans, 1991; and Rounds, 1986, for observations and analyses of ITAs in typical ITA positions in economics, science labs, and mathematics sections.) Researchers are just beginning to appreciate how much assignments vary from one department to another and how the dynamics of the setting and the participants seem to affect the communicative demands on TAs.

The University of Michigan's Performance Test

Format

In the 10 years I have been involved in the operation of a performance test for ITAs at the University of Michigan, the discourse tasks, the specification of the tasks, and the rating scheme have undergone continual alteration. The initial tests required only that the potential TA deliver a minilecture for a panel of evaluators composed of two staff members from the English Language Institute (ELI) and a faculty member from the department in which the graduate student might work. Over a 2-year period, based on a follow-up investigation (Kulik, Kulik, Cole, & Briggs, 1985) of how well those approved for TA duties performed as TAs and further analysis of TA responsibilities, the tasks were expanded to include questions from the audience during the minilesson, a warm-up background interview with one of the evaluators, a role play involving an office-hour-type problem, and a videotaped question-handling task.

We changed the ITA performance test tasks because including only a lesson presentation task frequently resulted in canned, rehearsed performances, particularly after an ITA skills improvement course. The speech sample did not adequately predict the range of functions related to actual performance as a TA. The office-hour role-play situations and listening task were added to the test procedure because of the relevance of assessing the one-on-one communication skills and aural comprehension facility of prospective TAs.

Generally, all the evaluators participate in the test. One of the ESL professionals usually conducts the initial background interview, but often the other evaluators ask additional questions for clarification or to seek other information. All the evaluators, particularly the representative from the prospective TA's department, ask field-specific questions during the lesson task. In the office-hour simulation, one of the ESL professionals (usually the youngest and the one who looks most like a student) pretends to be a student in the prospective TA's section and presents the ITA with two problems: one related to the subject matter presented by the TA in the lesson task, and the other a personal problem for which the "student" seeks advice.

Undergraduates from a student government organization have occasionally been included in the evaluation panel for some tests, but scheduling constraints have made it difficult to routinely include undergraduates except as speakers of the videotaped questions for the question-handling task. ITA tests are conducted throughout the school year, often on short notice. Getting even four people together—a faculty member from the prospective TA's department, two ELI staff, and a graduate student—prospective TA—has sometimes proven difficult. Practical considerations must sometimes override authenticity, but a follow-up survey of ITAs showed that most perceive the teaching simulations as reasonable. When the occasional ITA has obvious difficulty with the simulations, it is generally easy to determine whether the difficulty is the result of linguistic limitations or a matter of personality or style. In the latter cases, an ITA has an opportunity to demonstrate authentic language use in the opening interview in numerous procedural aspects of the test. One of the advantages of individual performance tests that last 20–25 minutes is that the evaluators have an opportunity to observe language use for an extended period of time.

Rating Instrument

Evaluators are encouraged to note salient features of task performance on an open-ended rating form. The ESL professionals are all experienced in ITA language assessment and/or instruction, and the department representative may have had prior experience with the test procedure. An open-ended note-taking instrument has worked well; it requires minimal training to use and encourages documentation that the evaluators can use later in deciding on the rating and to provide written feedback to the student and the department about test performance. TA tests are occasionally, but not routinely, audiotaped or videotaped.

Raters' Judgments

Research on second language proficiency assessment and from research on ITAs specifically has shown that raters will react differently to different nonnative speakers. As mentioned, Hinofotis et al. (1981) reported that undergraduates rated factors of test performance differently than ESL professionals did. However, what is particularly important for ITA tests is how different raters judge the overall performance of an ITA in deciding whether the prospective ITA should be approved for TA duties. Abraham and Plakans (1988) have reported that departments at their university received fewer complaints about the speaking ability of TAs after the introduction of a teaching simulation performance test. Briggs and Hofer (1991), examining end-of-term undergraduate ratings of new TAs in chemistry, economics, and mathematics, reported that ITAs on average were perceived as positively on teaching and clarity of material presentation as their U.S. counterparts were. All the ITAs in the study had participated in mandated ITA training and performance test screening, and, significantly, TA training for the U.S. TAs is also mandated at the large public university where the study was conducted.

Courchene and de Bagheera (1985), in a discussion of a theoretical framework for the development of performance tests, have noted that expert and naive judges may not view performance in the same way. The raters can be reminded to attempt to keep in mind how undergraduates might view a particular nonnative graduate student as a TA. Observation of live performance tests seems to encourage evaluators to focus on how something is said and what is said rather than only on the form. Because most TA tests are conducted for assignments in engineering, mathematics, or the sciences, the limited background knowledge of the ELI evaluators allows them to realistically assume the role of naive— sometimes perhaps too naive—undergraduates. Faculty representatives, however, are often quite adept in asking the type of question a student might ask about the material.

Judging Different Types of Language Use

Tests can be designed to include multisampling of interactive language use. Within the context of a university and the roles TAs assume, effective interactive language use, including good aural comprehension, appears crucial to job success. A warm-up oral interview lasting just a few minutes can let the evaluators and the ITA become accustomed to each other's articulation and voice quality. From the interview evaluators can also judge the ITA's transactional ability (providing background information), fluency, and intelligibility, and can note whether the ITA becomes an active participant in the oral interaction. In addition, an effective screening test needs evidence of an ITA's ability to produce extended heuristic discourse (language for teaching purposes).

Evaluators can distinguish between language use that consists only of stating propositions and facts and language use that is heuristic. Departmental evaluators often are impressed with people who show more heuristic discourse in the minilesson task. Less effective is display discourse, the kind of language more appropriate for a demonstration of how much one knows about a topic. Some ITAs attempt real interactive teaching styles in the lesson task, and departmental evaluators generally view such an approach favorably but do not necessarily expect an interactive teaching style. ITAs are expected to be able to grasp questions from the audience or negotiate understanding of the questions and to respond appropriately within the context of the task. Occasionally, department representatives notice what they term significant limitations in technical or semitechnical knowledge in a lesson or office-hour role interaction about subject matter presented in the ITA's lesson. However, such observations in isolation do not result in a candidate's not being approved for a TA position.

Yet, through the substance of the discourse, the user's world knowledge becomes evident in performance tests in which ITAs talk about discipline-specific subject matter. Such tests may tap into what Bachman (1990) called *strategic competence*: an aspect of communicative language ability that is a capacity mobilized in the context of language use. To communicate, a prospective ITA, like anyone using language to communicate, must use general knowledge structures along with language knowledge. Language tests that allow ITAs to demonstrate their communicative language ability will also allow them to demonstrate their knowledge of the real world. A test that does not allow ITAs to tap into their knowledge of the world may restrict them from demonstrating their communicative language ability.

An office-hour simulation and a task in which an ITA responds to typical undergraduate questions can provide further information about the ITA's interactive language use. Such tasks demonstrate an ITA's general grammatical (used in the broader sense of linguistic repertoire) and pragmatic (functional and sociolinguistic) ability as well as ability in language production.

An analysis of the evaluators' notes on some 350 ITA tests conducted in 1987 and 1988 revealed that individual evaluators made notes on a variety of aspects of an ITA's test performance. Comments fell into the following general categories:

- linguistic repertoire
- aural processing and comprehension
- speech production
- functional language use
- instructional context awareness
- interactive communicative behavior (verbal and nonverbal)
- behaviors to promote good communication
- behaviors for handling gaps in linguistic repertoire.

The categories deal with language use in a broad sense. The evaluators seemed to have observed communicative language ability in the test situation; the categories seem to reflect the performance of language competence (grammatical, textual, illocutionary, and sociolinguistic) as well as strategic competence.

Arriving at a Rating

To arrive at a consensus on a score or rating of overall performance on the test, the evaluators discuss their observations immediately following the test. The main question they consider is whether the particular graduate student's communicative abilities are adequate to perform TA duties in the department. Examinees receive an overall rating (5 is high, 1 is low, 4 is the minimally acceptable rating for a TA assignment). Scale descriptors of performance at different levels provide a criterion for reference in assigning various ratings. General descriptions were developed based on performance observed in the first few years of the test's administration.

Recently, the questions below were added to the evaluation rating form in an effort to focus raters' attention on aspects of communicative effectiveness so that ITAs not viewed as effective would not be approved for TA assignments:

Task 1 (oral interview about background)
1. After a few minutes, was the speech clear and intelligible?
2. Did the TA provide sufficient responses to the interviewers' questions?
3. Were the responses comprehensible?
4. Was the TA able to explain clearly his research or what he is studying?
5. Did the TA take the initiative and become a participant rather than simply a responder?

Task 2 (minilesson and audience questions)
1. Was the point of the lesson understandable?
2. Was the lesson engaging?
3. Did the lesson flow in a coherent way?
4. Did boardwork promote better communication?
5. Was contact maintained with the "audience"?
6. Were audience questions understood?
7. Were they responded to adequately?
8. Was the speech clear and intelligible?

Task 3 (office-hour role play)
1. Was the "student's" confusion about the subject matter understood?
2. If not, did the TA probe for clarification?
3. Was the problem eventually addressed?

4. Was the response clear, and did it vary from how the information might have been presented in the lesson?
5. Did the TA confirm that the response was being understood by the student?
6. Did the TA grasp the real nature of the student's personal problem?
7. Did the TA offer appropriate guidance for the context of the problem?
8. Was the TA's speech understandable?

Task 4 (handling videotaped questions)
1. Were at least 75% of the cues understood?
2. Were responses relatively quick and on-target in substance?
3. Did the responses show that the question had been correctly understood?
4. Did the TA grasp the colloquialisms and student talk in the cues?
5. Did the TA know when he had understood and when he had not?

Overall
1. Does the TA appear capable in role?
2. Would you want this person for your TA?

Raters continue to make open notes, but after each test task they are asked to consider individually whether they perceive performance in the task negatively or positively.

Preliminary analysis suggests that the questions served their intended purpose of helping evaluators arrive at valid decisions about the performance, but some raters commented that they did not always feel comfortable responding with a "yes" or "no" to the questions. The test developers initially decided not to use a Likert-type scale because the purpose of the questions was to help evaluators arrive at appropriate final decisions. Some evidence showed that in the past a few ITAs who had exhibited communication limitations in all the test tasks had in fact been approved for assignments. Follow-up on the students as TAs had indicated that most had frequent difficulties communicating with their students and supervisors. Consistent negative reactions by test evaluators predict negative reactions from undergraduates.

One intriguing aspect of rating test performance that has emerged is a recognition that using level descriptors is indeed problematic. The communicative ability necessary for working in a inorganic chemistry lab is different than that needed to explain problems in an introductory microeconomics recitation section. An examination of hundreds of reports and evaluators' notes from tests conducted in the past 3 years has confirmed this. The individual profile of one TA rated 4−, the minimal approval rating, may differ significantly from that of another rated 4 in another discipline. Thus general descriptions of test performance appear to serve only as guidelines, not as strict criteria. Profile descriptions by rating level need to be developed task by task and then related to instructional assignment discipline by discipline.

With reference to the salient categories on which evaluators most often take notes, speech production and language use along with limitations in linguistic repertoire appear most discernible in students rated low on the test and not approved for assignments. Other aspects of communicative language ability are most noted as positive attributes in the rating of those approved for assignments and as negative aspects of performance of those almost approved (a 3 rating) or those approved only for specific TA assignments (a 4 rating). Some prospective ITAs who give a reasonably coherent presentation may be rated 3 because of an overriding factor of speech production—fluency, intelligibility, or distracting prosodic features. Additionally, speech production may appear adequate in its transactional nature (getting the main message across), but the office-hour and question-handling tasks may reveal an inability to handle unpredictable one-on-one situations with facility.

Conclusion

Bachman (1990) and others have suggested that language testers should examine nontest language use when developing performance tests. In this case, the approach would be to examine effective use of language by TAs on the job as a basis for developing rating criteria. In fact, these criteria may already exist in the minds of the evaluators because, as mentioned, evidence exists that the procedure itself works. However, it may only work when evaluators know what various TA roles actually demand.

To make the criteria explicit requires using intuition about language use and examining the language tasks demanded of TAs and the level of facility at which TAs are expected to perform them. Myers and Plakans (1991) have shown that ITAs in science labs must communicate in challenging situations. Such research suggests that TAs working in lab settings must understand colloquial language use to be effective, must know how to give directives to maintain discipline, and must know how to reframe questions so that they serve an instructional role. Perhaps testers should focus their attention on how effective nonnative speakers actually communicate in their TA roles. Although native speaker performance can guide testers, a more realistic model appears to be effective nonnative speakers, particularly those from the linguistic and cultural backgrounds of the majority of current ITAs. Evidence shows that undergraduates' perceptions of ITAs vary depending on the perceived ethnographic background of the ITA (Brown, 1988).

One important benefit of performance tests for ITAs is that they can provide comprehensive information about an individual's spoken English. The information can be used to recommend appropriate language training and collectively to help decide the kinds of language courses needed and the focus of particular courses. Universities can develop courses that help prospective ITAs develop the communicative language abilities they need to work as TAs.

Performance tests that evaluate whether students have adequate communicative ability in English to assume TA duties work well if evaluators continually monitor and adjust how they test and what they look at in the tests. Evaluators apparently can recreate, at least to some extent, the language use situations the TA will encounter on the job. However, because there is much evidence that those situations vary from department to department and within departments, performance tests must contain flexible tasks. Scoring criteria need to be revised as evaluators learn more about communicative language ability, and ITA performance tests may lead to a better understanding of the communicative language ability needs of ITAs. Evaluators can incorporate theory and practice from varied sources to improve performance tests.

In training programs, evaluators who work with ITAs in teaching roles have the opportunity to determine whether the behavior observed in a test situation is actualized in real life. If test observations are accurate, then testing can help inform training, and test results can help evaluators focus their efforts on aspects of language use that are amenable to improvement; if test observations are inaccurate, evaluators can use what they learn about communicative effectiveness on the job to help redesign test tasks and the criteria used to make decisions.

Notes

1. A survey of U.S. universities by Johncock (1991) revealed that the SPEAK is used widely as a screening measure for ITAs, though the majority reported requiring additional oral testing procedures for ITAs.

2. The TSE and its institutional version, the SPEAK, were developed by the Educational Testing Service in response to the expressed needs of universities and other educational organizations for an instrument that assesses the speaking ability of nonnative speakers. That many institutions supplement the TSE and SPEAK with other measures suggests a practical recognition that pronunciation, grammar, fluency, and overall comprehensibility ratings based on audiotaped responses on a series of structured tasks do not completely assess the communicative ability of a prospective TA.

II
.
Discourse

■ 5 ■

Question-Based Discourse in Science Labs: Issues for ITAs

Cynthia L. Myers
Iowa State University

■

Traditionally, programs for training international teaching assistants (ITAs) have focused on a broad set of skills or strategies assumed helpful for success in the undergraduate classroom. ITA programs have typically incorporated cultural materials about the U.S. university environment, pedagogical methods, and linguistic training (Barnes, Finger, Hoekje, & Ruffin, 1989; Schneider & Stevens, 1987; Smith, 1987; Smith, Byrd, Constantinides, & Barrett, 1991). However, as yet no precise description exists of the skills TAs need for all the varied environments in which they teach. Pedagogical strategies appropriate for a recitation may not be appropriate for a lecture, and the academic culture and the resulting roles of teacher and student may also differ among the environments of office hour, lab, and discussion class. The discourse used in different pedagogical settings presents different challenges for an ITA. Ard (1989), for example, noted differences between the speech genres of college classrooms and the genres of textbooks or informal conversation, with which ITAs may be more familiar. Thus research into specific academic disciplines is needed to inform ITA training (Kaplan, 1989; Byrd & Constantinides, 1988).

Some researchers have begun to provide insights into academic disciplines. For instance, Rounds (1986, 1987a) has examined TAs teaching math recitation classes, and Byrd and Constantinides (1992) have described data collected from professors in the same field. Shaw (1985), who examined engineering professors, and Tanner (1991b), who compared native and nonnative TAs in chemistry labs, also have contributed to an understanding of specific academic discourse communities. Continued research in these areas can help more clearly define the specific needs of the ITA, teaching in a certain environment within the constraints of a certain field.

This study analyzes one such environment—the teaching lab—in

■ 83 ■

which the ITA's role differs from that in classroom teaching. The lab is of particular interest not only because it is a frequent assignment for ITAs, but because ITAs with marginal English proficiency have sometimes been allowed to serve as lab assistants but not as classroom teachers. Lab teaching, the assumption has been, is less demanding than classroom teaching; however, the demands of the lab are not always simple. Unlike the classroom, which tends to be "a constant, ritualized, stylized environment" (Stubbs, 1983, p. 63), the lab is diverse, and communication is not always predictable. Lab assistants must not only understand and be able to explain the procedure of an experiment, but also explain and enforce safety regulations (Barnes & van Naerssen, 1991), perform administrative responsibilities including managing time and people (Tanner, 1991b), have a working knowledge of the apparatus and the ability to describe it, be able to adjust apparatus that is malfunctioning, possess the flexibility and negotiating ability to answer frequent and poorly articulated student questions, and have the insight and initiative to formulate questions that will facilitate their students' learning. Thus the lab makes many demands on an ITA's linguistic and pedagogical abilities.

Background

The data described here were collected as part of a project designed to provide a clearer picture of the requirements for lab teaching (Myers & Plakans, 1990, 1991). Thirty-five ITAs were observed teaching labs in eight departments at Iowa State University, and their duties were catalogued. A few of the ITAs were recommended as particularly effective and experienced teachers, more were relatively inexperienced, and some were teaching for the first time. Most had passed the university screening program for nonnative TAs, though some had taken or were currently enrolled in sections of the ITA training program. Audiotapes of five of the labs taught by new ITAs were transcribed and analyzed as a way of closely examining lab discourse. (I describe the five ITAs observed in more detail in the section on TA discourse.)

From these data, question patterns in lab communication were chosen for analysis. The first section of the chapter describes features of student questions that pose difficulties for some ITAs, including the students' assumptions of shared context and the problem-solving nature of student talk. The second section discusses the ITAs' discourse, focusing on the functions of questions that lab assistants ask their students. Effective ITAs appear to use questions differently than do those who are less effective, both in quantity and in question type.

Student Discourse

In some labs, students frequently ask questions, often averaging more than one per minute in freshman or sophomore classes for nonmajors. Rounds (1990) found that students asked relatively few questions in math recitations—fewer than six per class period for four of her five observations. In labs, however, students asked many more questions: In the five tape-recorded labs studied, the number of student questions ranged from 56 to 168 during 90 minutes of taping. Because of the frequency of students' questions, lab assistants have an opportunity to interact one-on-one with their students and to personalize their teaching. But students' questions can challenge the inexperienced or less fluent ITA.

In the lab ITAs relinquish the control they have in a more traditional classroom setting. Lab assistants cannot fall back on the familiar three-part interaction, described by classroom researchers as initiation / reply / feedback (Sinclair & Coulthard, 1975), or initiation / reply / evaluation (Mehan, 1979b). Implicit in these descriptions of teacher-student interaction is the assumption that the teacher will control the discourse by introducing the topic and evaluating the students' responses. However, TAs in the lab do not control the topic of discourse as they might in the recitation or lecture; instead the students frequently initiate interaction and control the discourse topic. Lab assistants move from one student's questions to another's, and the questions demand that they shift rapidly from giving advice to giving instructions, from answering physical questions about the apparatus to responding to questions about course requirements, from offering praise to giving criticism. Unlike the lecture, the lab offers a dynamic interaction, a linguistic challenge for the ITA.

Perception of Shared Context

Discourse in an ordinary class or discussion section tends to be highly context embedded: The teacher and students share assumptions, for the most part, about what is being discussed. As a result, students' questions may be grammatically abbreviated and contain unspecified references. For example, McKenna (1987) noticed reduction, elision, and substitution in students' questions in a study of student-teacher interaction in lectures and review sessions for a phonetics course. Students often phrased questions in reduced form because of the "shared presuppositions about what was at the center of attention" (p. 193). Thus the topic of discussion in a recitation or lecture forms a context for student questions so that, when students interrupt with abbreviated questions, the teacher usually understands their questions in spite of their reduced form. More evidence for this is seen in videotaped data from an engineering recitation class (Douglas & Myers, 1990). As a TA in a fluid dynamics class was explaining *rotating flow field*, a student interrupted with, "Where do you find that?" The teacher inferred with no difficulty that the *that* referred to a rotating flow freeld and that the student wanted to know where the flow field could be found in the real world.

One might assume that this situation also exists in the lab. The context would be the experiment itself, as well as the apparatus, the microscopic slide, the computer screen, or the calculations. The difficulty for the ITA arises because discourse in the lab is not actually as context embedded as it appears: Questions tend to be disconnected, interrupted, and unpredictable rather than part of an extended dialogue in which context has been developed. The lab assistant must move from one student to another, each with a different problem, and students may not phrase their questions in a way that orients the lab assistant to the nature of those differences. Thus lab assistants must have in mind a variety of problems a student might be having and must negotiate until they are certain which problem it is. In the lab, the out-of-context question *Where do you find that?* may mean *I can't find the correct setting on the oscilloscope, Where should I look in the lab manual to find a description of the procedure?* or *Where can I find the right equation?* ITAs need to know which question the student is asking before they can respond adequately.

Although not all ITAs in the study had difficulty with this feature of lab discourse, some occasionally answered a different question from the one a student was asking or never entirely understood a question at all. For example, in the lab transcribed in Excerpt 1, the student was looking into a container containing both hydras, the tiny aquatic organisms he was supposed to observe under the microscope, and dead, brown *Daphnia*, the prey on which the hydra had been feeding.

[1] S: where d' ya see these things at—is it the brown things?
    T: the—do you remember the lab for nutritionable something like a filter feed—yeah *Daphnia* was in there—the last lab too
    S: so that's
    T: you know—the hydra you know has a tentacle right?
    S: yeah
    T: uh in which uh you know there are as I told you the nematocyst the nematocyst comes out—you know? to kill the prey here *Daphnia*
    S: where are they at in here?
    T: hydra?
    S: yeah
    T: in the bottle—so
    S: is it those little brown things?

> **T:** no no no—brown things is *Daphnia*—you know—just prey for /hydra
> **S2:** /just dead meat
> **T:** they dead already because—uh by the hydra—you know?

Although the ITA and student had a "shared presupposition" that they were discussing the contents of the container, the ITA failed to answer the student's question directly, assuming a different context for his explanation. The student's question, "Where d' ya see these things at?" meant *Where can I find the hydra?* or even *How can I remove the hydra from the jar?* The ITA's response, however, focused on the predator-prey relationship between the hydra and *Daphnia*. The student substituted *these things* for a more specific reference, and his assumption of shared context probably contributed to the ITA's comprehension difficulty.

Students' assumption of shared context is also evident in the absence of framing prefaces for their questions. In Plakans' (1987) research into questions asked in a teaching simulation test, nonnative teachers had less difficulty comprehending and answering questions introduced with phrases like *I've got a question about the final* or *May I ask you something about our homework?* This kind of framing preface is fairly common when students ask questions of teachers in the classroom, especially when they have to interrupt the teacher to ask a question. McKenna (1987) observed in lecture classes that students would signal the lecturer for a turn to talk and that their interruptions were often framed with apologetic comments like *Excuse me, I have a question. . . .*

The environment of the lab is very different from that of the lecture. Students do not apologize for interrupting, nor do they help orient the ITA by contextualizing their problems with phrases like *I have a question about the structure of the mesidermis* or *Could you tell me about the electrical setup here?* Instead students tend to blurt out what is bothering them as soon as they glimpse the TA nearing the bench and seldom use even general prefaces like *I've got a question* or *Could you tell me something?* In one transcribed lab, the only time a student used a preface during the 90 minutes of observation was when one said, "Can I borrow you for a minute?" The ITA didn't understand her.

Another function of the students' perception of shared context in the lab is the informality of communication there. Students speak to their lab partner about problems with the experiment in the same way they would talk about last night's basketball game; then they turn to talk to the ITA in the same register, again without contextualizing their comments for the TA. Slang and idioms are common.

In one zoology lab, a student asked the ITA, ". . . ya get a needle for the hydra? to poke that dude?" Uncomprehending, the ITA responded,

"Needle?" A few seconds later, after finding his dissecting needle, the same student said to his lab partner, "Here Tim, go for it—see what happens to that little bugger—poke him on the tentacles." Although the ITA attempted to join in the interaction ("Basically *Cnidaria* is a tentacle feeder—but I think that *Aurelia* is a filter feeder."), the students ignored him. Here the ITA responded to the words he knew, *needle* and *tentacles*, but did not succeed in entering into dialogue with the student. The ITA's formal register and his inability to put his comments in context did not match the informality of the students' speech.

Sometimes the informality of students' language provides an opportunity for the ITA to learn lexical items. In the lab transcribed in Excerpt 2 a student in a chemistry lab asked the ITA how to insert a large piece of filter paper into a small crucible. When the ITA struggled to find the words to tell her what to do, she helped him find the right expression.

[2] **S:** is this not right yet?
　　T: let me think—ah—ah stop—let's modify our setup—crumble—crumble—crumble? right? crumble—crumble your paper to
　　S: squish / it down?
　　T: 　　　　　/ to skiss it down
　　S2: do you want the paper above?
　　S1: like that?
　　T: like that—like like this—crumble
　　　　　/ oh crumble your sample
　　S1: / squish it?
　　S2: / all the paper in there?
　　T: skish? squiss?
　　S: squish [laughs]
　　T: squish—squish yeah squish—squish it
　　S: [laughs]
　　T: squish it into the into the crucible
　　S: squish is good

The ITA had to negotiate repeatedly to understand the word *squish* but a few minutes later suggested to another student that she should also "squish" her filter paper.

Student discourse tends to be informal regardless of the setting; ITAs teaching in discussion sections must also comprehend unfamiliar idioms and slang. However, the lab setting, with its task-oriented, pragmatic, roll-up-your-sleeves atmosphere, especially encourages an informal register and can challenge an ITA trying to communicate with students. Many nonnative TAs deal with the informality effectively, learning or at least comprehending their students' slang, but other ITAs have more difficulty. The informality of student talk is simply another aspect of lab discourse that reveals a perception of shared context on the part of the students.

Problem Solving

A second general feature of student discourse is the students' involvement in solving problems in the lab, and their talk is often stream of consciousness as they think aloud. This feature encourages question-answer sequences in which the students add information to the ITA's explanation or interrupt the ITA to suggest ideas or even to answer their own questions. The resulting discourse contains joint linguistic constructions created simultaneously across turns by both student and TA:

[3] **S:** what's the difference between burning and charring?
　　T: burning / is has
　　S:　　　　　/ starts on / fire?
　　T:　　　　　　　　　　/ has fire flame, but charring
　　　　/ just some
　　S: / turn black
　　T: turn black and maybe some gas gas is evolved

Here the student answered her own question while getting confirmation from the ITA that her assumptions were correct. Ideally, labs should work that way, the students arriving at their own accurate conclusions as they proceed through the experiment. However, students frequently make incorrect assumptions about the problems they are having. The students in a chemistry lab theorized about the reasons for the readings they were seeing on their voltmeter; their questions show them thinking aloud as they suggested reasons for their problem:

[4] **S1:** I had a question—OK?—we can't get this measured correctly
　　S2: I mean it jumps all over the place
　　T: yeah—I know—I can't understand why
　　S1: is that hooked up correctly?
　　T: / that is—yeah
　　S1: / do we have the right solutions?
　　T: yeah—why don't you let it settle for awhile and then it should uh it / should reach
　　S2:　　　　/ it should be quite a
　　　　bit lower than that?
　　T: yeah it should
　　S2: it still should be positive though, right?

T: positive?
S2: it should be, right?
T: no, because this is going to be your cathode, which is the nega-
tive, right? the cathode is the reduction

In any series of questions like that in Excerpt 4, some of the students'
assumptions may be accurate, some may be inaccurate, some may be
correct in some situations but incorrect in others, and some may be
accurate but not germane to the problem. ITAs may have difficulty with
several features of these question clusters: the speed with which the
students state their comments, the shifts from the physical to the theoretical realm, and the confusion of dealing with problems the ITA has not
yet worked out. In this lab the students' questions about reconciling their
theoretical assumptions with a voltmeter reading led the TA to discover
that his instructions for setting up the apparatus were incorrect. In
addition to simply comprehending and answering students' questions,
lab assistants may simultaneously be trying to solve a problem themselves.

Students sometimes ask a series of questions like those in Excerpt
4, expecting an answer after every question; at other times they ask a
rapid series of questions without stopping to give the ITA a chance to
answer. These questions are often embedded in a stream of discourse
and may be particularly challenging for an ITA with marginal listening
comprehension. Excerpts 5a, from a physics lab (Myers & Plakans, 1991),
and 5b, from a chemistry lab, illustrate this:

[5a] **S:** how would you do this one here—we put 'em together and
you can't find an image—this one—you can't get an image—
so you look into the lens—how do you find that image—you
look into the lens and try to find it or what? (p. 373)

[5b] **S:** before I moved it, it was four and now it's four-something
and now it's one-something—I mean it's just a whole—I mean
it's a huge difference in number—I mean I just don't understand why—I mean if there is a difference—what is the
right—what is the right place—do you want it out on the
end?—I don't know

Figuring out what the student is asking becomes more than a matter of
comprehension. The ITA must be skilled in negotiating and in restating
and clarifying to effectively understand students who lack the vocabulary
to describe equipment, processes, or reactions with precision.

Both the students' perception of shared context and the problem-
solving nature of their discourse make communication in the lab problematic for nonnative speakers. ITAs who are new to the United States

and those who have the weakest English proficiency are likely to have difficulty with students' questions in the lab; yet these ITAs are frequently assigned to the lab because it is perceived as an easier assignment than classroom teaching. Because of the importance of informal interaction in the lab, training should help new ITAs gain proficiency in interactional skills, especially in negotiating for comprehension. Methods for helping ITAs gain these skills are discussed in the final section.

TA Discourse

Much lab discourse is motivated by students' questions, but the content of these questions, especially in an introductory course, is often superficial. Students frequently ask about the mechanics of the lab: finding and assembling apparatus, getting the experiment to work, or making sure they are following directions properly. Much less frequently do students ask *why* the experiment is set up the way it is, *how* the experiment validates their theoretical knowledge of the discipline, or *what* the process of the experiment will teach them. In other words, introductory students tend to follow the lab manual like a cookbook, relying on the lab assistant only for troubleshooting and often not challenging themselves to figure out exactly what they are doing. A lab assistant who merely responds to students' questions, especially in an introductory course, may not be helping the students as much as an ITA who uses the lab as an opportunity to ask questions that probe students' understanding or that help the students integrate the process they are observing with the theory they have learned. The lab is a perfect place for this teaching dialogue to occur. The 35 ITAs in this study varied in how active they were in initiating interaction with students as well as in their ability to use questions effectively. In this section I explain the importance of TA questions and examine the kinds of questions the inexperienced ITAs asked in the five transcribed labs.

Significance of TA Questions

Interviews with lab supervisors revealed a common concern: that TAs be active, not passive (Peterson, 1989). One lab supervisor said, "We tell them not to hold up the wall." He wanted his lab assistants to circulate, ask questions, and be involved with the students rather than lean against the wall waiting for students to ask questions. Despite the supervisors' concerns, a lab assistant's role is less clearly defined than that of a lecturer or discussion leader. The structure of a standard classroom requires ITAs to take initiative: They propose boundaries for the topic under discussion, they give students permission to ask questions, and they can control how many and which questions they will answer. The format of the lab, however, does not require this initiative. The willingness or ability to take an active role in the lab was one important difference among the ITAs in the 35 observations. Some of the ITAs seldom initiated interaction and simply waited for students to determine whether interaction would occur. Similarly, Tanner (1991b) noted that the two less proficient nonnative-speaking TAs in his study "were often observed standing at one end of the lab, periodically looking out over the students" (p. 143). On the other hand, a few ITAs *were* active teachers, encouraging their students to think about the lab by posing frequent questions to them.

For instance, one chemistry ITA who had been recommended by his supervisor began his lab by saying, "I want to make this lab not too mechanical. So we put two things together and we all go home. That's boring." As he circulated among his students, he frequently pushed them to think about what they were doing. He stopped to watch a student adding a chemical to a solution and asked, "What causes that color? What is the most likely element that would cause that color?" When the student answered incorrectly, he continued to query her: "Sulfate is a different color than sulfur. So what else might cause the color?" After another wrong guess, he gave her a hint: "So what is that precipitate? . . . Iron oxalate. So what causes the color?" He left her with a bit of friendly advice: "So think about what causes the color change. That's the fun of it. Not the stirring, that's the boring part." This ITA approached the lab enthusiastically, encouraging his students to get the most out of it. An active use of questions characterized his teaching style and certainly contributed to his success as a lab assistant.

Classification of TA Questions

Classroom research has shown that teachers can improve the quality of students' participation by carefully choosing their questions (Andrews, 1980), and educational researchers have devised various classification schemes for teachers' questions, based on the cognitive effect those questions have on students (Bloom, 1956; Hyman, 1982). Tanner (1991a) noted the importance of incorporating research on asking questions into ITA training. ITA texts also devote space to discussing interaction (Byrd, Constantinides, & Pennington, 1989; Pica, Barnes, & Finger, 1990; Smith, Meyers, & Burkhalter, 1992). Because the lab is highly interactive, asking questions appears to be an important skill in effective teaching.

To examine differences in question patterns, I analyzed the questions used by five audiotaped ITAs. They were chosen because they were relatively inexperienced, in their first year of teaching. All were Asian males in their early 20s; ITA 1 was a native speaker of Chinese from Malaysia, and ITAs 2, 3, 4, and 5 were Korean. Their spoken English

Table 1 ▪ Classification of Questions

	ITA and SPEAK score				
	1	2	3	4	5
Question type	260	200	230	200	200
Echoic					
Comprehension Checks	24	10	1	10	3
Clarification Requests	7	6	6	3	7
Confirmation Checks	22	26	7	11	3
Epistemic					
Referential	47	23	26	8	13
Evaluative	28	41	2	5	2
Rhetorical	4	1	0	0	2
Other[a]	11	11	15	0	5
Total	143	118	57	37	35

Note. Categories from Kearsley (1976) and Long and Sato (1983). "Expressive" questions, used in Long and Sato's study, were not observed in the lab.
[a]Includes directives *(Why don't you turn up the burner?)*; criticisms *(Why didn't you read over the procedures first?)*; and incompletely phrased questions that could not be clearly classified.

proficiency (as measured by scores on the Speaking Proficiency in English Assessment Kit [SPEAK], the Educational Testing Service's locally administered test of spoken English) ranged from 200 to 260, with a SPEAK score of 200 permitting minimal teaching duties (a lab assignment) but requiring concurrent enrollment in a course for nonnative TAs. ITAs 1 and 3 taught freshman chemistry labs; ITA 2, an introductory physics lab; ITA 4, an introductory zoology lab; and ITA 5, organic chemistry. Table 1 shows the number of questions asked by the five ITAs.

None of the five ITAs was particularly passive: All circulated and commented on students' work in addition to answering students' questions. However, ITAs 1 and 2, with 143 and 118 total questions, based more of their interaction on asking questions. The other three lab assistants, with question totals of 57, 37, and 35, were available to answer students' questions but were less likely to involve a student with questions of their own.

The questions asked by the five ITAs were classified according to a modified version of Kearsley's (1976) taxonomy of question functions. The original taxonomy included four general categories: *echoic, epistemic, expressive,* and *social control.* The first two are common in classroom discourse, with echoic questions used for negotiating meaning and checking comprehension, and epistemic questions used for asking about the subject matter of the class. Long and Sato (1983) subdivided the echoic category into *clarification requests, comprehension checks,* and *confirmation checks,* and added a third general category, *rhetorical questions.* Table 1 categorizes the questions asked by each TA.

Echoic questions. Various second language acquisition researchers have described the effect of communication negotiation—specifically the modifications a native speaker makes when a nonnative speaker fails to understand—in providing a language learner with comprehensible input (Hatch, 1978; Long, 1981). A number of empirical studies have examined the effect of negotiation on nonnative speakers' comprehension of native speakers. (See, for example, Gass & Varonis, 1985; Pica, Young, & Doughty, 1987; Pica, 1989.) Other studies, like Yule's in this volume, have focused on negotiation between nonnative speakers (Varonis & Gass, 1985; Yule & Gregory, 1989; Yule & Macdonald, 1990). For nonnative lab assistants, the ability to negotiate effectively is a practical survival skill, as they must cope with the sometimes incomprehensible discourse of their students.

Typically, the most common devices for negotiating communication are echoic questions, in which a person asks for repetition, seeks confirmation that he or she understands something correctly, or asks for feedback to ascertain that he or she has been understood. In the lab an ITA used comprehension checks to ask if a student had understood what the ITA had said: *Got that? Any problems with that? Understand?* ITAs used clarification requests to ask for repetition or to indicate that they had not understood something their students had said: *What? Huh?* and *Would you repeat that?* Confirmation checks were complete or partial repetitions of a student's words stated with rising intonation. These checks asked students to confirm that the ITA had heard them correctly; for example:

S: It's positive, isn't it?
T: Positive?

ITA 1, the most linguistically competent of the five, asked the most echoic questions. He seldom had trouble comprehending his students but used echoic questions to clarify poorly worded or unfocused comments from them, as illustrated in Excerpt 6.

[6] **S1:** I understand that—but does our main
    S2: ours aren't consistent—that's what I'm saying
    T: yeah—it is not consistent because this is not

> **S2:** in any place? I couldn't understand why the difference in numbers is so great
> **S1:** that's a whole different number—I mean—I don't—I don't—know
> **T:** so what you're saying is when you move this around you're going to have a different?
> **S:** yeah—if I hook it up closer to the water

The ITA rephrased the student's ideas in the confirmation check, "so what you're saying is. . . ." He also restated the student's words with, "yeah, it is not consistent because. . . ." Even though he understood the student, he used paraphrase and echoic questions to keep the dialogue moving, as if to say, "Keep talking. I hear you."

Similarly, ITA 2 used echoic questions effectively to negotiate for meaning:

> **[7] S:** can you explain why it's doing this? the ray entering the block—refracts—away from the normal to the surface
> **T:** what is your question?
> **S:** I s-- we see why it does that but why—I mean we see that it does that—but why does it do that?
> **T:** why—why does it bend toward the normal?
> **S:** yah
> **T:** uh—that's because of the difference of index of refraction /
> **S:**   / OK
> **T:**   / between air and
> **S:** is that the same thing for why this does that away from   it?
> **T:** yes—that's the same reason but depending on from where to where the beam goes there's a change in angle/
> **S:**   / OK
> **T:**   / direction of the angle

ITA 2 begins with a simple clarification request, "What is your question?" when he doesn't understand the student and continues to negotiate by asking for confirmation ("Why does it bend toward the normal?") and with a partial rephrasing of the student's words ("yes—that's the same reason"). This conversational use of echoic questions was a common feature of the discourse of ITAs 1 and 2. Like the subjects in Yule and MacDonald's (1990) study in which each participant tried to "make sense of the other's referential world" (p. 550), the two ITAs were able to relate to their students and perceive the experiment from the students' perspective.

On the other hand, ITAs 3, 4, and 5 used relatively few echoic questions, despite situations in which they clearly did not understand their students. Excerpt 8 shows a situation in which ITA 5 failed to negotiate successfully when he didn't understand a student.

[8] **S:** when we shut it off—we have to take the hose off here first—
no wait—how is that again? take the hose off this here first
T: what?
S: when we shut it off—in order for it not—you know—we have to take the hose off here first—don't we?
T: water goes through here—is correct?
S: yeah—water goes in through there
T: uh
S: but when it's all done—should we take this off of here before we shut the water off?
T: uh
S: oh no—we take this off first
T: OK—after shut off water then remove this

In this excerpt the ITA used the clarification request, "What?" but did not continue to negotiate until he understood completely. The student, who wanted to know the correct procedure for removing a hose, was asking whether she should turn off the water before or after removing the hose. The ITA was not certain exactly what she was asking and made the unnecessary comment, "water goes through here," a fact that the student already knew. More effective at that point would have been a specific clarification request like *What do you want to know about the hose?* or confirmation checks such as *Take the hose off first?* or *Take what off first?* in which the function word *what* is substituted for *the hose*. The ITA could have improved his communication with students by using echoic questions more skillfully.

In Excerpt 9 ITA 3 also had difficulty understanding a student's question. The lab manual did not indicate whether the students were supposed to use a regular Bunsen burner or a larger Meeker burner in the first step of the procedure, and the student questioned the ITA about this point. Although the student both built in repetition as she rephrased her question and used a confirmation check herself when the ITA's response was ambiguous, communication was not negotiated successfully.

[9] **S:** I was just—do you want us to use the Meeker burner when we weigh the crucible to start out with as well?
T: what?
S: when we start out we're supposed to weigh the crucible twice—once while it's cool and then once again when when it's hot—are we supposed to use the Meeker burner to get it hot?

> **T:** no I don't think so
> **S:** no—just the regular burner? or it doesn't matter
> **T:** obtain the vacant weight of the crucible

The ITA did not paraphrase or repeat any part of the student's question in a confirmation check. His use of *I don't think so* revealed his uncertainty about what she had said. Several minutes earlier the ITA had told another student, "Use the Meeker burner to obtain the vacant weight of crucible," yet when this student asked whether she should use the Meeker burner, he answered, "No, I don't think so."

In some situations an ITA needs to use echoic questions to negotiate meaning successfully. Yet even when ITAs are linguistically proficient and can comprehend their students accurately, they may find that echoic questions will help them communicate more effectively with students.

Epistemic questions. Unlike echoic questions, which negotiate comprehension, epistemic questions are those a lab assistant consciously uses to move the experiment ahead, check on students' comprehension, and probe students' thinking. The two most common types of epistemic questions seen in the data, *referential questions* and *evaluative questions*, can be considered the "content" questions TAs use in the lab. (The other category noted by Long and Sato, *rhetorical questions*, consists of those the teacher asked and then immediately answered without waiting for a student to respond. Infrequent in lab discourse, they functioned more like discourse markers in the ITA's speech than as true questions meant to engage the student. They will not be discussed further in this chapter.)

Referential questions are information-seeking questions, common in casual discourse. In the lab they frequently concerned lab procedures or apparatus: *Do you have any matches in your drawer? Have you completed step one? Where did you get that number?*

Referential questions move the business of the lab forward: They ascertain how much the students have done rather than whether they understand what they have done. A lab assistant may have to ask many referential questions if the experiment is complicated or if the students are having trouble getting the results they expect. Questions like *Did you try heating it? Have you tested the switches?* and *Did you find the structure in the microscope?* were frequent and necessary in several labs. The 47 referential questions asked by ITA 1, for instance, dealt with the students' problems in making the experiment work. However, an exclusive use of referential questions may indicate that the lab assistant is primarily taking the role of troubleshooter rather than teacher. For example, the 26 referential questions asked by ITA 3 included many questions like these: *Is there a volunteer to get matches from storeroom? Was it broken? You have crucible?* These questions showed the ITA's concern that the students were simply carrying out the lab assignment; although necessary, they didn't contribute to a teaching dialogue in the way that carefully chosen evaluative questions could.

Evaluative questions, on the other hand, requested information already known by the ITA. Their purpose was to check students' understanding of the subject matter or to encourage them to think more deeply about a topic. Examples included *Why is that crystallizing? Can you tell me which is being oxidized and which is being reduced?* and *Why do we need that constant in the equation?* For the purposes of this study, the category included both simple convergent checks on student understanding, like *Is the anode connected to black or red?*, as well as divergent questions like *Why do you think the manual suggested this method?*

In Long and Sato's study (1983), evaluative "display" questions were used frequently by ESL teachers but were almost nonexistent in casual conversation. Particularly noting narrowly focused display questions like *What is the capital of Peru?*, they cautioned ESL teachers against overemploying a question form that students will not encounter in real communication. Poorly chosen evaluative questions can certainly be of limited use, if not insulting to students' intelligence, and in the ESL classroom, where communicative use of the language is a teaching goal, a teacher's evaluative questions may not provide learners with the communicative practice they need. However, the goals in a university science lab are different: Students are communicating not to develop skill in a language but to understand the factual content of the discipline. A teacher's questions in the lab ought to push students to more fully understand and apply the theory that underlies the experiment. Well-chosen evaluative questions, especially those requiring divergent thinking, can serve this function. *Why is that solution orange?* or *What's the reason for the discrepancy between the values in the book and your data?* are the kinds of questions ITAs can use effectively to actively engage their students.

The five audiotaped ITAs in this study used evaluative questions differently, with ITAs 1 and 2 employing them more frequently than the other three. In Lab 1 students called on the ITA almost constantly; although he seldom needed to initiate interaction with them, when asked a question he frequently responded with another question, leading the students to think about the issue at hand. These two excerpts from a lab taught by ITA 1 illustrate this:

[10a] S: our one—one is way off—but the other ones have been clear
       T: so what do you think have gone wrong?

[10b] S: so you just subtract the—find the difference between those?

> **T:** for example—the rate of copper and cadmium—OK?—
> which one is oxidation and which one is reduction in this
> case?

Rather than simply answering the students' questions, ITA 1 tried to get the students to think about their problems. During the lab he asked 28 evaluative questions, almost always in response to a student's question.

ITA 2 also actively asked his students questions to get them to think about the lab, using 41 evaluative questions. He often initiated interaction with questions like *Does it go toward this line or away from that line?* and *The index of refraction should be greater than one or smaller than one—what do you think?* ITAs 1 and 2 encouraged student involvement and problem solving. Both effectively used evaluative questions to probe students' understanding.

The other three ITAs used evaluative questions less frequently: ITAs 3 and 5 each asked only two in 90 minutes of taping. Although these ITAs answered students' questions and made comments about students' lab technique, they were less likely to engage in a teaching dialogue and essentially never responded to a student's questions with questions of their own. Their limited speaking proficiency may have contributed to the low number of questions, but it is unlikely to have been the only cause, as ITA 2, who also had a SPEAK score of 200, asked the most evaluative questions. Perhaps this skill—asking a type of question that is so rare in conversational settings—is a learned skill, one that training can teach.

Effectiveness of ITAs

Were ITAs 1 and 2 more effective in the lab? Unfortunately, the study did not include a collection of student evaluations, interviews with students, or a comparison of final test scores as checks on student achievement and satisfaction. A longitudinal study of a few ITAs in which student data are collected would yield a clearer picture of students' responses to ITAs. In the brief observations of the five ITAs, however, students did appear to respond positively to ITAs 1 and 2. Students seemed to like them: A student of ITA 1 told the observer what a good lab assistant he was, and another referred to ITA 2 as "buddy" as he was leaving the lab. Students called on both ITAs frequently and referred to them by name. The frequent questions asked by these ITAs may have helped to create a rapport with their students.

ITAs 3, 4, and 5 appeared less effective than ITAs 1 and 2. Students of ITAs 3 and 5 did not engage the lab assistants in small talk and ignored the ITAs unless they needed help; some of ITA 4's students were openly hostile. These lab assistants tended to issue short directives rather than asking questions, and when they engaged their students with questions, they asked almost exclusively about procedural matters.

A limitation of the study is that the five ITAs were teaching different labs in different disciplines and that each was observed only once. The limited data yield impressions rather than definitive conclusions, and more research is needed to clarify the relationship between lab assistants' questioning and students' responses to them.

ITA Instruction

This study and others that increase knowledge of varied teaching environments should help program planners increase the relevance of curricula for ITA development. Pedagogical effectiveness is a complex matter, one based on personality and linguistic proficiency as well as on training, but the lab observations clearly showed the importance of interaction. Lab assistants need to be good listeners and skilled negotiators to follow students' often complex and confusing questions, and they need to be able to ask effective teaching questions to stimulate their students' thinking. These goals, though not contradictory to the usual pedagogical, cultural, and linguistic goals of ITA programs, may sometimes be slighted with a focus on improving the lecturing abilities of the ITA or, in Brown and Yule's terms (1983), on the "transactional" rather than the "interactional."

ITAs can become aware of the need for negotiation by looking at transcripts from labs in which communication has somehow stalled. ITAs in the course become animated in discussing short "problem transcripts" illustrating situations in which ITAs are not communicating effectively with their students in the lab. The class discusses the transcripts, and students pinpoint where communication broke down and suggest alternative responses the ITA could have used to more effectively negotiate for meaning. Having the ITAs in the training class suggest alternative echoic questions can broaden their own strategic repertoire of responses beyond *What?* or *Pardon me?* Axelson and Madden (this volume) suggest other ways to use lab transcriptions.

Analysis of breakdowns in communication is a first step, but actual practice in negotiating communication should also be an important part of ITA training. ITA trainees can practice negotiation strategies in dyads in any kind of paired task in which one student has information and the other must negotiate to get it, whether the task involves following a map (as in Yule's chapter in this volume), completing a diagram, labeling a drawing, or even taking dictation of sentences with technical terms from each other's fields.

The possibilities for developing paired exercises are limitless. A chemistry ITA, for example, can instruct an ITA from a nonscientific field in labeling a drawing of assembled lab apparatus, and a biology student can instruct a physics student in drawing and labeling a cell. Especially when the pairs are composed of ITAs from different disciplines, unfamiliar terminology usually mandates a good deal of negotiation, and the concrete nature of the tasks allows the TAs to check the success of their negotiations by comparing the diagram they have labeled or the sketch they have drawn with their partner's original, accurately labeled picture. ITAs can find a variety of appropriate illustrations in the textbooks they use in their teaching, or they can create their own labeled drawings for class practice. In this volume Yule makes additional recommendations for pairing students of varying ability levels and for designing exercises in which one student is perceived as leader. Also, if U.S. students are available to participate in these exercises, ITAs can benefit from practicing negotiation with native speakers. Schneider and Stevens (1991) and Davies, Tyler, and Koran (1989) have discussed other ways to involve U.S. undergraduates in ITA training.

Teaching ITAs to restate and paraphrase in order to help them understand their students is another skill that they can practice in the classroom. In one activity the ITAs work in groups of three, taking turns playing the role of lab assistant, student, and recorder. As the lab assistant explains a procedure, the "student" is required to interrupt with questions. Before answering, the ITA must restate or paraphrase the student's question to practice negotiating, and the "recorder" writes down for later analysis all clarification requests and confirmation checks the ITA has used. Another version of the exercise eliminates the recorder and employs a cassette tape for the same function.

The second general skill, asking appropriate teaching questions, can also be approached in many ways. ITAs can preview a lesson in their lab manual and formulate a list of appropriate questions. This analysis can allow ITAs to plan what general concepts they need to emphasize as well as to predict which concepts or techniques will cause the students problems. If ITAs are already teaching in a lab, they can tape record a lab, transcribe the questions that they have asked their students, and classify the questions into general functional categories: questions that invite communication, that negotiate for meaning (echoic questions), that focus on procedure (referential questions), and that probe students' understanding (evaluative questions). From their own analysis ITAs can discover whether they are limiting their questions to a narrow function and brainstorm ideas for questions that could serve alternate functions. If ITAs are not currently teaching a lab, they can be given a partial lab transcript or work with a short videotaped segment featuring another ITA to analyze the ITA's questions and to offer suggestions for improving them. Focusing attention on asking questions helps ITAs become aware of the varied functions questions can fulfill.

Naturally, asking and answering questions should be important parts of any ITA curriculum, and ITAs who will not be teaching in labs can benefit from the practice. But for those who will teach in the lab, effective interaction and an understanding of the ways to use teaching questions is primary. With a certain amount of flexibility, training programs can meet these needs.

Note

This chapter is a revised and expanded version of a paper presented at the 24th Annual TESOL Convention, San Francisco, CA, March 1990. I thank Barbara Plakans for her support and encouragement and for her helpful comments on an early draft. Additionally, I appreciate the insights and suggestions of my colleagues Dan Douglas, Roberta Abraham, and Felicity Douglas; the chapter is better for their input. I am also indebted to Ruth Johnson and Janet Searls for help with data collection and transcription.

6

Student Questions: When, Where, Why, and How Many

Patricia L. Rounds
University of Oregon

■

Frequent and fruitful interaction between students and teacher has been shown to be a highly valued feature of U.S. university classrooms. Bailey (1984) first illustrated this empirically in the development of her typology of teaching assistants (TAs). The "entertaining allies" and the "inspiring cheerleaders," those who were interactive, one of the group, and communicated personal interest in their students as individuals, were the most highly rated teachers. Rounds (1986) also found that those TAs who evidenced a high degree of group membership and who ran classes as if they were conversations (albeit lopsided) rather than monologues more closely fit what U.S. students expected and valued in classrooms.

An essential ingredient in developing interactivity is asking students questions and responding to their questions. The ability to respond to students' questions is thus part of communicative competence for international teaching assistants (ITAs), and teaching materials designed specifically for ITA training address this area of communicative competence. For example, Byrd, Constantinides, and Pennington (1989) devoted three sections of their *Foreign Teaching Assistant's Manual* to the topic of asking questions and answering student's questions. They also included a reference guide to question types and exercises in which ITAs observe classes, record question-answer sequences, and subsequently analyze them. Pica, Barnes, and Finger (1990) discussed the topic of responding to student questions and devised exercises in which ITAs analyze different scenarios featuring student questions. Moreover, several of the testing procedures used nationally to screen nonnative English speakers for TA positions recognize the importance of this area of discourse interaction. For example, two sections of the Speaking Proficiency in English Assessment Kit (SPEAK) require examinees to respond to questions put to them on tape. The Ohio State University's mock teaching test, Iowa State University's Taped Evaluation of Assistants' Classroom

Handling (TEACH), and the University of Michigan's ITA screening tool all require examinees to respond to direct questioning.

Responding to student questions nevertheless remains one of the most problematic areas for ITAs, one that they constantly remark on as a source of anxiety. Their anxiety stems from the fact that students' questions are difficult to predict, unlike a lecture, which an ITA can thoroughly plan and carry out. When teachers enter classrooms, they have very little idea what the students will ask. Experienced teachers may be able to predict some questions but surely not all of them. Students' questions thus represent a great unknown for teachers and perhaps even a greater unknown for ITAs who have limited speaking and listening abilities.

The goal of this chapter is to investigate the kinds of questions students ask as a way of increasing the understanding of questioning in the university classroom and providing a basis for developing a model of ITA communicative competence with regard to questioning. I address several questions: What is known about the act of questioning as a discourse phenomenon? What is known about student questions—that is, what guidance does the literature provide as a basis for developing a pedagogical program in this area? Does the literature offer any information about what kinds of questions students are likely to ask? In answering these questions, my aim is, first, to describe the discourse of student questioning and, second, to use this analysis as a basis for developing empirically sound pedagogical materials for ITA training. A second goal is to understand more fully the U.S. student-teacher relationship that has been developing as a result of the freedom that U.S. students have to ask teachers questions in the public forum of the classroom.

The Act of Questioning

The Theoretical Perspective

Goody (1978) pointed out, "The most general thing we can say about a question is that it compels, requires, may even demand, a response" (p. 23). The response constitutes an instance of interaction. As Goody further noted, questions are like the exchange of gifts—they bind two parties in reciprocity. Perhaps because of the power of questions in social situations, a large and growing body of literature is concerned with the study and practice of questioning. These materials include theoretical models in philosophy, logic, linguistics, anthropology, and artificial intelligence. Applied studies examine interactions between counselor and client, lawyer and witness, doctor and patient, and teacher and student. No unified literature exists on questioning, but separate traditions are found within various disciplines; these represent different ways of knowing. All these literatures stand unrelated to one another; the works cited in one study often do not refer to one another.

Within the relatively well-studied area of the interaction involved in teacher-student questioning, the focus has been almost exclusively on the kinds of questions teachers can use to optimize certain kinds of intellectual thought in their students. As Carlson (1983) pointed out, the aim of question-answer sequences is pedagogical: to arrive at a common understanding of the topic. Through question-answer sequences the teacher brings the information to the floor and makes sure that everyone agrees on the answer.

Questions can also be viewed as one means of achieving the highly valued interactional classroom. Rounds (1986, 1987b) has characterized the classroom as an example of a social encounter, an arena for face-to-face interaction. Yet, at least for many university classes, classroom talk is not a dialogue in form because the teacher holds the floor to an extent that is off-norm for ordinary conversation. Classroom discourse deviates from the monologue-dialogue dichotomy in that it can be shown to exhibit facets of both. From an interactive perspective, the teacher can ask questions and allow students to do so in order to establish a pattern of verbal exchanges that change the floor, however briefly—a pattern fundamental to face-to-face interaction and inherently dialogic.

Viewing classroom interactivity from the point of view of students' questions is by and large uncharted territory. The literature that does exist is primarily interested in developing educational programs guided by student questions. Dillon (1986a, 1986b) points out that a student's question displays knowledge and understanding particular to the questioner. Thus it provides the teacher with an excellent window into the students' understanding. Dillon has constructed a framework for conceptualizing question asking as an act in three parts: a presupposition, a question, and an answer.

Dillon's framework leads to a clearer understanding of the range of tasks a teacher must perform because they are inherent in the act of questioning by students. A *presupposition* is a proposition that the student asserts to be true by virtue of asking the question. If the teacher thinks the proposition is true, he or she can reinforce the student's knowledge status and proceed with answering the question; if the teacher thinks the proposition is false, he or she can correct the student's knowledge and eliminate the question. Thus, via the question the teacher can estimate and intervene in the student's knowledge and understanding of the topic at hand; in this way a question reveals the nature and extent of that student's knowledge. For example, suppose a student in a mathematics class asks, "Shouldn't this come out to be one-half the quantity minus t to the negative one-half?" By examining the student's proposed solution, the teacher can try to determine whether it is a correct alternate expression of the answer, in which case he or she can demonstrate to the student how to arrive at the other expression or explain why the teacher didn't give that expression. If the student's answer is incorrect, the teacher can try to work back through the solution to pinpoint where the student erred. Dillon also suggested that, through the study of student questioning behavior and the sequencing of questions and the systematization of question-answer knowledge, instruction can become genuinely and inevitably individualized.

Dillon's framework clearly illustrates the formidable task the teacher faces with each student question. However, he does not address the key first step for nonnative speakers, which is that the teacher needs to understand the question. Although it may not be so for Dillon's work, this step is critically important for ITAs, on whom it places considerable comprehension demands. Every time a student asks a question, the possibility of misunderstanding or not understanding exists.

Furthermore, a concern for information or for clarification of a misunderstanding is a necessary implication only of a genuine act of questioning. The questioner may already know the answer—such as in cross-examination of criminal witnesses—and may have a different agenda for asking questions. Similarly, there is no reason to expect that every student question is a genuine act of questioning. The classroom is a forum for social as well as educationally oriented interaction (Erickson, 1982; Rounds, 1986), and questions can serve this dual function, too. McKeachie (1978) noted, for example, that questions during the first class have a hidden agenda, such as finding out if the teacher is flexible, sincere about helping the students, easily rattled, or able to handle criticism. Such uses of questions reveal much about the social relationships established in classrooms.

The Empirical Perspective

This section examines and compares two data samples. McKenna (1987) studies student behavior in university phonetics classes in order to develop some basis for advising foreign students on appropriate classroom behavior. She constructed a typology of student questions based on a corpus of 244 questions recorded during 33 lectures (henceforth *McKenna data*). Here I present data from five different university mathematics classes taught by international and U.S. TAs, a total of 30 questions (henceforth *Rounds data*). The subject matter of these data is somewhat comparable as both classes were technical: The phonetics professor concentrated on how to form sounds; the mathematics TAs concentrated on how to perform certain mathematical operations. The two sets of data differ significantly, however, in the profiles of the teachers. The

Table 1 ▪ Number of Student Questions per Teacher

Teacher	Number of student questions
Native speaker	
A	5
G	15
Nonnative speaker	
J	6
M	4
L	0

McKenna data came from classes taught by an elderly, highly respected professor; the Rounds data, from classes taught exclusively by graduate TAs. Both sets of data were collected at the same large midwestern university.

Based on both sets of data, a response to the research question, *How many questions can an ITA expect in a typical class?* would be about six to eight—six based on the Rounds data and eight based on the McKenna data. Table 1 shows, however, that in the Rounds data the questions are not equally distributed. Three of the TAs receive the average number of questions; one TA, L, does not generate any student questions; and another, G, generates 15.

These data seem to show that students' questions are a relatively minor part of mathematics classroom discourse. One reason for this surfaced in follow-up discussions with the students in these classes: pressure. One source of pressure is one's peers, as one student volunteered: "A lot of times I want to ask questions in the class but . . . I'm sorta scared to ask them." Another source of pressure is their fear of losing face or causing the teacher to lose face: "A lot of people have that, you know, complex, that, if I ask a question he's gonna, you know, I didn't do my homework last night . . . or I don't think he's a good enough teacher, or something like this. . . . It's just a lot of people are afraid to ask questions." Or another student: "If you ask a question in class like something a teacher isn't explaining good enough. . . . I know you shouldn't feel this way . . . but you sort of feel that the teacher is going to get on your case because you're not learning well enough for him, because he's doing his job as a teacher." Both comments were volunteered by students in L's class, where no questions were asked.

This reluctance to ask or distaste for asking questions is also evident in students' reactions to the teachers' solicitation, "Any questions?" In the classes I observed, there were 14 elicitations for questions. Twelve led to no response or simply to a request for the teacher to work out another problem. Only two elicited genuine questions. What do students do when they don't understand? "If I have a question, I just make a note of it in my notes and go home and read the book," said one student.

McKenna's typology (see Table 2) divided questions into four categories: *clarification, interpretation check, digression,* and *challenge.* The Rounds data (Table 2) added two more categories: *ask teacher to perform* and *answer question.* In questions in the *clarification* category, the most highly represented in both data samples, students ask for information to be repeated, such as *I just wanted to clarify that sequences are different from coarticulation* (McKenna, 1987), or ask for more information, such as *In our normal* b *is that fully voiced?* (McKenna, 1987).

For McKenna the next most highly represented category is *interpretation check,* such as *You've just moved the tongue back, right?* (McKenna, 1987). However, no tokens were classified as such in the Rounds data. In mathematics, students may have more difficulty interpreting the teacher's words, or they may not need to, as they can usually rely on mathematical symbols to disambiguate a statement. For questions of type 2b in Table 2 (*illustrate given information*), students may find it more difficult to illustrate an abstract mathematical concept than a concept in phonetics, or it may be unnecessary as a mathematical problem generally illustrates the concepts immediately. A student would have to draw an analogy to another theoretical concept, which is more difficult than drawing an analogy between, for example, a given sound and a sound in one's native language in phonetics. Such differences in questioning behavior are another argument for making distinctions between academic discourse communities (Byrd & Constantinides, 1988). Selinker and Douglas (1985, 1989a) have argued that interlanguage variation is associated with discourse domain, and the present analysis suggests that different academic domains motivate differential discourses or genres (Swales, 1990).

Digression questions, such as *I was just curious, we haven't run across the* ch *sound yet* (McKenna, 1987), were not as common in mathematics classes as in the phonetics classes. There were 11 instances of digression questions in McKenna's data sample of 33 classes, or one digression for every three classes, whereas in the mathematics data there was one digression in six classes. Because McKenna's data all come from the same professor's classes, it is hard to tell whether it is easier to digress in phonetics than mathematics or whether that particular phonetics professor welcomed digression. Digression questions are particularly problematic for ITAs. First, they are more difficult to comprehend because they are not contextually supported. Second, responding to them offers a tactical problem for all teachers. Davis (1973), for example, noted that such questions may lead the teacher far afield, away from the day's lesson plan and into either unknown or unplanned territory. Also, time always

Table 2 ▪ Number of Student Questions, by Type

Type of question	McKenna data (244 questions)		Rounds data (30 questions)	
1. Clarification		(36%)		(50%)
a. Repeat information (information not understood or heard)	22	(9%)	3	(10%)
b. Request additional information (student asks for more information)	66	(27%)	12	(40%)
2. Interpretation check		(26.6%)		(0%)
a. Rephrase information (student tries to interpret teacher's words	42	(17.2%)	0	
b. Illustrate given information (student tries to exemplify a concept)	23	(9.4%)	0	
3. Digression	11	(4.5%)	1	(3%)
4. Challenge	4	(1.6%)	6	(20%)
5. Ask teacher to perform	—		2	(6.7%)
6. Answer question	—		3	(10%)

Note. The Rounds data contained three additional utterances that could be identified as questions via intonation and discourse function but that could not be understood; hence they were not classifiable.

presses. ITAs find it challenging to improvise and are exceedingly conscious of the difficulty of covering all the required material in the time allotted. They often see digressions as a hindrance rather than as an opportunity to break out of the script.

In training, the ITA is often taught a variety of means to set aside or ignore such questions in order to get through the curriculum. However, the ITA may carry out this sidestepping at the cost of blunting the student's ability to see connections between apparently unrelated matters. Further, the teacher may teach the students that questions are wrong unless they are asked at the right moment, that teachers "have the Big Picture and the student ought to sit back and simply follow the dots" (Davis, 1973, p. 81). Perhaps the teacher needs to be a little more humble in deciding what is or is not relevant and to remember that the clock means more to the teacher than to the student.

The first three categories—clarifications, interpretation checks, and digressions—represent "genuine acts of questioning," but challenge questions represent another act. In the Rounds data, a challenge sequence starts with a question, but not a naive question or one delineating a presupposition of not knowing. Such questions often begin with negative forms like *Shouldn't that be . . .?* or *Shouldn't this come out to . . .?* The responses to such questions are rather lengthy justifications and reasons for having taken certain steps in working out problems.

The excerpt below illustrates a typical challenge sequence. G had difficulty explaining the problem clearly, and one student felt she had to double-check his explanation. At the point where the excerpt begins, G has just finished explaining a problem.

TA: . . . so that's gonna be the expression that's the derivative. Questions on that? . . . Any other que-

S: can you simplify that more?

TA: um simplify this?

S: shouldn't this come out to be one half the quantity minus t to the negative one half?

TA: um . . . that's an equivalent form I'm not sure that that um . . . if you like, you know, rational exponents that's certainly a legitimate question

S: shouldn't that be positive one half though?

TA: sh-

S: one half the quantity one minus t to the negative one half if you use the chain rule to find the derivative . . . that should be positive one half?

TA: ummm . . . no no I think it's right I think it's right as it is umm if you had well the chain rule, see there's ways of doing this that we haven't got to yet, an one of these things . . . let's not worry about it at this point, I think that's right it's possible there's a sign mistake, but I don't think so

The outcome of this interaction appears to be that the TA has not gained the student's confidence that the answer is correct. Repeated episodes such as this one have the potential to undermine the students' confidence in the teacher's ability to give them correct information. When students see their performance in the course put on the line because of constant uncertainty about what they are told, they are bound to become unhappy with the class. A kind of folk wisdom says that students enjoy challenging their teacher, but this seems not to be true for all students. A student in G's class comments, ". . . that (challenging the teacher) wears after a while. It's fun sorta . . . it was kinda, fun you know, it's almost challenging, but to somebody who hasn't had calculus or who doesn't enjoy math to that extent it's aggravating and discouraging as opposed to fun." Some students feel that it is the teacher's job to teach and expect the teacher to be accurate and correct. Moreover, G appears to have injured his own self-confidence, that is, he appears to question the accuracy of his own work.

Furthermore, in challenge situations the teacher is placed in a defensive position, having to justify actions taken, or in a position of having to admit error. Both of these situations represent awkward and culturally sensitive occasions for ITAs who are accustomed to a different model of classroom decorum.

The two additional categories in Table 2 (5 and 6) were motivated by the mathematics classes in the data. An *ask teacher to perform* question is a request for the teacher to work through a certain problem. It is not a genuine act of questioning, as it does not ask for information. An example occurs when J asks if there are any questions and a student responds, "Not on this problem, but would you set up (problem number) 19?"

Category 6, *answer question*, represents a situation in which a student answers a teacher's question with question intonation, signaling that the student is not entirely sure of the answer. For example, when J is discussing a problem, he asks the class if anyone knows "the value of the function for this x?" A student responds, "pi over three?" This type of question can become problematic for nonnative speakers of English because it does not have the syntactic form of a question; furthermore, it occurs at a place in the discourse where the teacher expects an answer, not a question. In fact, the act relies entirely on intonation to signal intent. If ITAs do not control intonationally carried discourse signals, the potential for missing the question is substantial; they may not be able to pick up the subtle insecurity that the student voices by the question intonation.

Implications for ITA Training

Classrooms are a potential forum for cross-cultural miscommunication: Gumperz, Jupp, and Roberts (1979), in delineating the differences that contribute to miscommunication, have pointed out that the participants in the communication come together with different cultural assumptions. Pica, Barnes, and Finger (1990) contrast the educational system that most ITAs are accustomed to—a system in which instructors read their notes to large classes, are generally unavailable to students, and know none of them by name—with the U.S. system, which they characterize as interactive—a system in which students expect their teachers to know their names, answer their questions, meet them when they need help, motivate them for learning, and show concern about their progress. Constantino (1987) reported that many ITAs find the interactive mode of teaching very uncomfortable and prefer straightforward lecturing without any student feedback. Especially during their first months in the United States, many ITAs feel that asking questions is a rude interruption and a show of disrespect on the part of the students. If ITAs are uncomfortable with this aspect of U.S. culture, they will find it difficult to attend to and respond appropriately to their students' questions.

Through data-based studies like McKenna's (1987) and the analysis presented here, ITAs can learn about student questioning behavior. They can learn that in some 'contexts students just will not ask many questions and that in most questions students will ask for information to be repeated or for additional information. Because repeating often means adding to the original phrasing, students must learn oral paraphrasing techniques. ITAs will also find that often students try to rephrase information the teacher has offered to ensure that they understand, and that students like to present examples as checks on their understanding. The latter also reinforces the general pedagogical usefulness of examples and reminds TAs to offer many everyday examples to illustrate complex, theoretical concepts. Students will occasionally attempt to digress; if ITAs are concerned about handling digressions, they can learn to identify them, learn techniques for avoiding them, and learn when they should be taken up. Perhaps the most difficult situation is the challenge sequence. If challenge questions arise frequently in an ITA's class, it is a clear sign that the ITA has a serious problem with teaching style. Often students' dissatisfaction is caused by what they interpret as a teacher's lack of thoroughness. For example, teachers may be more concerned with illustrating a particular concept than with completely finishing a problem or taking care that they are absolutely accurate. At this point it is worthwhile for ITAs to review their teaching style to determine whether they are fulfilling their students' needs for completeness.

ITAs can learn strategies to control the occurrence and flow of questions. First, it is reasonable to ask students to hold questions if the ITA is in the middle of an explanation, but it is essential to open the floor to questions at some point. When the floor is open to questions, ITAs must recognize the role of "wait time," a little patience for student questions to materialize. Most current studies of teacher-student interaction have included response opportunity as a category of teacher behavior. Research in science teaching has shown, for example, that longer teacher wait time results in more student questions, more questions by slow students, greater variety in student thought, and greater student achievement (Rowe, 1973, 1974). Furthermore, Rowe (1974) found that if wait time is increased, certain characteristics of teacher input, such as an improved ability to respond to student questions, change. As an added bonus, increased wait time might give ITAs more time to process the colloquial variety of English they have been listening to. Finally, students expect teachers to provide opportunities for their questions. As one student in M's class explained, "When he asks questions . . . he doesn't

wait that long. . . . I feel that if he coaxed us more we might ask questions.
. . . I have the feeling he knows we don't quite understand."

Gumperz, Jupp, and Roberts (1979) have pointed out that different
ways of organizing information contribute to miscommunication. Research such as that presented in Connor and Kaplan (1987) has begun
to document differences in cross-cultural rhetoric. Such differences materialize in the classroom when ITAs feel they have explained well or
responded adequately to a question only to have students react in a way
that indicates they are not satisfied or have not understood. ITA and
student are at an impasse, with the ITA completely at a loss to understand
the difficulty and no way out of the difficulty. First, ITAs can be reminded
that studies like this one indicate that it is completely normal for students
to ask for rephrasing of information and not simply a reaction to the
ITA's nonnativeness. Second, they can be reminded of the usefulness
of a few good examples to explain their way out of many difficult areas.

Finally, Gumperz, Jupp, and Roberts (1979) noted that different
ways of speaking contribute to miscommunication. ITAs identify these
major stumbling blocks to understanding questions: Students use slang
and unknown words; students speak fast; students don't pronounce
clearly; students pause or rephrase their questions so much that the
question is lost; students form their questions poorly, often because they
are searching for a way to verbalize their difficulty. In addition, Byrd,
Constantinides, and Pennington (1989) have pointed out that students
do not always use the ordinary, grammatical question forms language
learners are trained to expect. Sometimes students will use oral language
forms such as *How is it that . . .?* or *How can it be that . . .?* Sometimes a
question will be indicated only by a rising tone of voice, by a statement
of the student's understanding and an expectation of correction if the
understanding is inaccurate, or by nonverbal behaviors such as a puzzled
look.

The difficulties caused by students' informal or ill-formed questions
are a concern for ITAs and help build the case for ongoing training in
listening comprehension to develop strategies for improving accuracy in
listening. Furthermore, these difficulties speak to a need for ITAs to
develop a stronger ability to exploit their linguistic environment in order
to begin to pick up on the latest slang or the jargon students regularly
use to talk about the classroom.

McKeachie (1978) has recommended the technique of "problem
posting" if teachers wish to avoid answering questions immediately because they want to lay more groundwork or because they don't wish to
reinforce or to engage in a colloquy with a questioner whose concerns
are not likely to contribute toward achieving the goals of the whole class.
The teacher can say something like, *Let's see if we can get all the questions*

out so that we can see what they are and how to handle them. If it is the first class, the teacher might say, *Let's see what problems you'd like to have us tackle during the course. What sorts of concerns do you think that we might deal with?* The instructor's task then becomes that of understanding and recording briefly on the blackboard the problems contributed by the group. Such a technique is useful for ITAs because in writing the question they can focus on unknown lexical items and have them explained in the context of the question.

Conclusion

ITAs should not be forced to reject their belief systems regarding appropriate classroom behavior but to modify them. Through training, ITAs need to come to understand clearly that questions are not rude and disrespectful but embody the behaviors that teachers in U.S. society work to instill into the learner: attention, thinking, expressing; motivation and readiness; participation and action. The question represents a perfect opening for teaching, because inquiry is already under way and learning already sought. Furthermore, as pointed out, questions are a first step in developing a dialogic learning context. When questions are viewed from this perspective, it is easy to see why questioning behavior is so highly valued in the U.S. educational system.

Ard (1987) suggested that observation can provide ITAs with some insight into why classrooms are as they are and why people behave as they do. This is a valuable first step. ITAs sit in U.S. university classrooms fairly often, but their presence does not ensure that they have developed any organized characterization of these classrooms. Also, the graduate course is not always the best model for their own teaching efforts. ITAs can and should become intelligent observers of classes similar to those they will work in. Nevertheless, however useful it is for ITAs to observe and to view videotapes of discussions, labs, office hours, and so on to develop a systematic understanding of these educational contexts, simply talking about educationally based behaviors such as asking questions, or telling the ITA what the situation is, is not sufficient. The challenge for ITA trainers is to build the training course around a central core of activity in which the second language learner performs the tasks associated with the particular area of classroom-based communicative competence, either in a real or a simulated context.

Finally, the ITA trainer may need to become an advocate for ITAs on campus. McKeachie (1978) suggested that handling a discussion section is sometimes more difficult than giving a lecture. Lectures often present fact and interpretation; a discussion should be a time for developing skills in application and problem solving rather than interpreting the lecture. The difficulties TAs have with running discussion sections are apt to be that they are not well enough acquainted with the materials the lecturers have covered. They may have read the sections in the textbook but have difficulty with the multiple synonymous versions they might have to verbalize in answering students' questions. A revolutionary, but linguistically more reasonable, arrangement is one that takes into consideration the ITAs' limited English proficiency. Such an arrangement might have the TAs give the highly organized monologic lecture and have the professors handle the discussion and problem-solving sections. This change will probably never happen, but at least ITA trainers can move toward recommending roles that exploit the strengths rather than expose the weaknesses of ITAs.

■ 7 ■

Effective Role-Play Situations and Focused Feedback:
A Case for Pragmatic Analysis in the Classroom

Andrea E. Tyler
University of Florida

■

This chapter focuses on using a pragmatic analysis of speaker goals and intentions as a framework for structuring role-play scenarios and giving appropriate feedback in response to the role plays. The purpose of the role plays is to help international teaching assistants (ITAs) develop and practice effective communication strategies in key problematic situations they are likely to encounter in the U.S. undergraduate classroom. The ITAs explore their options for negotiating the exchange in a relatively safe, nonthreatening environment where they can examine the consequences of various communication strategies.

No teacher, no matter how confident and skillful, will be able to avoid all conflict with students. Conflict situations are not pleasant, and even experienced, native-speaking teachers find them difficult. ITAs tend to find these problematic situations particularly difficult to negotiate, at least in part because they are emotionally charged and involve a complex, conflicting set of goals for the participants. ITA trainers can analyze the situations in terms of goals that are appropriate for the participants and the moves by which they can realize these goals. Based on this analysis, ITA trainers can identify less emotionally charged, more easily negotiated subcomponents of the problem and use them to develop a series of role-play situations that give the ITAs practice in handling crucial aspects of the problematic situation. Once the ITAs have become familiar with the subcomponents, they can successfully take on the more difficult exchange.

The methodology I discuss draws on earlier work in role plays (Clark, 1980; Hinds, 1973; Maley & Duff, 1978; Moffett, 1967; Munby, 1978; Rodriguez & White, 1983; Stern, 1983), as well as the work of people involved in sociodrama (Chesler & Fox, 1966; Scarcella, 1983; Shaftel & Shaftel, 1967), and particularly on DiPietro's *Strategic Interactions* (1987), which emphasizes conflicts in participants' roles. These authors have offered lucid justifications for the use of role plays in developing language skills and overall communicative competence. I refer the reader with general questions on the efficacy of role plays to them. The work of Douglas and Myers (1989), which explores the usefulness of using video in conjunction with role plays, has also influenced the methodology. On a more theoretical level, my thinking has been influenced by the work of scholars in pragmatics (especially Green, 1989; Grice, 1975; Reddy, 1979; Sperber & Wilson, 1986), which emphasizes that human communication is always in some sense indirect. This theoretical perspective sees all communication as a delicate negotiation in which the main work is determining the goals and intentions of one's interlocutor and finding appropriate, effective ways to signal one's own goals and intentions back.

The approach presented here departs from earlier work in role plays in the following ways:

1. The role playing begins with a consideration of the participants' goals and intentions, with emphasis on what is appropriate within the cultural situation.
2. In the enactment of the role play itself, native-speaking undergraduates play the roles of native-speaking interlocutors.
3. The native-speaking participants provide feedback on how well the ITAs communicated their intentions and met their goals.
4. The feedback that the nonnative speakers receive is aimed primarily at realizing goals and intentions, managing discourse strategies, and building schema, and only secondarily on specific elements of the linguistic code.
5. Nonnative players are given the chance to replay the role play immediately after receiving feedback.
6. The role plays build on one another, becoming gradually more challenging.

In the next section I introduce the approach through an analysis of an actual problem situation. A series of role plays developed from the analysis exemplifies the method for constructing the role-play situations. Finally, I discuss analyses of transcripts of videotaped enactments of the role-play situations in terms of appropriate feedback for the participants.

The Difficult Exchange

At the University of Florida, where this methodology was developed, all ITAs who score between 220 and 250 on the comprehensibility section of the Speaking Proficiency in English Assessment Kit (SPEAK) are required to take a training class during their first semester of teaching.

As part of that class, ITAs are observed in their classrooms biweekly; observations are often videotaped. Subsequently, the instructor and the ITA meet privately to discuss the observation and review the videotape. The ITAs are also required to keep a teaching journal throughout the semester. The difficult exchanges that form the basis of the role plays are based on incidents reported in the ITA's teaching journals or occurring during classroom observations.

Several factors contribute to making these exchanges difficult. First, they are unexpected: The ITA has never before considered either the entire situation or some important aspect of it. Second, the exchanges seem to be highly charged emotionally. Often the student begins the exchange with a great deal of emotion, or something the student says triggers strong emotions in the ITA. Third, the exchanges involve conflicting goals. The student is usually asking for something the ITA does not feel he or she can give. The requests often involve potential challenges to the ITA's authority. Moreover, the teacher may have goals that are potentially in conflict and need careful balancing.

One of the most dramatic examples of a difficult situation occurred in a first semester physics lab I observed. The first few minutes of the lab were uneventful. While the students took a quiz, the ITA passed back graded homework assignments. Not all the students did well. One student got fewer than half the points on the homework assignment. The quiz was followed by a brief introduction to the lab for the day. At the end of his introductory remarks, the ITA encouraged everyone to set to work as they had several steps to complete in a limited amount of time. He announced that he would be coming around to make sure everyone was off to the right start.

At that point, the student mentioned above approached the ITA and asked why he had received such a low grade on his homework assignment. The quality of his voice (which was cracking and quavery) as well as his agitated body movements suggested that he was quite upset. The ITA engaged the student in a long discussion (approximately 10 minutes) about the grade. Eventually the discussion turned to the issue of cheating. The ITA openly accused the student of cheating on a quiz— a charge the student vigorously denied. As the exchange progressed, both parties became more and more agitated. The other students in class, although trying to pursue the assigned experiment, could not help but overhear the exchange and evidenced discomfort, particularly during the discussion of cheating. The exchange ended rather badly with the ITA asserting that the grading was fair and the student responding, "I've been reamed."

Within a day of the exchange, I reviewed the videotape with the ITA. The comments throughout the analysis sections of this chapter that indicate the ITA's interpretation, intentions, and goals are based on the ITA's statements during the review session.

Any teacher might have found the situation of a student frustrated with his low homework grade and suspected of cheating a prickly one. Although there is no perfect, easy way to handle the entire problem, the ITA could have prevented the extremity of the situation outlined above with a few basic moves if he been able to see the alternatives available to him. Role plays in the ITA training class can help provide this perspective. The purpose of the role plays is to train ITAs in assessing the situation, understanding appropriate goals within the situation, seeing a range of alternatives, and developing the communication skills necessary to act on the alternative they prefer.

Analyzing the Situation

A role-play session begins with the introduction of the difficult exchange to the class. Playing a videotape of the exchange is usually the most effective introduction. (In the case under discussion, I used a videotape of the exchange accompanied by a transcript.) If a videotape is not available, the instructor summarizes the situation. Several role plays have become part of the regular curriculum; in these cases, the ITA involved in the exchange is not present for the class discussion. Usually at least once a semester, an ITA who is a member of the class encounters a difficult situation that forms the basis of a role-play session. In this situation, the ITA joins the instructor in explaining the exchange and giving information about his or her perceptions of the exchange. The instructor always discusses the situation with the ITA before class and receives permission to share the experience with the class.

After the instructor introduces the situation, the class identifies the elements that make the exchange difficult. As part of this discussion, the instructor describes the ITA's goals, intentions, and interpretations; the class discusses how these affect the exchange. In the situation described above, a number of factors make the exchange problematic. First, the student is in a highly charged, emotional state. The video reveals a good deal of agitation in the student's body language and voice quality. Even in the first few sentences, his voice is quavery and cracking; he frequently shifts positions and rocks back and forth. The ITA involved in the exchange is only vaguely aware that the student is upset. In most classes, several members of class miss the signals that reveal the student's emotional state, suggesting that many ITAs may misassess student's intentions and may often not be aware of how volatile a situation is. Moreover, failure to recognize the student's emotional state may result in the ITA's not making moves that would calm the student and indicate sympathy. An important part of the discussion, then, is pointing out these emotional signals.

Another difficulty is that the student is asking for something the

ITA is not prepared to give him. On the surface, the student asks for an explanation of the grade; however, his goal is to have his grade raised. The ITA, on the other hand, is convinced that he has graded the assignment appropriately.

Third, the ITA is balancing a complex set of potentially conflicting goals. For instance, the ITA wants to maintain his authority and credibility and at the same time show sympathy for the student's problem. Letting one of these goals dominate could disrupt the exchange. In this exchange, the ITA attempts to maintain his credibility by trying to make all the student's errors clear. In the class discussion, the instructor notes that the goal of maintaining credibility dominates to the point that the ITA even lectures the student on what type of paper to use. The class's attention is focused on the student's facial expressions and verbal responses, which suggest that he felt embarrassed by the remarks about the paper. The instructor also notes that this discussion marks a downward turn in the exchange, with the student responding with greater sarcasm and hostility from that point on.

Another problem area is the discourse management strategies adopted by the ITA. In particular, the decision to allow the exchange to take place during class is a communication misstep with many negative repercussions. Carrying out the exchange in front of an audience puts both participants under extra pressure to perform and brings out many aspects of saving face that are much less of an issue in a private conversation. The ITA is aware that he is ignoring other students and the work he should be attending to, which makes him more anxious. Not surprisingly, the additional stress and anxiety adversely affect the ITA's linguistic production, creating more emotion and more confusion. The question of face may also affect the power dynamics, leading the student to challenge the teacher's authority. The student's initial move to question the grade is already a potential challenge to the ITA's judgment or credibility. Within the exchange the student openly challenges the ITA's knowledge of the assignment. As the ITA's linguistic control deteriorates, the student corrects the ITA's English, again challenging the credibility and authority of the teacher (Tyler & Davies, 1990a).

After identifying some of the elements that make the situation difficult, the next step is to identify appropriate goals for the ITA. As a teacher in a U.S. classroom, the ITA needs to remain in authority without being overly authoritarian. His instructional aim is to ensure that the students have the opportunity to cover the material scheduled for the day. To do so he must be free to assist the students as they carry out their experiments and to maintain an atmosphere in which learning can take place with a minimum of distractions. To accomplish these goals, he should postpone the discussion the student requested. On a personal level, the ITA wants to retain the respect of his students. He does not want to provide a forum within the classroom for challenges to his authority. Again, postponing the discussion is important to meeting this goal. In regard to the student, the ITA wants to appear knowledgeable about the assignment itself and about why he has marked the assignment as he has. Thus, while refusing the request to discuss the grade during class, he must appear willing to discuss the problem. He does not want to appear to be trying to avoid the student. To accomplish this and to respond to the emotions displayed by the student, the teacher needs to appear somewhat sympathetic without committing to changing the grade. Finally, the ITA wants to keep conflict with this student to a minimum and avoid a difficult relationship for the remainder of the semester. Avoiding public embarrassment or humiliation is important in meeting this long-term goal, so the ITA wants to avoid a public discussion of grades.

After identifying the goals, the class may briefly discuss what the ITA might say to accomplish them. I suggest that this discussion be quite limited, just enough to give the ITAs a broad outline and the general tenor of a successful exchange. The instructor might suggest a few sentences such as *I can understand why you might be concerned*; *I thought you might want to discuss this*; or *I'd be happy to discuss the assignment with you. Let's make an appointment to do that so you can get on with the experiment.*

The Subcomponents and the Nested Situations

Experience has taught that initially the dynamics involved in difficult exchanges are too complex for ITAs to successfully negotiate in toto, even after a thorough discussion. ITAs need practice with strategically similar but less threatening situations before they are ready to take on the difficult exchange. The purpose of developing a series of role plays, then, is to introduce the ITAs to strategically similar but less emotionally charged scenarios, gradually building to the difficult exchange.

In developing the series of role plays, the instructor must determine the key move(s) for the ITA to accomplish in order to successfully negotiate the exchange. The first scenario should allow the ITAs to practice a basic move with a minimum of the complicating emotions and conflicts involved in the original difficult situation. The subsequent role plays progress from emotionally neutral situations to more emotionally charged, confrontational ones. As a group, the role plays can be seen as a series of approximations, with each one moving closer to the difficult, emotionally charged situation. By participating in the series of role plays, the ITAs have the opportunity to gain familiarity with the basic move within a range of situations. In the later role plays, the ITAs engage in more emotional, threatening exchanges using the basic move as a kind of scaffold for organizing and guiding their response (Bruner, 1981a, 1985; Vygotsky, 1978, 1987).

Under the analysis presented above, the key to successfully negotiating the exchange is for the ITA to indicate simultaneously a general willingness to discuss the student's problem and the idea that the current moment is not an appropriate time to do so. The first role play in the series represents a simplified scenario involving the basic move of postponing a discussion but without the emotional issues of the grade and the potential involvement of other students found in the original exchange.

A series of seven scenarios was developed for this exchange. For the first five the ITA's role stays essentially the same. The basic scenario is that the class has just finished. The ITA has an important test across campus in 15 minutes and needs to leave quickly. A student approaches and expresses a need to talk to the ITA. The ITA must quickly let the student know that he or she is willing to work with the student but that this is not an appropriate time.

The student's role varies throughout the first five scenarios. In the first two, the student simply wants to clarify some aspects of an assignment due in a day or two. Role play 3 introduces the issue of grading. Role plays 4 and 5 add steadily escalating emotions over the grade. Role plays 6 and 7 switch the setting to the middle of class, where the rest of the class is potentially involved. Role play 7 is intended to represent all the difficulties involved in the original exchange outlined above. (The complete scenarios appear in Appendix A.)

Enacting the Role Plays

Native-Speaking Interlocutors

Two to four native English-speaking undergraduates play the part of undergraduates in the role plays. The involvement of native speakers in the role plays is vital. Work in interethnic miscommunication (Erickson & Schultz, 1982; Gumperz, Jupp, & Roberts, 1979; Gumperz, 1982a, 1982b; Scollon & Scollon, 1981) has demonstrated that many sources of communication breakdown between interlocutors from different cultural or linguistic backgrounds are subtle and not readily accessible to the participants. For instance, Erickson and Schultz (1982) have documented that such slight differences as how interlocutors nod their heads can change the interpretation of a statement and eventually the entire tenor of the exchange. The interlocutors were often aware that the exchanges had not gone as they expected, but they had no insight into the differences in nodding styles and their effect on the exchange. These more

subtle areas include many aspects of schema and conventionalized implicatures associated with particular phrases or syntactic constructions as
well as paralinguistic phenomena. For instance, the implicatures associated with *What's your problem?* are quite different than those associated
with *What's the problem?* (See Tyler & Davies, 1990a, for further discussion.) An ITA may be able to produce grammatically correct English,
but the requisite understanding of the possible range of acceptable,
legitimate responses, of the constraints of the U.S. university classroom,
and of the pragmatics involved in the exchange requires native speakers.
The presence of the native-speaking undergraduates creates an authenticity and sense of immediacy that could never be achieved by having
another ITA play the role of an undergraduate. Moreover, the undergraduates' interpretation of the exchange and feedback to the ITA are
an essential part of the debriefing.

Identifying Appropriate Goals

Prior to enacting the role play, the class briefly discusses the appropriate
goals for the ITA. The chief goals identified with this series of role plays
are to get away from the student quickly and to indicate that the ITA
is willing to meet with the student later if necessary. A number of strategies can be employed to accomplish these goals. For instance, one recommended strategy for showing willingness to discuss the problem is to
make a definite appointment rather just postponing the discussion to
some later, unspecified time.

A Sample Enactment and Feedback

The following discussion of appropriate feedback centers on one ITA's
enactment of the second scenario in the series. The native speaker plays
the role of a somewhat pushy student who wants information about an
assignment due the following day. The ITA begins the role play with a
general announcement that she wanted to end class a little early because
she has an important appointment. She apologizes, saying, "I have an
appointment in 5 minutes. I'm so sorry for that." The student advances,
saying he has some quick questions about a research paper due the
following day. The student then asks a long series of detailed questions
about citations and the proper form for the bibliography, ending with
a negotiation over turning the assignment in late. The enactment ends
after approximately 5 minutes with the native speaker turning to the
camera and saying, "I'm running out of questions." Throughout the role
play, the ITA faces the student squarely, smiling and answering the
student's questions. After the third question, the ITA makes a tentative
move to delay the questions by setting up an appointment, but the student
deflects the move, saying that he has to take his sister to the hospital.

The ITA acquiesces with a smile. (A transcript of the enactment appears in Appendix B.)

The feedback begins with a quick review of the ITA's goals in this scenario and the question, "Did the ITA reach those goals?" First, the native-speaking interlocutor is asked to interpret the ITA's intentions and goals based on the performance. After the role play in question, the native speaker said that the ITA appeared knowledgeable and willing to give the student time but that she did not seem committed to postponing the interview or leaving quickly. He noted that, even in her first statement, the ITA apologized for having an appointment, which seemed to put her in a weak position. If she had ended her initial statement with something like *I'd be glad to see any of you today after X time, but I cannot talk now,* she would have put herself in a much stronger position to postpone his questions. He added that he felt he could have kept her in the classroom indefinitely.

The other members of the class and the instructor pointed out that the ITA employed a good strategy at the beginning of the enactment, that of announcing to the class that she had an important appointment and had to leave early. Her goal was frustrated when she allowed the student to ask his questions rather than politely cutting him off. The class noted that although the ITA said during the exchange that she needed to go, she did not forcefully articulate these sentiments or support them with body language. The ITA responded that she felt unsure of what was polite in the situation, that is, how strongly she could assert her need to leave without offending the student. She noted that apologizing for having to leave seemed more polite than just announcing she had to leave. The other students suggested several simple, alternative strategies; instead of squarely facing the student, leaving her books on the desk, and making no movement toward the door, she could pointedly look at her watch, gather up her books as she talked, and invite the student to walk with her on her way to her appointment.

It is important for the ITA to receive balanced information in the feedback session, that is, to point out the strengths as well as the weaknesses of the enactment. If students do not receive positive reinforcement for what works, they may abandon a perfectly good strategy. Before moving on, both participants are given an opportunity to discuss any confusion or feelings that might have arisen during the enactment. At this point, the interlocutors often ask about phrases they did not understand.

Reenacting the Scenario

Depending on how the first enactment goes, the class may move on to the next scenario or try the same scenario again. In this case, because the ITA failed to accomplish the basic goal of postponing the discussion, she was given the chance to play the role again.

Allowing the same student to immediately replay the role play has many benefits. Most ITAs are able to perform significantly better in terms of reaching their goals after receiving pragmatic feedback. Also, many tend to improve their grammatical and lexical production. (See Davies & Tyler, 1989; Tyler & Davies, 1990b, for discussion of this phenomenon.) The reenactment, then, usually provides an immediate boost to the ITA's confidence.

No two enactments are ever the same, even if the participants and the scenario are unchanged. Seeing how a relatively minor shift in strategy or execution of a strategy can affect the interaction is valuable training for the whole class. (In this case, the difference between beginning with an apology or not had an important effect on the tone of the exchange.) If at all possible, the instructor tries to use a different native-speaking interlocutor in the second enactment. (In the reenactment discussed below, a different native-speaking interlocutor played the role of the student.) Changing the interlocutor highlights how the dynamics of an exchange change with individual personalities and minor variations in the interpretation of the role. Observing these variations begins to give ITAs a sense of the range of potential native-speaker responses and takes them away from relying on a pat, memorized response. The reenactment provides practice of the key move in a familiar but somewhat different circumstance so that ITAs can see the structure beneath the varying surface manifestations of the general situation. Finally, reenactments emphasize flexibility by exposing the class to alternative strategies they can successfully use in the general situation.

In the second enactment, the ITA again begins by announcing that she has an appointment in 5 minutes. However, this time as she makes the announcement, the ITA also steps toward the door. The student quickly approaches, saying that she has questions about the material to be covered in tomorrow's quiz. The ITA responds, "Can you walk with me because I have to go to my office first?" The student answers that she needs more time than that, acknowledging that she has several questions. The ITA then asserts that she must go and offers to discuss the questions over the phone. The student rejects this, and they negotiate an appointment for later in the afternoon. (A full transcript of the enactment appears in Appendix C.)

In the second enactment, the ITA came closer to meeting the goals of quickly postponing the discussion while still indicating a willingness to work with the student. The second role play lasted approximately half as long as the first. The native-speaking interlocutor stated that the ITA showed a willingness to discuss her questions and general sympathy for the student by offering several alternative times for discussing the material. The ITA retained the strategy of beginning with an announcement that she had an appointment in order to try to head off any discussion. This time the strategy worked more successfully because she did not undercut herself with an apology. Her strategy of suggesting that the student walk with her immediately forced the student to determine that there was not enough time to have her questions answered. Although the student rebuffed the ITA's first suggestion to discuss the problems over the phone, the two interlocutors were able to set a definite time to meet later in the day. Generally, the ITA was praised for the increased control she showed. The class pointed out that her body language was still somewhat passive and that she might have been able to shorten the exchange even more if she had gathered up her books and started walking to the door as she carried on the conversation.

After the reenactment, the class is ready to move on to the next scenario. The role plays are videotaped; the tapes are reviewed in one-on-one sessions between the instructor and the ITA. At this point the instructor may discuss grammar or pronunciation points. For instance, in this case the ITA was encouraged to use *Sorry about that* rather than *Sorry for that*. Use of modals, as in *You have to do that* versus *You'd better do that*, were also discussed.

Conclusion

The role plays have become a regular part of the curriculum in the University of Florida's ITA training program. Comments on the class evaluations consistently indicate that the ITAs find the role plays valuable and engaging. Each semester brings more anecdotes from ITAs indicating that role playing difficult exchanges arm them with the confidence, understanding of the norms of expected behavior, and foreknowledge that allow them to more successfully negotiate difficult situations. In addition, analyzing speaker goals and intentions, along with pragmatic feedback, sensitizes the ITAs to the types of subtle missteps that lead to miscommunication and thus provides them with valuable tools for recognizing and repairing a misstep before the exchange breaks down.

Appendix A: The Scenarios

For the first five scenarios, the ITA's role stays the same.

TA

You are at the end of the class. Normally you are willing to stay around and talk to the students for a few minutes, but today you are in a hurry. You have a big test starting in 15 minutes in a building on the other side of campus. You need to leave class quickly in order to make it to the test on time. You have a regular office hour scheduled for tomorrow.

Student

1. The class is just ending and you would like to talk to the teacher now. You have some questions about an assignment that is due next week. You think you only need about 15 minutes or so to get things sorted out. You would rather not wait for office hours, which are scheduled for tomorrow, but you will if you have to.

2. The class is just ending and you want to talk to the teacher now. You have an assignment due tomorrow and you have several questions about it. You'd like to start working on it as soon as possible. You are a fairly insistent person.

3. The class is just ending and you want to talk to the teacher now. You just got an assignment back and you did not do as well on it as you originally expected. Getting a good grade in this class is important to you. You accept that the teacher has graded you fairly, but you are quite worried about the assignment due next week. You want to get started on it as soon as possible and feel you can't do any work until you've sorted things out with the teacher.

4. The class is just ending and you want to talk to the teacher now. You just got a test back and you didn't do as well as you had hoped. You feel there might be some points the teacher failed to give you, that perhaps the teacher was being too much of a stickler. You're generally a cooperative student; you do not want to offend the teacher, so you are not willing to push too hard.

5. The class is just ending and you want to talk to the teacher now. You just got a test back and you are quite upset at your grade. You were really hoping to get an A and you got a C. You feel some of the questions were ambiguous; others asked about applications that were not directly covered in the book. You looked at the paper of a student next to you, who got a B+ for what seems like almost the same answers.

Now the role plays shift to a qualitatively more difficult negotiation—one that takes place in the middle of the class and thus potentially involves the whole class as the audience.

TA

You've just finished your introduction to the day's material and instructed the students to begin working on their own. They must finish the assignment by the end of the class today. You know most of them will need some help from you, especially getting started. At the beginning of today's class, you handed back graded homework and quizzes. There were a range of scores with some students doing very well and others not so well. You see a student approaching with the returned quiz and homework in hand.

Student

6. It's the middle of class. The teacher has just finished a formal presentation and now the students are supposed to work on their own. You just got a test back and you're somewhat upset about it. You'd like the teacher to explain some of the points you missed now. You are a generally cooperative student.
7. It's the middle of class. The teacher has just finished a formal presentation and now the students are supposed to work on their own. You just got a test back and you're upset. You feel like the test was graded unfairly. If possible you'd like to get the teacher to change the grade now.

Appendix B: Transcript of the First Enactment

The numbered lines in italics contain a loose description of the most relevant facial expressions and body language that accompany the verbal exchange. A blank line indicates continuation of the most recently mentioned expression. The paralinguistic information focuses primarily on the ITA. The accompanying verbal exchange occurs on the line immediately below.

I (Instructor)
S (Student)

Role Play 1a

1 I is standing behind desk with both hands on the desk, leaning.
I: OK. So class has to be finish early today because I have
2 I slightly smiling.
I: appointment in 5 minutes. So I'm so sorry for that . . .
3 S walks up to and around the back of the desk. Positions
S: Let me catch you quickly while you leave. I've got an
4 himself between the ITA and door. I turns to S, smiling.
S: appointment too. I know the paper's due tomorrow.
5 I smiling and nodding. Body is very still.
I: Yes.

6 I's expression more serious.
S: And I've got some real quick questions about how to finish the paper.
7 I's expression serious, concerned.
I: Uhum.
8
S: I don't know where to cite my primary source material in the foot-
notes.
9 I gives slight nod. Concerned but friendly expression.
I: Uhm.
S: Should I put them at the beginning or at the end?
10 I smiling, shakes head. Small hand gestures.
I: No, that depends on yourself. If you think it's better to put
11 I smiling.
I: at the beginning, you can put at beginning. If you think it's
12
I: better in the end, then you can do that.
13 I's expression more serious. Body remains quite still.
S: OK. Also I'm not sure about um I used about 15 books for the
research.
14
I: Uhuh.
15
S: And I want to make sure I list them in the right order and I
16
S: also want to make sure, should I list periodical articles or
17
S: should I just list the books?
18 I gives slight shake of head. Very quick glance at watch.
I: I think is a big question. Because I have no more time, so if
19 I smiling
I: you can see me after this class.
20
S: Yeah, I've I've got an appointment. My sister's going to the
21
S: hospital. I've got to take her to the hospital. I just need to ya know
22 I looks serious
I: Do you have any time today?
23
S: Well, you know when you go to the hospital, you can get stuck
24
S: for hours. I'm really not sure how long it'll be.
25 I laughs. Glances at her watch.
I: Because I have to go in 5 minutes.
26

S: Yeah. I just need to know. Should we cite periodical articles
27
S: or just books. I'm I'm not sure on this.
28 *I looks serious. Nods.*
I: Yes, You can cite just books.
29
S: OK and also if we read part of a book, can we cite the whole book?
30 *I nods, looks serious.*
I: Yes, better put the whole book and the name of the book and
31
S: OK. Also I also I need to know do we need to double space footnotes?
32 *I looks puzzled.*
I: Your question, excuse me?
33
S: No, double space footnotes? Put footnotes in. Skip two lines and then
do another line.
34 *I smiles broadly. Nods vigorously.*
I: Yes, better do that. You'd better do that.
35 *I smiling.*
S: Also, we need do we need a title page?
36 *I smiling.*
I: Yes.
37
S: And we need to page number every page?
38 *I smiling and nodding.*
I: Yes, probably better do that.
39
S: OK. Do we need to put it in a binder?
40 *I smiling.*
I: Yeah.
41
S: OK. And we need to get this to you tomorrow, what by 5 o'clock?
42
I: Before 5 o'clock. OK?
43 *S rubbing chin.*
S: OK. OK. Wait a second. I think I've got a couple more
44 *S cleaning sleep from his eyes.*
S: questions. Also you want a bibliography?
45 *I more serious. Thrusts head forward and then retracts.*
I: Please do that.
46
S: It needs to be alphabetized?
47 *I smiling.*
I: Uhum.

48
S: OK. I've got someone typing it so it may be like a couple days
49
S: late. Uh. Is that a real big problem?
50 I serious. Holding head very still.
I: It is a big problem. I think you'd better give me it tomorrow.
51
S: And if it's like a day late, is that going to be a big problem?
52 I looks quite serious.
I: Ya. I think so.
53
S: OK.
54 I shakes head slightly.
I: Cuz if everyone waits
55
S: I've got someone typing it. I figure it's just a bibliography
56
S: and the paper's done. The research is done.
57 I laughs.
I: Probably can cancel some of that.
58 S turns to camera, smiling.
S: OK. I'm running out of questions.

Appendix C: Second Enactment

I (Instructor)
S (Student)

1 I is facing the class, standing behind the desk.
I: OK. So class is finished today. So I have to go. Because I
2 I sidesteps to the corner of the desk closest to the door.
I: have an appointment in 5 minutes. So
3 S approaches desk. I smiles. I serious.
S: Before you leave, I know we're having a quiz tomorrow and I
4
S: didn't understand the things you went over today for our quiz tomorrow.
5
I: Uhuh.
6
S: Would you just go over this with me really quick?
7 I holding arms straight, raises both arms a few inches from the sides of her body and rotates hands slightly. Serious.

I: Can you walk with me because I have to go to my office first.
8
I: If you can walk with me, we can talk together.
9
S: Um that's really not going to give us enough time, though cuz
10
S: I have like . . . the last 5 questions that you went over, I
11
S: really don't understand.
12 I Knits brows.
I: So you have a lot of them?
13
S: Excuse me.
14 I Serious.
I: Do you have a lot of questions?
15
S: Ya. I do. I didn't understand the last five.
16 I raises arms, almost a shrug. Serious expression.
I: So we because I really have to go so why don't I give
17
I: you my phone number. Probably you can call me tonight. So I
18
I: will be home tonight.
19
S: How how are we going to be able to do it on the phone,
20
S: though? You know because
21
I: Because you have your book, I have my book and so probably we
22
I: can discuss it on the phone.
23
S: There's no way we could do it in class?
24 I smiling.
I: Uhm . . . If you have another time today, maybe we can arrange
another time.
25
S: Ahah. Could we do it next period?
26 I shakes head. Looks serious.
I: Next period. Because I have appointment probably cost about
27
I: hour and a half. So next, next
28
S: No, I can't come then, um

29 I serious but friendly.
I: How about later today? How about 10th period or 9th period?
30
S: OK.
31 I smiles broadly.
I: Is that ok?
32
S: Ya, that's ok.
33 I smiling.
I: OK.

■ 8 ■

The Functional Language of the U.S. TA During Office Hours

Beverley J. McChesney
Stanford University

■

Undergraduate students in the United States go to see professors and teaching assistants (TAs) during their regular posted university office hours for help of various kinds; the office hour has come to be regarded as a resource not unlike the library or tutorial center. International teaching assistants (ITAs) spend a good portion of their assistantship time helping students individually, yet most ITA courses to date have focused primarily on the in-class tasks of teaching and reviewing with a group. To assist ITAs in using nativelike speech behavior in office hours, trainers need to examine that speech systematically. In an attempt to characterize the language of native English-speaking TAs in office hours, this study will examine audiotapes of instructors (14 of TAs and 14 of professors) with students at a major university.[1] Six social science departments and three engineering departments are represented in the tapes. All but one of the TAs and most of the students are native speakers. In certain cases, contrasts between TAs' and professors' speech will help to clarify their different roles.

Office hours, in which visits are one-on-one as well as student initiated, require different language use than the classroom. Studies of classroom discourse, such as Sinclair and Coulthard (1975), have examined student-teacher discourse in the group classroom setting but not the one-on-one, student-initiated language of the office hour. To analyze this discourse, a number of questions need to be asked. How do TAs talk with students? Is it different from professors' talk? Who controls these student-initiated exchanges? More specifically, how do TAs direct, encourage, correct, remind, and give study advice? And what student talk do TAs need to deal with? Language use in office hours, as in other conversation, depends not only on the purpose of the exchange but on the rank and relationship of the participants, their perceptions of their roles, their level of confidence, and their individual styles.

Office hours can be better understood by answering these questions: Why do students go to office hours, and for what purposes do they see TAs as opposed to professors? In the 28 conversations, the following seven purposes of visit were identified:

TAs
1. homework
2. preparation for exams
3. term paper advice

Professors
4. information on courses
5. completion of requirements
6. waivers and exemptions
7. projects and papers.

TAs exist to relieve professors of the routine tasks of assisting students with homework and preparation for examinations. Students see both professors and TAs to seek out role models and to choose courses and majors; however, most requests for TAs' time concern daily course work and short-term study advice.

In this chapter I describe and analyze four features of office-hour talk. The first, directing students' learning, covers the area traditionally associated with teaching by explaining, transmitting information, and leading step-by-step. The second, encouraging and reinforcing, is an indication of how the TA relates to the individual in a setting that offers more opportunities for this than a class does. The third has two parts: correcting students' mistakes and reminding them of terms or points taught earlier. These two related functions demonstrate the skill of the TA in linking prior to present work. The fourth, giving students advice on good technique and exam preparation, is one that tests the judgment as well as the knowledge of the TA.

Directing Students' Learning

During office hours, TAs direct students' learning not by presenting new material but by meeting individual students' needs. TAs respond to questions, look at attempts to solve problems, discuss assignments, and give hints on how to succeed in the courses. The degree of active direction by the TAs is relative to the students' preparation and ability to direct their own learning; with different students, TAs play various roles: drill instructor, memory prompter, sounding board, or supporter. Whatever style is required, TAs may play a central role in the process of learning for those students who seek them out. This section analyzes how directive or nondirective TAs are by examining the amount of talk they engage in, the type of questions they ask, and the dynamics of topic shifting. When appropriate, I contrast TAs' language and style with that of professors.

Sacks, Schegloff, and Jefferson (1974) examined turn taking as an indication of control in conversations. According to their study, at certain points in a conversation an opportunity arises for a new turn to begin. On a first-come, first-served basis, either the current speaker continues or another person begins. If five or more people are involved, as in a class, a complex situation that requires regulation can arise. Conversely, turn taking is relatively smooth and easy when only two people are involved. When those two are a TA and a student interacting in the relative privacy of an office for the purpose of increasing the student's understanding of course material, it is comparatively simple for either one to take a turn. In this sample, the data suggest that TAs often dominate the conversations but that students have ample opportunity for turns. As long as students have opportunities to take turns and shift topics, they can direct the course of the conversation and thus the course of their own learning. By the same token, TAs can take or extend turns to make helpful suggestions. Whether the students are undergraduates or graduates, the amount of instructor talk appears to vary according to the purpose of the visit, the rank of the instructor, and individual style. In conversations about the requirements of the major, professors talk twice as much as students, whereas in conversations about possible waivers of courses, students talk as much as professors. Table 1 shows the average words per turn (wpt) in the TAs' and professors' conversations. For the purpose of this study, a turn is a unit bounded by the other speaker's voice, regardless of syntactic units or continuing topics.

Comparing the mean wpt for students talking with professors and TAs reveals that the ratio of talk between students and professors (1:1.3) is closer than that between students and TAs (1:2.2). The ratio of instructor talk to student talk is no doubt affected by other variables, such as length of total conversation, native language, gender, and degree level of the students.

The correlation between purpose of visit and length of turn is clear. When a student asks for information or direction, a professor naturally talks more in, for example, conversations on requirements in majors. A student reporting on progress or difficulty in a project naturally talks more. TAs, in contrast, tend to talk as much as two times more than students when working on homework sets or helping students prepare for exams. It is interesting to note that two of the most interactive conversations concern mathematics. In these, the TAs and students have turns

Table 1 ▪ Average Words per Turn, by Purpose of Visit to TAs and Professors

Purpose of visit	Words per turn		Turns each
	TA[a]	Student[b]	
Discuss homework	35.2	10.7	37
	22.2	5.4	20
	16.6	8.8	87
	12.5	8.7	55
	10.7	5.3	43
	10.3	12.6	70
	10.3	8.6	81
	8.3[c]	9.6	124
Prepare for exam	27.6	10.8	12
	26.5	5.7	88
	25.3	6.0	85
	17.2	7.9	67
	10.0	11.1	432
Discuss term paper topic	30.5	8.1	12
	Professor[d]	Student[e]	
Discuss other university courses	25.6	10.2	22
Clarify project	20.9	8.7	46
Get feedback on final exam	20.5	14.5	70
Discuss requirements in major			
Conversation 1	20.1	9.6	155
Conversation 2	19.2	8.8	79
Conversation 3	17.9	9.4	46
Conversation 4	14.0	7.6	65
Discuss grant proposal	15.3	10.8	16
Discuss credit for courses outside department			
Conversation 1	12.4	13.8	40
Conversation 2	12.1	12.4	60
Update student's training	11.5	10.7	112
Discuss difficulty in writing	11.4	17.7	60
Ask about project or favor	10.3	16.1	104
Apologize	5.4	12.0	25

[a]By chance all the TAs dealing with homework were male, and all those dealing with exam preparation were female. The TA who dealt with a term paper topic was male. [b]By chance all but one of the students were male. Nine were undergraduates; five were graduate students. Two were nonnative speakers. [c]This TA was a nonnative speaker. [d]In 10 conversations the professors were male; in 4, female. [e]Eight males and six females.

of almost equal length and the students speak a bit more than the TAs do. With a sample of this size it is not possible to know whether the degree of interaction is due to the needs of the field, the purpose of the visit, or the ability of the TAs.

The 1-hour conversation (432 turns) of a mathematics TA and a student preparing for a calculus exam affords an opportunity to hear a TA and a student solving problems and to see how the learning is directed within each problem. The student comes in saying he has a lot of trouble with many of the problems; in fact, he does not know how to start the first one. The TA demonstrates her ability to help him learn; that is, she gives quite a bit of direction when needed and encourages him to take the initiative when possible. Embedded in the overall conversation are seven sections in which the TA and student focus on individual problems. Looking at the seven problem solutions in greater detail reveals a pattern: as Table 2 shows, increased length of turn fluctuates between TAs and students. In Problems 1, 3, and 7 the TA has fewer wpt.

The TA verbally directs the student when needed, as in Problems 1 and 3, but tries as much as possible to sit back and let the student lead, as in Problems 2, 4, 5, and 6. Problem 7 is a little unusual in that the TA gives relatively lengthy, technical explanations four times; otherwise, in that conversation the TA attempts to serve as quiet resource person rather than as recitation director. Within Problems 1 and 3, those in which the student feels particularly lost, a clear pattern in the TA's strategies and language emerges. Consider the beginning of one of the problem solutions in Excerpt 1:

[1] **S:** Uh, I have no idea how to start that.
    TA: Yeah, yeah you do. Why . . . I mean, look at it.
    S: Well, I mean . . . I think that I want to change all these. I want to . . . get these into sines . . . and cosines.
    TA: You're taking the limit , as x goes to zero.
    S: Zero . . . x squared, secant 2x . . . cosecant 3x
    TA: The limit x goes to zero. Now what does . . .
    S: Well, . . .
    TA: I mean, what's, what's going on? What's secant?

The student attempts to solve the problem; if necessary the TA assures him that he is capable of doing it. When the student runs into difficulty, the TA in some cases gives him a definition or rule of thumb but more often asks questions. Specifically, the TA asks a lot of *wh-* questions to steer him in the right direction. A few such questions from Problems 1 and 3 follow:

Table 2 ▪ **Average Words per Turn for TA and Student Preparing for an Examination**

		Average words per turn	
Problem	Turns each[a]	TA (female)	Student (male)
1	65	10.7	9.5
2	35	9.2	10.4
3	64	12.9	7.8
4	67	6.8	10.6
5	9	2.8	10.8
6	35	10.3	10.5
7	90	10.2	8.6

[a]Greetings, transitions, and partings not included.

Problem 1
- I mean, what's . . . what's going on? What's secant?
- I want you to say, what's cosine of 4x as x goes to zero?
- What's happening to cosine x?
- What were you going to say? So, what's the problem?
- What do you have to multiply by?
- You're supposed to have 2 on the bottom, so what do you have to do?

Problem 3
- So, what are the critical points?
- The critical point is, what does it do with the derivative?
- What did you find the critical points for?
- So on this picture which one would it be?
- How do you know, on the picture?
- Why do you want to cross that one out?

When the TA directs the learning actively, the TA's turns are longer and the questions more frequent. In the other cases, the TA achieves what she sets out to do by talking less; that is, she gives the student the floor. The student takes the initiative and asks the TA questions as he goes through the problems step by step.

To further understand the use of TA questions in directing learning, I used Kearsley's (1976) typology of question patterns. This typology, which Long and Sato (1983) modified and applied to the second language classroom, includes four categories that apply to TA-student interaction in office hours:

1. echoic: confirms comprehension
2. referential: asks for information the TA needs
3. evaluative: asks for thinking and response when the TA knows the answer
4. rhetorical: the TA asks and answers to direct.

Other researchers in ITA discourse have applied question typologies to their data (Myers, this volume; McKenna, 1987). This typology allows a more detailed examination of the math TA's questions above. Echoic questions and referential questions are not found in Problems 1 and 3, those in which the students had difficulties. The several evaluative questions that do occur function as "directors" in the sense that the TA leads the student step-by-step through difficult material by questioning the student at each step, thereby prompting the student to verbalize each point before continuing. Problems 1 and 3 contain evaluative questions such as "What's happening to cosine x?" and "So, what are the critical points?" In fact, evaluative questions such as these appear to be one of the primary keys to effectiveness when the TA can focus on one student at a time. A few rhetorical questions, such as "The critical point is, what does it do with the derivative?" are also present, functioning in the same way that they do in the classroom. Conversations on problems in which the student takes the lead and the TA takes a back seat as resource person (2, 4, 5, and 6) contain more echoic questions but fewer questions of all the other kinds. Table 3 contains a summary of the question types found in the math problem solutions. This question use is in marked contrast to the questions observed in four conversations between a professor and students. The purposes of those visits to the professor, which are much more general than TA-student problem solving, include discussions of requirements for the major and training or research beyond course work. Those conversations feature few echoic and rhetorical questions, 45 referential questions, and no evaluative questions at all. This contrast between the speech of TAs and that of professors is a reminder of how varied the functions of teaching and advising are.

To see how students direct learning, it is necessary to look at the number and type of questions that students ask. Rounds (1990) reported that math students ask very few questions in class, that is, generally not more than six per class. Myers (this volume), however, reported that students ask many questions in science laboratories, from 35 to 143 in the 90-minute labs in her data. In office hours, the number of direct *wh-* and yes/no questions (including question or statement word order, tag questions, and "phrase, right?") also varies greatly. As an indication of frequency, the three conversations that last from 20 to 60 minutes contain approximately one direct student question per minute.

As might be expected, students are likely to ask questions that request

Table 3 ▪ **Types of Questions Asked by TA in Six Math Problem Solutions**

	TA as director		TA as resource person			
Problem	1	3	2	4	5	6
Turns	65	64	35	67	9	35
Question type						
Echoic	0	0	0	2	1	1
Referential	1	2	1	1	0	0
Evaluative	6	8	1	0	0	2
Rhetorical	3	1	1	0	0	0

direction from TAs, expressing their areas of confusion and attempting to deal with new concepts and methods. In the data students ask 50% more direct questions than the TAs do; among their questions, there are nearly three times more yes/no than *wh-* questions. The students' questions not only demonstrate their ability to guess, to confirm, to challenge, and to conclude, but also give a snapshot of informal give-and-take with TAs. The examples of their questions below illustrate their active participation in learning:

- Is that what you want me to . . . ?
- Can I do that?
- May I skip this term?
- On my next part, would I write dx?
- Wouldn't you end up with 2 over here if it was even?
- Why can't you use the regular . . . umm . . . partition formulas on this?
- Then how do you start . . . how do you make sure that the last one's gonna be 1 over . . . ?
- And this is the expected value?
- Just write it in like that?
- So I have to plug in these?
- There's no other . . . there's no easy way to do this one?
- You have to do it both ways, right?

Students also solicit information and help by asking questions in indirect ways. These questions are not only numerous but no doubt somewhat difficult for nonnative-speaking TAs to comprehend. The following examples illustrate these indirect questions:

1. I was wondering if you could give me a little guidance on the term paper . . . .
2. I don't quite understand what these things stand for: symmetrical barter, fiat . . . money system, things like that.
3. I guess the only other question I had is like how familiar with the formulas should we be?
4. Yeah, so I expect that we're going to have to find the yield to maturity, or at least know how to for a coupon bond, for a fixed payment, and I'm not sure I know how to use the charts.

In cases such as 3 above, the student may be formulating the question only as it comes out, whereas in 4 the student is probing for exam content. Both require interpretation and response from the TA, just as direct questions do.

Myers (this volume) notes that ITAs have an easier time comprehending and responding appropriately to student questions that are preceded by framing statements so that they share the student's context. Unlike in the laboratory, in the office hour the TA and student usually focus on topics together for the duration of the conversation. Thus framing prefaces are less necessary than they are in the laboratory and tend to come only at the beginning of conversations. As such they are the students' way to set both the agenda and the boundaries for the conversations, thereby directing their own learning. The following are examples of framing prefaces found in the conversations:

- Could I ask you specifically about the limits. When you . . . have some questions about the study sheet that you gave . . . you gave us yesterday. Okay . . . uhh, first of all, I don't . . . .
- Fractional reserve banking . . . I couldn't find that in the literature.
- It's for that, uh . . . that section right before the miscellaneous problems.
- I was just looking over my notes, and what you were saying today, and I thought maybe I could get a few of your thoughts on, umm, civil liberties. . . .

Finally, topic shifting in the classroom is an indicator of the instructor's control and direction. In these student-initiated office-hour conversations, however, the students tend to be the ones to shift topics, whether they are speaking with TAs or with professors. Excerpt 2, which illustrates one such shift, occurs in a conversation on interpretation of the concept of free speech in political science. The TA is finishing an explanation; the student, satisfied with the explanation, takes the floor to shift to his next question:

[2] **TA:** There are any one of a number of ways of transferring the kind of vague ideas into . . . concepts . . . that. . . .

    S: Sure. That makes a lot of sense. And, just a question I was . . . just wondering . . . about is, a lot of the specifics, do you think that we really should be worried about that?

These transcripts suggest that during office hours TAs generally respond to rather than initiate topics.

The answer to the question of how directive or nondirective U.S. TAs are in office hours has three parts. First, TAs take over if the students do not know what to do, and they limit their talk if the students are making attempts to solve problems. Next, they use evaluative *wh*-questions to prompt students to think and respond. And finally, they allow students to set the direction of conversations.

Encouraging and Reinforcing Students' Attempts

As seen in the previous section, TAs often have a more informal and shorter-term relationship with students than professors do, closer to a peer relationship. Accordingly, TAs may be less likely to provide positive reinforcement than professors are. In the data from the TAs' and professors' conversations, this appears to be true, although an important difference exists between the purposes of the visits. Table 4 shows the percentage of instructors' turns that include some form of positive reinforcement. Positive reinforcement phrases occur in 10% or more of the turns in 10 of the professors' 14 conversations, but at the same rate in only 3 of the TAs' 14 conversations. TAs may not perceive that they have a responsibility to encourage and praise students unless they have been trained to do so. Much praise and encouragement, in fact, might distance TAs from students, thereby emphasizing their difference in rank. However, the TAs who use a good deal of positive reinforcement appear worthy of imitation. Among the professors, the two who gave more reinforcement than the others did appear to the observer to be the most supportive overall. In the conversations professors and TAs use the following one-word comments: *good, perfect, right, um-hmm, uh-huh, great, exactly*. Schegloff (1981) discusses the function of words such as *uh-huh* as topic continuers, signals that the listener will pass up potential content turns in order for the first speaker to continue. These continuers serve two functions for TAs: (a) to signal continued attention and interest and (b) to signal reinforcement of and agreement with what the speaker is saying. In some utterances only one function may be intended, but both may be perceived. Use of these continuers is very common in most of the TAs' conversations.

Table 4 · Positive Reinforcement Expressed by Professors and TAs

Purpose of visit	Turns including reinforcement (%)
Professor with student	
Get information on other university course	18.2
Clarify project	26.1
Get feedback on final exam	14.3
Discuss requirements in major	
Conversation 1	9.0
Conversation 2	3.8
Conversation 3	32.6
Conversation 4	0.0
Discuss grant proposal	6.2
Discuss credit for courses outside department	
Conversation 1	12.5
Conversation 2	36.7
Update student's training	17.0
Discuss difficulty in writing	11.7
Discuss project or favor	16.3
Apologize	28.2
TA with student	
Discuss homework	
Conversation 1	2.7
Conversation 2	0.0
Conversation 3	12.6
Conversation 4	5.4
Conversation 5	7.0
Conversation 6	14.3
Conversation 7	6.2
Conversation 8	8.9
Prepare for exam	
Conversation 1	0.0
Conversation 2	2.3
Conversation 3	4.7
Conversation 4	1.5
Conversation 5	28.2
Discuss term paper topic	8.3

Examples of positive reinforcement phrases and sentences are these: *Looks good*; *This is not hard at all. It just looks scary*; and *You did fine*. In Excerpt 3, the TA moves from longer phrases of guidance to one-word or short phrases of support, approval, and reinforcement.

[3] **S:** If we have x over sine . . . sine 3x, we want to make the top 3x.

TA: So this cosine 4x over cosine 2x, we don't worry about.

S: Just leave that, yeah.

TA: So then we say . . .

S: We've got x over sine 3x, let's leave it that way.

TA: Okay.

S: Sorry . . . times x over sine 4x.

TA: Right.

S: Okay. So let's make both of those . . . make this one 2, make this one 4.

TA: Um-hmm.

S: Multiply . . . uh, we have to multiply this bottom by 3 here, the bottom by 4.

TA: Um-hmm.

S: And the tops were both 1, so we'll keep them that way.

TA: So we're . . . so we're . . . right, so 1 over 3.

S: Right, so we don't have to do anything there. And then, this goes to . . . this is . . . going to one.

TA: Um-hmm.

S: This is going to 1 . . .

TA: Um-hmm.

S: So we have . . . 1/3,

TA: Yep.

S: 1/4, so we got 1/12.

TA: Right. Exactly.

S: Yeah.

TA: So don't be scared.

S: I guess not. I solved that.

Note how the TA varies her token continuers. According to Schegloff, variation may be done subconsciously to show interest. Schegloff's notion is supported by the observation that two of the professors who seem very supportive in a total of five conversations use continuers frequently, with variety. ITAs need to recognize and use these tokens to show their interest, which in turn encourages students in their problem solving.

Despite the importance of phrases for reinforcement, measuring positive reinforcement only in terms of words and phrases is inadequate because it neglects intonation as an expression of support. In fact, the warmth of any conversational exchange in English depends heavily on use of positive intonation patterns. Without going into an analysis of its use, I simply report that the TAs in this study did demonstrate their concern through their intonation.

Correcting and Reminding

Up to this point I have discussed how TAs direct students' learning, encourage students, and reinforce. Even when TAs are skilled in these areas, however, learning is sometimes not straightforward; for whatever reasons, students may still not understand or may be inaccurate in their work. How do TAs deal with students' mistakes?

In the data, when TAs correct students' errors or misunderstandings, they do so frankly, without many overt signals of politeness. Possibly they feel they need to do so in order to be particularly clear. Relatively formal linguistic signals of politeness when correcting may tend to distance TAs from students in the same way that formal expressions of praise do. Consider, for example, the mathematics conversation discussed at length earlier; in Excerpts 4 and 5 below from the same conversation the (female) TA tries to make sure that the (male) student does not make an error in the equation. When he makes the error, she tells him what not to do and then repeats her hint.

[4] **TA:** You want the whole top to be zero.
  S: So, . . . right.
  TA: You don't make them both . . . you don't make them both zero . . . you make the . . . whole thing zero.

[5] **TA:** Now, just look at what you've done . . . and check it. You know, we spent a lot of time on the derivative. I don't want you to . . .
  S: Oh . . .
  TA: Right.

In Excerpt 5 the TA's tone is definitely patient and kind as she tells the student to check what he has done. She is careful not to give the answer but to give the student a hint and time to find it himself. Later in that session when the student gives a wrong answer, the TA does not hesitate to tell him bluntly (in Excerpt 6) that it is wrong. Given the context of a 1-hour help session, her correction seems in order, whereas if it had occurred within their first 5 minutes of work, it might have seemed harsh.

[6] **TA:** Now what's the derivative of the second now? See?
S: Wh--
TA: With respect to x. See, y is a function of x.
S: 2xy. I don't know.
TA: Our second is just this y.
S: Right. The derivative of that is 1.
TA: No, no, no. The derivative with respect to y is 1, but the derivative with respect to x is just dydx. We don't know what it is. It's dydx.
S: Umm . . .
TA: Right?
S: I guess.

In addition to corrections, the office-hour TA needs to remind students of class discussions, textbook chapters, or other readings to help them understand and to prepare for exams. Rounds (1987a) pointed out in her study of mathematics classes that good TAs link current points with prior experience in class or in the textbooks. At times, as in Excerpts 7 and 8 below, TAs remind students of terms used by the professor or in the field as a whole. At other times, such as in Excerpt 9, they may caution students about procedure.

[7] **S:** So you have a commodity substitute for money.
TA: Right, and I think Professor McDonald called it commodity money.

[8] **TA:** In this special case, we do tend to use the term reflexes, which I don't think is used . . .
S: I don't recall it.
TA: . . . in the book, but the daughter language shows reflexes of the original sound in . . . the mother language.

[9] **S:** Where'd you get this from?
TA: If you're looking at Mannik and . . .
S: . . . supplement . . .
TA: . . . supplement, then be careful because sometimes what we've set up as the columns are rows, so be careful.

Another expression of the reminding function found in the office hour is the restatement of generalizations and rules that the student seems to have forgotten. In Excerpt 10 below the TA uses *you know* as a token of respect when repeating a generalization.

[10] **TA:** Now, strictly speaking, you know, a critical point is a point of a function.

   S: Right.

And in Excerpt 11 the TA observes the student closely to see how he is changing the equation; then she points out that the operation is "very standard procedure."

[11] **TA:** So, remember what you did there, 'cause you've got this x prime, and you . . . looked back, then you know what . . .

   S: I was all confused.

   TA: . . . were your critical points. See, bring . . .

   S: change it down . . .

   TA: and then . . . common denominator.

   S: Okay.

   TA: Very standard procedure for a lot of these problems, like that.

   S: When I look at this, I'll remember . . . critical points.

   To be helpful, a TA must correct and remind. Guidance on particular problems or assignments is, after all, the most frequent purpose of students' visits. These data contained fewer examples of correcting and reminding than I had anticipated. Possibly TAs have to learn this teaching skill. ITAs should be trained to perform these functions while expressing respect for what the student already knows.

Giving Study Advice

Giving students general study advice and helping them to prepare for exams are central functions of the TA office hour. Help ranges from individual study hints to predictions of exam coverage. Sometimes a TA advises by putting himself or herself in the student's position, as if to say "if I were you"; for example, in Excerpt 12 a TA introduces a mnemonic device:

[12] **TA:** Now, cosecant; what I . . . the way I remember this is . . . well, . . . secant starts . . . with s, and you sort of think sine.

   S: Um-hmm.

   TA: So . . . and cosecant, you'd think would be cosine. But it's just the opposite.

   S: Oh, that's right.

Two other TAs provide more general advice on procedure:

[13] TA: This is . . . this is kinda strange. When this happens, implicit ones like this, you have to solve for whatever you can solve for. So here, we want to . . .

[14] TA: It really is a case of, you know, going through it and writing down each stage and just going through it mechanically, because if you try and do a couple of stages in your head, you usually get mixed up. It's much better just to write it down, the whole thing.

S: Umm . . . yeah.

TAs often say that students come to their offices in greater numbers immediately before midterm and final exams. What kind of help do they need and want? A review of the five conversations in which students are preparing for exams shows that the students' needs fall into six categories: (a) handouts and review, (b) clarification of class notes, (c) clarification of puzzling concepts, (d) problem-solving guidance, (e) confirmation of readiness, and (f) information on exam coverage. Students are very frank about asking what will be on the exam, and TAs are direct in their responses. Notice the degree of assistance offered by a political science TA:

[15] S: And just a question I was just wondering about is . . . a lot of the specifics of the constitution, do you think that we should be worried about that?

TA: As long as you understand basically what they're talking 'bout . . . if you . . . understand the concept of due process . . .

S: Umm . . .

TA: If you understand the concept of privacy, you know, and that there are different ways of . . . if you have a notion that there are three different places that that comes from, and why.

S: Um-hmm.

TA: You know, just kind of vaguely . . . not vaguely, but you don't have to be a . . . constitutional lawyer to explain it.

In Excerpts 16 and 17 an economics TA provides information on exam ground rules and the relative importance of various resources.

[16] TA: And you don't need to bring a programmable calculator to class, because if you can't write down the formula, you get no points for getting the answer.

S: Oh, really.

TA: So, . . .

S: So, I gotta learn those.

[17] **S:** Is there stuff that wasn't covered in lecture that we should know? Like, there's something in there about the CIR model, . . . the efficiency frontier and indifference curves, but then he goes on to talk about standard deviation, expected value. . . .

TA: I would know it only . . . pay attention to it only inasmuch as it helps you understand what we did in class. He does, he does a pretty good explanation of the Fisher model.

S: Right.

TA: He does a more detailed explanation of that, of the diversification, and it's worth. . . . I don't think it's worth plowing through John Hudson's handout to be able to reproduce it, but it's certainly worth understanding what the ideas are. And other than that, the other thing I would look at in Van Horn is the term, . . . "structure of interest rates." He talks about that in what I think is a little bit clearer way than Mishkin. I mean, it almost sounds like Mishkin is afraid to make it complicated, and Van Horn's a little bit more clear because he's not afraid to say this is a complicated thing, but that's . . . I would only worry about it to the extent that it helps you.

S: So it's not like he's gonna . . . he'll mostly test us on what he covered in lecture?

TA: I think so.

The advice on the economics exam in Excerpt 17 is particularly extensive and revealing about the content of the coming exam. One wonders if the faculty member has approved this level of "help." TAs need to be careful to tell enough but not too much about an exam and not to mislead. For example, when the student summarizes his probing with the final question, "He'll mostly test us on what he covered in lecture?", the TA responds, "I think so." This may well lead the undergraduate to review only the class notes. In cases such as this, TAs have a responsibility to be sure of what they can and should say even though they may not have seen the exam. Because this is an area in which inexperienced TAs need training, ITA trainers need to know more about it. A survey of professors and TAs on their policies and practices regarding statements that "leak" exam coverage individually during office hours would be very helpful— and it would be valuable to have more recordings of instructors giving such information.

Summary and Recommendations

Office hours are a time when TAs, like professors, have the opportunity to observe the learning strategies of one student at a time and to assist with areas that the student identifies. This does not mean that U.S. TAs are carbon copies of U.S. professors in their office-hour interactions. On the contrary, they bridge a gap between professors and students; because TAs themselves are students, they are in some respects more able to reach and help students than professors are. The two areas in which TAs usually give short-term assistance are homework and exam preparation. In view of the fact that their talk varies according to their task, U.S. TAs' language use and behavior in office hours can be characterized as follows:

- They direct students actively by telling them what to do, or observe and comment in order to encourage the students to engage in self-directed learning.
- They ask many evaluative *wh-* questions to break problems into manageable steps.
- They respond to many student questions, as many as one direct question per minute.
- They respond to rather than initiate topics.
- They praise or provide other positive reinforcement
- They correct and remind students directly, without many overt signals of politeness.
- They control the degree of information that students have about impending examinations.

Compared with professors, TAs often talk more and appear to be more direct.

These findings lead to a number of recommendations for ITA course curricula. First, courses should pay attention to office hours as a setting and task different from both classrooms and undergraduate laboratories. Courses should encourage ITAs to analyze their own and recorded interactions with students in an attempt to focus on an appropriate communication style. Second, ITAs should practice asking and answering questions of the types found in the conversations reviewed here. In particular, ITAs should practice asking *wh-* questions to direct students' learning, and they should be ready to relinquish the lead when students want to take that role. Third, ITAs should discuss effective teaching and learning strategies in the one-on-one situation, with attention to how ITAs' strategies might need to differ from those of U.S. TAs.

Briefly stated, office hours give TAs a chance to assist students in a setting that is less threatening to ITAs than the classroom is. If done well, office-hour assistance not only enhances the experience of the students in the course but provides opportunities for ITAs to communicate with U.S. students in meaningful and memorable ways.

Note

1. Collection of a portion of the data was made possible as part of an international student training grant, a Cooperative Grant, administered by the National Association for Foreign Student Affairs for the United States Information Agency.

■ 9 ■

Discourse Strategies for ITAs Across Instructional Contexts

Elizabeth R. Axelson
University of Michigan

Carolyn G. Madden
University of Michigan

■

The linguistic study of language in the classroom is a branch of discourse analysis . . . it has relevance to a number of educational problems, and can be an instrument of clarification if it is developed appropriately. The process of learning and teaching is realized through language to a significant extent. . . . By using a generally applicable method of linguistic description, the distinctive features of classroom discourse show up in perspective. We can thus approach questions like how similar or different is it from other types of discourse, particularly those which are important in teaching and learning. (Sinclair, 1987, p. 1)

The involvement of applied linguists in the training of international teaching assistants (ITAs) has led to a continued concern with the analysis of both the language of the learner, that is, the ITA, and the target language of the discourse communities to which the ITAs are assigned. An emphasis on classroom discourse and behavior has been present in the research on ITA training focusing on a range of issues, such as the discipline-specific language of the math classroom (Rounds, 1987a; Byrd & Constantinides, 1988), the analysis of spoken discourse and nonverbal behavior in the classroom (Hinofotis & Bailey, 1981; vom Saal, 1987; Tyler, Jefferies, & Davies, 1988), as well as a discussion of classroom materials used to enhance the effectiveness of presentation skills (Douglas & Myers, 1989; Boyd, 1989a; Axelson & Madden, 1990). Myers and Plakans (1991), Young (1989a), and others, however, have recently cited the need for a more thorough understanding of the language and strategies ITAs require to enhance their nonlecturing skills. Myers and Plakans (1991) have stated that at Iowa State University, "the most common teaching responsibility of the ITAs . . . is not classroom teaching, but serving as laboratory assistants" (p. 368), and a cursory investigation at the University of Michigan revealed a similar finding. Nelson's research (1990), similarly to the early Bailey article (1984), addressed the undergraduate perspective indicating that even in the classroom, U.S. college students prefer TAs who use interactive and interpersonal teaching behaviors. Smith (1989a) summarized the language needs for ITAs by stating, "answering questions is a far more typical task than lecturing; more emphasis should be given to assignments developing interactive skills and attention needs to be given to issues beyond presentation skills."

These findings suggest the need to investigate the discourse of these contexts as well as to understand the difficulties ITAs may have in performing effectively. For example, in a small but significant finding of Douglas and Selinker (this volume), an ITA inappropriately incorporated a lecture style of discourse into an interactive context, suggesting that trainers should focus on the varying discourse strategies needed for effective communication across contexts. Myers and Plakans (1991) additionally pointed out that, because university administrations have assumed that "less skill—linguistic, cultural and pedagogical—is required in handling a lab section than in leading a recitation or discussion section or teaching a class" (p. 368), lab assignments are often given to ITAs with marginal proficiency. In addition, the practice at universities has been to give office-hour assignments to ITAs with less than adequate instructional language. An initial investigation of a number of laboratory assignments and office-hour situations indicates, however, that their interactive nature is far from easy to manage. The following is an excerpt from a statistics office hour between an ITA and a U.S. undergraduate:

[1] **TA:** . . . come on in. Have a seat please.
   S: All right. I came to talk about,
   TA: Yeah,
   S: not so much for the last homework but myself in class.
   TA: mm-hm
   S: Um . . . I don't know if you've noticed that I mean I've I
       don't, come to . . . lab
   TA: Right
   S: as often as I should
   TA: Right, right
   S: and I haven't been turning my homeworks in, as often as I
       should, I do them but I don't always turn them in.
   TA: . . . mm-hm . . .
   S: It's just that, I don't come to lab, because I get frustrated,
       and like I don't
   TA: About, about the

S: the materials

TA: . . . unh-huh . . .

S: . . . and because like I don't, I'm not, I don't think I'm grasping it very quickly,

TA: . . . mm-hm . . .

S: . . . so if I don't understand it, then I'll be like, "aw, forget it, I don't need to go" . . .

TA: . . . mm-hm . . .

S: . . . and, it c- . . . , you know, I don't realize that, it's gonna be explained to me in lecture—because I have lecture right after lab . . .

TA: . . . mm-hm . . .

S: . . . but, um, and I didn't want you to think that I was just blowing off the class, and just—I mean like I know I need to do a lot of work . . .

TA: . . . mm-hm . . .

S: . . . but, I know that if I, you know, work hard I can't—I can pass the class at least . . .

The dialogue continues for a few more interactions with the ITA nodding, mm-hmming, listening, and finally responding to the issue fairly appropriately and effectively. However, a closer analysis of the body language and the linguistic content of the student's monologue suggests that interpreting the form and the content of the message might create some difficulty for a nonnative speaker with marginal proficiency and, further, that an effective and linguistically appropriate response to such a message might not be within the grasp of an ITA. For example, is the student looking for a better grade? Does she want to drop the class? Is she sincere? Is the ITA responding with the reassurance the student needs? Does the ITA understand some of the phrases, such as "blowing off the class" or "grasping it very quickly"?

In a volume of the *Annual Review of Applied Linguistics* devoted entirely to discourse analysis and its importance in the understanding of language, language learning, and language training, Riggenbach, in "Discourse Analysis and Spoken Language Instruction" (1990), focused attention on "ways in which discourse analysis itself can be useful for language learners as a tool for speaking and listening instruction" (p. 152). Riggenbach further stated that a most recent concern for language teachers is how to design instructional tasks and activities that allow the learner to focus on accuracy but that also incorporate some of the communication practices found to be effective and appealing. Riggenbach suggested that two instructional levels exist: at the micro level, the teacher and learner are concerned with grammatical structures in context, and at the macro level, with the sociocultural appropriateness of various related utterances for accomplishing particular speech acts in a given setting. If we accept Shaw and Garate's (1984) premise that "trainees arrive with a good command of the grammatical, lexical and semantic system of the language . . . a general competence in the language," then the goal of ITA programs is to address language at the macro level of instruction.

This chapter addresses the issue of appropriateness and context of the language of ITAs in laboratory, office-hour, and classroom situations. We continue the efforts of Axelson and Madden (1990) and Young (1989a) in specifying the details of target language discourse categories appropriate to these academic contexts as well as to provide an informed and organized syllabus of these categories. We take a closer look at these categories and their manifestations from native and nonnative instructors, emphasizing the similarities and differences across contexts in content, style, form, and purpose. Finally, we summarize our findings in order to enable trainers to bring the information to the ITAs so as to provide organized and meaningful choices that will enrich the discourse repertoire of ITAs.

Methodology

We came to the task of identifying discourse categories from two directions. The first was the observation of what teachers actually do in their classrooms, office hours, and labs. As we watched videotapes of TAs and professors in these settings, we made transcripts, notes and lists, which included direct quotes as well as entries such as *greetings, emphasis, explaining*, and *responding to questions*. At that stage we clearly needed a further theoretical framework, one to help in organizing our observations, for as Sinclair (1987) has pointed out, "Without proper safeguards for the unwary, selections from the vast stream of verbal activity can be made to satisfy almost any preformed notion of the learning or teaching process" (p. 1). Sinclair's research (1987) speaks to the general-purpose English Language Institute classroom. Nevertheless, his interest in comparing different kinds of classroom discourse to understand the purpose of discourse and how it is shaped by the social context forms a meaningful context for the study of TA discourse. His research constructs a framework for investigating how TAs use discourse to meet the obligations of instructing and supporting the learning of university students.

Sinclair offers an analytical framework of three levels, which he calls *moves, transactions* or *exchanges*, and *discourse categories*. The first and third levels proved instrumental in organizing our data. The moves, Sinclair's first level, are the actual speech events, and his third level, discourse categories, defines the purpose of the move. For example, in office hours a TA makes the following move: "Thank you. That's what I wanted to know. Now what is it here?" His purposes, as it appears to us, are to acknowledge the student's answer and to move on to the next step in the problem. Thus, one discourse category is *moving on to the next step in a problem*. We emphasize that no neat one-to-one correspondence exists between moves and discourse categories. Rather, the match is many-to-many. For example, in the classroom, a mathematics TA says, "Well, I'm almost there. I'm looking for f of x. I don't quite have f of x. But I can solve for f of x squared." The purpose of these comments may be like those just quoted above, to move on to the next step in the math problem. In addition, the narrative style of the remarks is a part of establishing an informal atmosphere and facilitating student understanding. Moves thus can serve more than one purpose and therefore belong in more than one discourse category.

Beyond Sinclair's discourse categories, there seems to be a level of *pedagogical objectives* that is served by a number of these categories. For example, greetings and small talk before class, informal style, using student names and inclusive pronouns, and softening the blow when responding to students' wrong answers all seem to be part of an overarching objective *creating the right atmosphere for student learning*. We have organized the discourse categories across contexts according to these overall objectives in Table 1.

The lists in the table are shaped both by our observations and by video- and audiotaping of actual academic encounters in the classroom, lab, and office hour. We are keenly aware that many other possible kinds of interactions in these settings simply may not have occurred during our observations and are therefore not represented here. The lists remain fluid, open to modification in response to new observations and interpretations. This awareness notwithstanding, the global view they provide helps us to see where significant similarities and differences may lie. For example, the teacher frontedness of the classroom stands out in contrast to the emphasis on student "doing" in the other two settings. Thus, the general goal of facilitating learning is categorized differentially as *facilitating student performance/problem solving* in the lab, *facilitating student problem solving* in the office hour, and the contrasting *facilitating student understanding of material* in the classroom. A glance at Table 1 also indicates, for example, that *creating the right atmosphere* is an objective of all three contexts, although the language, manner, and extent of creating the right atmosphere vary.[1] These particular objectives and the varying categories across contexts underscore the diverse language and style TAs need to control and pay attention to and the depth of linguistic skills

Table 1 • Pedagogical Objectives and Discourse Categories

Discourse Categories in the Lab

1. *Creating the right atmosphere*
   a. using side sequences: *banter, small ialk, humor*
   b. giving clear instructions
   c. encouraging atmosphere of equality
   d. using informal style
   e. acknowledging other students' needs for attention
2. *Circulating to provide assistance*
   a. initiating interrelations with lab partners *(also a feature of creating the right atmosphere)*
   b. finding out how individuals are doing when they haven't asked for help
   c. responding to student-initiated interaction: *matching level of response to level of question*
   d. responding to competing claims for attention
3. *Facilitating student performance/problem solving*
   a. stating purpose: why are we doing this experiment?
   b. setting up independent work
   c. time keeping
   d. giving instructions while demonstrating procedures
   e. giving instructions while circulating
   f. giving changes to instructions, interpreting lab manual or instructor's instructions
   g. giving reasons
   h. giving reminders, linking old and new material
   i. warning and cautioning
   j. reassuring
   k. congratulating
4. *Responding to student comments on returned lab reports, reactions to grades, student justifications for miscalculations*
5. *Negotiating with, complaining to, and assisting other TAs*
   a. complaints
   b. negotiations

Discourse Categories in the Office Hour

1. *Creating the right atmosphere: framing the interaction*
   a. greetings
   b. small talk
   c. names and inclusive pronouns
   d. tension-breaking side sequences
   e. informal style
   f. praise, congratulations, reassurance
   g. acknowledgment of the presence of other students waiting: *part of managing turnover, but also could be a tension breaker, closer, or form of congratulations*
   h. closings

Table 1 ▪ *Continued*

2. *Making transitions*
   a. initiating a new exchange
   b. responding to the student's initiation of an exchange
   c. moving on to the next step in a problem
3. *Reassuring*
   a. making sympathetic remarks
   b. rewarding responses to right answers
   c. softening the blow in response to wrong answers
4. *Facilitating student problem solving*
   a. eliciting questions and problems
   b. step-by-step questioning
   c. simplifying the question or breaking it down when the student is unable to respond
   d. warning the student s/he is on the wrong track or should know the answer
   e. encouraging students to continue with the task
   f. linking old and new material
   g. giving tips, advice, warnings, reminders; emphasizing important points
   h. giving information
   i. giving reasons
   j. congratulating
5. *Modeling problem solving*
   a. thinking out loud
   b. demonstrating
   c. pointing out a problem-solving technique
   d. checking comprehension

Discourse Categories in the Classroom
1. *Creating the right atmosphere*
   a. greeting and making small talk before class
   b. using informal, narrative style, humor, local references
   c. using students' names
   d. using inclusive pronouns *(atmosphere of equality)*
   e. handling students' wrong answers: softening the blow, praising, reassuring
   f. maintaining contact while writing on the board
   g. using body language
2. *Facilitating student understanding of material*
   a. giving interesting, clear introductions
   b. restating, paraphrasing, using synonyms
   c. using examples, leading to examples, analogies, metaphors
   d. using informal, narrative references
   e. linking: relating new and old work

Continued

Table 1 • *Continued*

---

    f. emphasizing important points
    g. using transitions, moving to the next point, motivating the next step, labeling the steps
    h. provoking students to think
    i. eliciting opinions, guesses, ideas
    j. simplifying questions
    k. presenting information
    l. offering warnings, reminders
    m. giving advice
    n. concluding, wrapping up, summarizing
    o. encouraging students to handle their own mistakes
3. *Managing the classroom*
    a. making announcements
    b. running out of time, revising your plan as you go
    c. deferring response to student questions *(also contributes to the right atmosphere)*
    d. managing student turn taking

---

necessary for effective TA interaction with undergraduates. In this chapter we focus on two of the most salient objectives of TAs—creating the right atmosphere and facilitating learning.[2]

Creating the Right Atmosphere

Evidence suggests that students strongly prefer an interactive, informal, personalized, and supportive atmosphere, particularly in TA-run sessions (Bailey, 1983; Nelson, 1990). At the University of Michigan, for example, a 1990 survey of undergraduates found that "less than 5% are very satisfied and only another 15% are at least somewhat satisfied with the level of personal attention they are receiving at the university" (*A Michigan Education*, 1990, p. 97). Furthermore, an environment with these characteristics actually facilitates the learning of U.S. undergraduates. This objective of creating an informal, personalized, interactive environment therefore appears to be an important one for ITAs. The question remains, however, how to accomplish it. Some strategies already mentioned are greetings and small talk, using students' names and inclusive pronouns, and responding uncondemningly when students offer incorrect answers. Are these strategies employed in all teaching contexts? Are they equally important? Are there others? A look across the environment of labs, office hours, and classrooms will help to answer these questions. Table 2 elaborates on the information provided in Table 1 by including examples of the moves observed across contexts that contribute to an appropriate atmosphere.

Styles of Interaction

As Myers and Plakans (1991) have pointed out, the lab has many characteristics that distinguish it from the classroom. Notably, the tone is largely set by students in their interactions with their lab partners. A highly informal style of slang-laden banter seems typically to accompany lab work in introductory-level courses. For example, during one of our observations in a chemistry lab, a student referred to a small spatula as a *pooper scooper*. Needless to say, the ITA to whom this remark was addressed did not understand the reference. Furthermore, students seem to avoid technical terms, using expressions like *the little top adapter thing* or *one of those little rings* instead. Thus, the TA has an intense need to adopt an appropriate, informal style in order to stay afloat—to participate in interactions with students, to get and maintain their attention, to deal with what the TA does not understand, and to push the students' thinking about what they are doing. Moreover, the TA must be able to take control where appropriate, setting a tone that maintains safety and responds to emergencies in a potentially dangerous setting. Thus, for example, an ITA who has been swapping jokes with members of his class switches to a louder, more authoritative voice and to the form of direct commands when saying, "Something's burning? Change it, because the acid may dissolve the rubber. And wash your hands."

In contrast to the lab, both the office hour and the classroom offer the TA considerably more control over the style of interaction. In the latter cases, the TA can adopt a more formal tone without the risk of falling outside the mainstream of an appropriate interactive style. Although students still tend to dislike the TA who acts like a "little professor," they tolerate a wider range of styles in these settings. For instance, we have observed a very popular ITA using the service encounter language, "What can I do for you?", and the rather imperious invitation to enter the office, "Come, James." The slight strangeness and variability of his tone is overlooked by the student, who cannot mistake the genuine welcome and interest expressed in the ITA's tone of voice, intonation, and body language.

In the lab, interactions tend to be short and numerous, and occur without the framing of greetings and closings. Rather, the TA asks directly, "How's it going?" or the student initiates the interaction with a question or comment regarding the experiment under way. By contrast, in office hours the absence of the framing of greetings, small talk and closings would be a source of enormous social discomfort for the student.

Table 2 · Creating the Right Atmosphere for Student Learning

Creating the Right Atmosphere in the Lab
Relaxed enough to be productive, unintimidating but not so casual that students are sloppy or unsafe
1. *Using side sequences:* banter, small talk, humor
   TA: Don't you want to keep it?
   S: Take it home and eat it? OK. If I want to kill someone.
   TA: Sugar for the coffee. Or for your cakes.
   S: Do you travel much?
   TA: Yeah. From Baits to the Chemistry Building and back again.
2. *Giving clear instructions:* safety precautions
   S: I smell something burning . . .
   TA: Something's burning? Change it, because the acid may dissolve the rubber. And wash your hands.
3. *Encouraging an atmosphere of equality*
   "Well, I'll try to help you."
   "I'm like you. This is the first time I did this."
4. *Using informal style*
   "How's it going?"
   "[male damsel flies] cruise up and down the stream"
5. *Acknowledging other students' needs for attention*
   "uh, just uh wait a moment, OK"

Creating the Right Amosphere in the Office Hour
Framing the interaction
1. *Greeting*
   "Hi Tonio. Glad you made it on time."
   "Ah, James! What can I do for you? Are you feeling better?"
2. *Making small talk*
   "How are your courses going? . . . I remember you had an exam yesterday."
3. *Using names and inclusive pronouns*
4. *Using tension-breaking side sequences*
   a. *change to the narrative tone*: "This guy always gets you in trouble because you always forget him."
   b. *change of subject*: "Is that my book or yours?"
5. *Using informal style*
   "This guy always gets you in trouble."
6. *Giving praise, congratulations, reassurance*
   "Right, that's exactly right."
   "All right, you're close, getting close"
   "So you wrote down what's given and what to find. Excellent."
7. *Acknowledging the presence of other students waiting* (part of managing turnover, but also could be a tension breaker, a closer, a form of congratulations)

Table 2 • *Continued*

"Go catch that last guy that came out. He had all the answers."
"If there's anybody else out there, send them in."

8. *Closing*

S: All right, OK . . . I'd like it easier.

TA: OK.

S: OK. Good enough.

TA: Go catch that last guy that came out. He had all the answers.

S: OK. Thanks.

TA: Uh huh.

"Good. So you feel you've got a handle on that now. Good."

Creating the Right Atmosphere in the Classroom

1. *Using greetings and small talk before class*
"How did you do it?"[to a student with crutches and cast] ". . . Surgery?
Really?"

2. *Using informal, narrative style, humor, local references*
"an' he mentioned before about the monarch butterflies . . . and they get
protection by some of them tasting bad an' hanging out in big groups. You
know, if one of 'em gets eaten then the birds that eat 'em learn real quickly
that they taste awful and they make you feel bad. . . ."
"Well, I'm almost there. I'm looking for f of x. I don't quite have f of x.
But I can solve for f of x squared."
"You've heard of Angelo's Restaurant, right? . . . On Sunday mornings I
pass by and I see long queues. It's packed. Yeah, it's packed. But, uh, if
you open another restaurant, will it still . . . what happens to Angelo's Restaurant?"

3. *Using students' names*
"Yes, Doug?" [in response to raised hand]

4. *Using inclusive pronouns (creating an atmosphere of equality)*
"So, OK, that is our basic assumption. Let's draw some differences and sim-
ilarities in terms of market."
"We're asked to find f of 4. And what we're given is. . . ."
"It turns out we got lucky as far as dosage goes. . . ."

5. *Handling students' wrong answers: softening the blow, praising, reassuring*
"I think you'll find that a little complicated."
"Um . . . we could, but it wouldn't be useful. . . . So what you're thinking
wouldn't work very well."

6. *Maintaining contact while writing on the board*
Turning profile to the audience, talking while writing

7. *Using body language*
Open stance, eye contact, movement, gestures

Here the issue of welcome is much more salient, as is the question of defining when the encounter is over. Indeed, we have observed that, in the case of an ITA who did not initiate these moves in office hours, the self-confident students who visited him provided this interactional framework themselves.

[2] **S:** You wanna practice on me? [pause]
I'm Mike. [pause]
What's yr name?
TA: Cheng.
S: Well, let's see [pausing while taking a seat and unloading book bag]. I need help with about a million things . . . Chapter 2
TA: 2
S: 2.4
TA: 2.4 [pause] What is your problem? You mean you have problem in all of these?

In the classroom, greetings and preclass small talk may be skipped. The TA may simply come in and start. As in the lab, welcome does not appear to be an issue, and the TA-student encounter may be personalized in other ways.

Side Sequences

Office hours are distinguished by one-on-one encounters, which may be intense. In this situation, the use of small-talk side sequences to break the tension can be an important ingredient in sustaining a comfortable atmosphere. For example, when a student is struggling with the material, a TA may shift the tone of the conversation to a more informal one, or may change the subject temporarily, to allow the student to regain confidence and composure. For example, we have observed an ITA remarking to a student who has experienced frustration with a problem, "In the very beginning I didn't catch its meaning, but I ask someone." By mentioning his own lack of understanding and telling how he remedied it, the ITA provides some common ground and reassurance for the student. Moreover, when the tension mounts and the TA makes no move to break it, the student may offer a tension-breaking aside, as in this dialogue:

[3] **S:** It's kind of hot in here, huh?
TA: Yeah, actually suppose the value . . .
S: Fun stuff.
TA: So actually we just find T value, to contain the T value.

Side sequences also occur in the lab but function somewhat differently, to incorporate the TA into the style established by lab partners. No doubt, this informal tone or shift of the topic away from the experiment to questions about the TA's personal life and adventures also helps to diffuse some tension about such discomforts as fear of chemicals (as when a student says, "If this thing explodes, I'm toast!") or hesitancy in studying live organisms. These tensions are considerably less likely to develop in the classroom. In one incident we observed, the bulb in an overhead projector burned out just as the professor was about to embark on a carefully prepared series of overhead illustrations. Tension mounted in the classroom as he lifted the lid of the machine. At this point, he made a joke, demonstrating his own poise in the situation, which released the tension in the room. Other imaginable cases in which a side sequence would perform this function are in response to teacher error or confusion. However, we have not seen such events in our observations of TAs.

Use of Names

ITAs are commonly advised to learn and use students' names, but there appears to be some variability in the use of names in different teaching contexts. In the lab, for example, students' names appear to be used somewhat infrequently. Students, on the other hand, constantly use TAs' names to get their attention. Thus in the lab ITAs must offer a clear and pronounceable name for students to use. In the office hour, using a student's name is a valuable tool in creating an atmosphere of welcome. In the example of greetings given above, the ITA uses the student's name effectively. In the example that follows, the ITA appears to understand the value of using a name but may not actually know the student's name. He says, somewhat awkwardly, "Hi. It's you!" Likewise, names seem useful in the classroom when the TA wishes to stimulate and encourage student participation. For example, an ITA says, "Yes, Doug?" to call on a student who has raised his hand. In this case, names seem to counteract the impersonal atmosphere of the teacher-fronted classroom.

Turn Taking

Managing student turn taking is potentially an issue in all three teaching settings. It appears in our lists for office hours, where it is called *acknowledging the presence of other students waiting*, for labs, where it appears as *acknowledging other students' needs for attention*, and under a different pedagogical category, *managing the classroom*, for the classroom. In the lab, students compete for attention, sometimes with a high sense of urgency, calling the TA's name, thrusting forward with bits of equipment ("Here. You fix it!"), and crowding around. The TA needs language in this situation to allay the fears and frustrations of those waiting. For example, one ITA said "Uh, just uh wait a moment, OK." Often, however, it appears that ITAs do not have a repertoire of effective responses in this situation. They conscientiously attempt to meet the demands of their students without saying anything about the situation. In one case, a student requested help, but the TA responded to another student's request without acknowledging the request of the first student. Her frustration is evident in her response to the situation:

[4] **S:** Feng, I need help.
    [TA walks away, in response to someone else's request for help]
    S: [aloud, to no one in particular] So he leaves.

Expressions like *Hang on a minute* and *I'll get to you in a minute* would be particularly useful here. In office hours, when students may be waiting for the TA's attention and the TA may not be able to see that they are waiting, the task of managing turns is different. We have seen a math TA who welcomed all students into his office when they arrived. At one session just before the final, at least nine students crowded into his office at once. He used a rotation system, allowing each a turn to raise an issue or problem, which he then dealt with for the benefit of the whole group. In another case, an engineering TA took students one at a time but made frequent references to those who might be waiting. Indeed, in one office hour he incorporated managing the line into greetings, small talk, praise and closings, saying such things as "Are you next?" "Why don't you stick around for half the people out in the hallway?" "Send the next guy in if you would." "Go catch that last guy that came out. He had all the answers." Turns in the classroom are again much more under the control of the teacher, who may praise (*Good!*), give a closure signal (*OK*), paraphrase the comment, ask another question, use body language such as moving toward the next speaker, or call on someone else to signal that the student's turn is over. The classroom teacher also needs to be able to defer a student question for another time and decide who needs to have an opportunity to respond or to question when numerous hands go up. These skills are a major part of classroom management and contribute to the right atmosphere as well.

Praise

Praise, congratulations, and reassurance seem to be particularly appropriate and prevalent in office-hour interactions. In office hours, the student is called upon to reveal weaknesses and struggle with inabilities. Thus the TA's support encourages the student to continue with what may be an uncomfortable task. TAs use such expressions as *right, perfect, exactly, yeah, good,* and *excellent* in response to the efforts students make in problem solving. A particularly effective move is that in which the TA summarizes what the student has done correctly and then praises it: *So you wrote down what's given and what to find. Excellent.* The fact that we see little praise, congratulation, or reassurance in the classroom corresponds to the fact that students do less there. We do not see them solving problems or taking many risks. When they do, however, this feature of TA behavior—handling students' wrong answers, softening the blow, praising, and reassuring—becomes very important because the student risks failure in front of other students. Thus teachers often respond to students' responses to questions with the same range of reassuring words listed above for office hours. Moreover, TAs use strategies to soften the blow when responding to incorrect answers in class. For example, when a TA says *I think you'll find that a little complicated,* he or she is not saying *You are wrong,* but *Your response is OK but could be better,* saving the student from complete embarrassment. If praise is a function of risk-taking behavior on the part of the student, one would expect to find it lavishly applied in the lab, where students are called on to perform new and sometimes frightening procedures. Nevertheless, they appear to be reassured by the actions of the TA rather than by words. The tone of bravado adopted by students may also preclude overtly reassuring remarks from the TA.

Different Contexts, Different Strategies

The foregoing discussion demonstrates the need to differentiate teaching contexts when considering appropriate means to create a positive atmosphere for student learning. In the lab, the features of TA discourse that appear to be most salient in creating the right atmosphere for learning are an informal style compatible with that established by the students and an ability to use language to acknowledge the needs of students who are waiting for attention. The framing of interactions and the use of names appear to be of little importance in this context. By contrast, in the office hour, framing the interaction through greetings, small talk, and closings is essential, as is the use of student names, to establish welcome. Furthermore, the discourse categories of praise, congratulations, and reassurance and of side sequences to break tension are important, as the student is called on to expose weaknesses during the interaction. In the office hour, as in the lab, it is useful to acknowledge students who are waiting for attention, but the moves employed to do so are different in each setting. The discourse categories and moves used to create an atmosphere conducive to learning in the classroom reflect the more teacher-centered, less interactive nature of most classroom teaching. In this setting, TAs may skip greetings and small talk, moving directly to announcements and the lesson. They may adopt a more formal tone here than elsewhere, relying on such strategies as the use of inclusive pronouns to personalize the interaction. Finally, in the classroom, use of students' names takes on real importance, as do praise and supportive responses to students' contributions when students are called upon to take risks in front of their fellow students.

As this summary illustrates, within the overarching pedagogical objective of creating the right atmosphere for learning, both discourse categories and language moves vary with the context of teaching. Some discourse categories are important within one setting but not in another. Similarly, the moves used to accomplish a discourse category may differ from one setting to another. The analysis confirms that the TA needs a varied and sophisticated repertoire of linguistic skills to accomplish the pedagogical objective of creating the right atmosphere, which in itself merely sets the stage for the main event, learning. In the next section we continue to explore the range and variability of discourse categories and moves associated with different teaching contexts by looking at a pedagogical objective in the foreground of learning, that of facilitating problem solving.

Facilitating Problem Solving

Problem solving, an essential skill for all students in an academic environment, involves being able to analyze, identify constraints, gather information, and generate and test hypotheses. It is a goal-oriented skill (Kurfiss, 1988) and is particularly critical in the fields where the majority of ITAs are assigned: chemistry, physics, mathematics, and engineering. Facilitating problem solving is an essential part of any teaching context, but it is primary in the context of the office hour. Hence, as seen in Table 3, *facilitating problem solving* is a unique pedagogical category in the office hour, shared with *facilitating student performance* for the lab, and diffused over the discourse categories under *facilitating student understanding of material* in the classroom. As these different categorizations suggest, problem solving is handled differently in the three teaching contexts.

The Lab

The relationship of discourse and purpose of instructional context is complex. For example, both the office-hour and the lab TA focus attention on individual students. However, problem solving in the lab usually relates to the successful completion of an experiment not to the content of the subject matter. Issues of safety, performance, measurements, time management, and so on are the content of most exchanges. The TA is

Table 3 · Facilitating Student Learning

Facilitating Student Performance and Problem Solving in the Lab

1. *Stating the purpose:* Why are we doing this experiment?
2. *Setting up independent work, telling enough but not too much, using classroom lecture skills*
3. *Keeping the time*
   "Well, if you have already gone ahead of time, you can go if you like."
   S: Should we leave these 'til 3:15? We don't know when it began to boil because we were in there.
   TA: It may have begun boiling 10–15 minutes after you went to the instrument room. So that can give you an idea.
4. *Giving instructions while demonstrating procedures:* show and tell
   "You're gonna . . ."
   "Never put it in a beaker, put it in a flask."
5. *Giving instructions while circulating*
   "You have to identify the mole's characteristic peaks."
   "So try to close the flask when you finish weighing."
   S: I smell something burning . . . .
   TA: Something's burning? Change it, because the acid may dissolve the rubber. And wash your hands.
6. *Changing instructions, interpreting lab manual or instructor's instructions*
7. *Giving reasons*
   "I turn up your thermostat because it wasn't boiling. It looks like 8 is right for it to boil."
   S: She said don't wash this with water because it wasn't very pure.
   TA: Mmm, you can use distilled water. But water is not going to dissolve the organic compounds. So you can't use water to clean something that contains. . . .
8. *Reminding, linking old and new material*
   "I wanta remind you . . . just like I told you."
9. *Giving warnings, cautions*
   "What did I just do wrong?"
   "Make sure you understand it before you leave tonight."
   "Of course, you're not going to die, but if you do it very often. . . ."
10. *Reassuring*
    S: How does that look?
    TA: It looks fine. . . . If the peaks are very sharp and very clear like this one, it means . . . uh . . . looks good [disturbance]. The peaks are very clear.
    S: Is this enough?
    TA: Yeah, I think so. Oh, the spectra are really nice.
11. *Congratulating*
    ". . . Oh, the spectra are really nice."

Continued

Table 3 • *Continued*

Facilitating Student Problem Solving in the Office Hour
1. *Eliciting questions and problems*
   "So where'd you go wrong?"
2. Using step-by-step questioning
3. *Simplifying the question or breaking it down when the student is unable to respond*
   "It's off until when? When will our voltage be like this?"
   TA: . . . and what was VC1 at steady state?
   S: V . . . (doesn't know the answer)
   TA: See, so what is the current at the steady state? The current, what is the current here?
4. *Warning students that they are on the wrong track or should know the answer*
   "No. The book doesn't say it's 4 volts. What is V2 in that case, is what I'm asking."
   "Why do you say there's no I?"
   "I don't understand your question."
   "That's easy enough." (could also be reassurance in some contexts)
5. *Encouraging students to continue with the task*
   "Just tell me what you're thinking."
6. *Linking old and new material*
   "So we take the same approach that I said to take last time."
7. *Giving tips; offering advice, warnings, and reminders; emphasizing important points*
   "Sketch it on a graph."
   "The correct answer is the correct answer."
   "Well, always attack these diode problems by what is the circuit when the diode is on and what is the circuit when the diode is off. OK?"
   "You don't ever ignore a resistor. Never. OK? Never ignore a circuit component. OK? So, what's V2 here?"
8. *Giving information*
   "Let's see. . . . We're saying that at T2 = 0 we chose the switch. . . ."
9. *Giving reasons*
   "So that's why the voltage is . . . because the capacitor charges up and stores all the energy for the circuit and it's got V across it."
10. *Congratulating*
    "Why don't you stick around and help those people out in the hallway?"

Facilitating Students' Understanding of Material in the Classroom
1. *Giving interesting, clear introductions*
   "Today, what I want to do. . . ."
   "OK, so I guess we're ready to start. First of all let me, uh, remind . . . ."
2. *Restating, paraphrasing, using synonyms (could be for clarification or verification)*
   ". . . you get a series, a complicated series of nuclear reactions, of thermo-nuclear reactions, . . ."
   "The key word's replace. Using a substitution."

Table 3 ▪ *Continued*

S: Maker.

TA: Price maker. Right, price maker.

3. *Using examples; leading to examples, analogies, and metaphors*

"You expect that animals will learn . . . what's good to eat an' what's not good to eat at a young age. A lot of other animals depend on that. Um, like the centipedes or millipedes that Brian was talking about today depends on animals learning that it's bad to eat . . . ."

4. *Using informal, narrative references*

"An' he mentioned before about the monarch butterflies . . . and they get protection by some of them tasting bad an' hanging out in big groups. You know, if one of 'em gets eaten then the birds that eat 'em learn real quickly that they taste awful and they make you feel bad. . . ."

"Well, I'm almost there. I'm looking for f of x. I don't quite have f of x. But I can solve for f of x squared."

5. *Linking:* relating new and old work

". . . let's look at part B. It's slightly more complicated. You have an integral from 0 to x squared not just x, of f of. . . . And the question is the same, find f of 4. [pause] Well, what should we do?"

"Start out the same way, right."

"You're gonna have to use the formula I gave you yesterday, the general formula, which says that. . . ."

"Notice the difference with the other 2 parts is that. . . ."

"First of all, let me remind. . . ."

6. *Emphasizing important points:* using repetition, stress, pseudo-cleft; using questions for reinforcement

"The key word's replace. Using a substitution."

"So what we're gonna do here is. . . ."

"So that's a question that commonly appears on tests."

7. *Making transitions, moving to the next point, showing the relationship between points, motivating the next step, labeling the steps*

"And so. . . ." "And then . . . ," "And now if you differentiate you get. . . ."

"So I get a quarter. OK? If you want you can check that you. . . ."

"First of all. . . ."

8. *Provoking students' thinking:* using questions

"What would be another set of directions that would land you in that same point?"

"Let me ask you this: If you imagine all possible coordinates, r must be either what or what?"

"What is another thing that'll do the job?"

TA: But uh if you open another restaurant, will it still . . . what happens to Angelo's Restaurant?

Continued

Table 3 · *Continued*

S: It'll still be packed.
TA: It'll still be packed. Why is it packed?

9. *Eliciting opinions, guesses, ideas*
"So [writes on the board] find f of 4. Do you have any ideas how to go about it?" [pause]

10. *Simplifying questions*
"Do you have any ideas how to go about it? [pause] We want to calculate f of something, right? . . . So the real question is can we find f of . . . f of x. The general formula for f."

11. *Presenting information*
TA: Why do you think restaurants are monopolistic competition?
S: Because they're basically selling the same product. Maybe just slightly different specific products. Let's say you're going out for a burger. It's generally going to cost about the same price and generally contains the same ingredients. And that's about it.
TA: Right. So it fulfills all of these. It can affect its own price, not necessarily the whole industry. Anybody can open a restaurant and compete for the whatever stake there is. It's differentiated—Bob Evans is different from Bill Knapps and different from Lobster, uh, what, Red Lobster, and etc., etc. Uh, many firms. OK? So that's it.

12. *Offering warnings, reminders*
"This is where it could cause problems."
"Now all the stuff in Chapters 13 and 14 are very readable . . . . That is, you can read for yourselves . . . . I will go through it faster speeding bullet."

13. *Giving advice*
"I want to remind you that . . . ." "That's the form . . . ."
"We set it up and the next thing to do is . . . ."

14. *Concluding, wrapping up, summarizing*
"OK, there you are. Looking at the markets, there are four of them here. Perfect competition, monopolistic competition . . . ."

15. *Handling your own mistakes*
"[pause] Oh. Oh oh oh. I forgot to say one thing . . . ."

---

responsible for stating the purpose of the experiment and guiding the students toward completing the task. Characteristically, the lab TA uses a direct discourse style to give instructions, reasons, and warnings:

■ You have to identify the mole's characteristic peaks.
■ . . . so try to close the flask when you finish weighing.
■ . . . mm you can use distilled water. But water is not going to dissolve the organic compounds. So you can't use water to clean something that contains . . . .
■ Never put it in a beaker, put it in a flask.

■ Make sure you understand it before you leave tonight.

Rarely do lab TAs provoke students' thinking about the possible problems, outcome, or significance of the experiments. In fact, in Excerpt 5 an ITA engages in small talk and is offered an opportunity to help a student but apparently fails to understand the meaning of a student's response.

[5] **TA:** How's it going?
   S: It's going all right. I really don't know what I'm doing here but . . .
   TA: [doesn't say anything, just stands by observing for a while]

Interpreting the TA's response as inadequate is, however, not the only possibility. Myers and Plakans (1991) have pointed out that the role of the lab TA is somewhat ambiguous. Lab assistants are trained to focus their energies and language on the issues of safety and performance but only superficially on an understanding or discovery of the issues. An example such as the one above causes us to question whether opportunities for more problem solving are missed in the lab, particularly when the TA apparently has plenty of time to move around and ask more probing questions. However, ITAs frequently report that they are instructed to take a hands-off approach in the lab. Byrd and Constantinides (1988) have suggested that trainers exercise caution in teaching TAs to follow the philosophy of ESL learning and teaching. But trainers recognize the need for ITAs to teach undergraduates critical thinking skills and problem-solving abilities. This area seems to be one in which language and effective pedagogy are inextricably linked, where the function—the macro level of instruction—can serve both the linguistic needs of the ITA and the learning needs of an undergraduate. The issue here is language, training, and the negotiation of ITA performance between trainers and departments.

The Office Hour

Defining the role of the TA in the office hour is less ambiguous, however. Although students come to office hours for many reasons (see McChesney, this volume), one of the main reasons is to seek help in solving often difficult problems. Table 3 shows that this is no easy task. Some of the essential characteristics of facilitating good problem solving that we have identified are eliciting questions and problems, step-by-step questioning, simplifying the question, breaking it down when the student is unable to respond, and warning students that they are on the wrong track. The linguistic dexterity required to accomplish these goals is challenging at the very least. A glance at the office-hour moves in Table 3 indicates that, although the language is not lengthy and is often simple, it is dynamic, probing, analytical, responsive to the needs of the student, and functionally diverse. The following summary of the questions from an exchange between a physics TA and an undergraduate student shows the structural simplicity of questions as well as the diversity of their function.

Moves	*Functions*
"What's B asking for?" "So what is it that they're asking for?" "In your own words, how would you . . . ?" "So the current is increasing. What can you say about it?"	Asking for a paraphrase, asking student to demonstrate understanding of the problem
"OK, so you have the rate at which energy is being stored. So how do you express that?"	Confirming, breaking it down Asking for factual information
"How do you find the rate at which energy is being stored from the energy itself?"	Pushing on to the next step
"During *what* time?"	Intonation suggests something is missing
"So you have the energy in the conductor?"	Intonation encourages student to go on
"Well now, this is the energy and you just told me you're looking for the rate of change, the derivative?"	Intonation underscores potential problem
"So what don't you know in this part?" "So the circuit is connected at time, so what does it start out at?"	Breaking the problem down, underscoring where learning needs to take place

The transcript of this particular interaction is characterized by many questions: Some facilitate learning by asking for paraphrases, asking for the student to demonstrate an understanding of the problem, and some prompt a factual response or seek the manipulation of data. The TA also uses intonation and emphasis frequently and effectively, such as, "During *what* time?" to signal a warning that something else is needed, to encourage the student to go on, and to underscore potential problems.

The ability to see potential problems is related to familiarity with subject matter and attention to the student's thinking process, and the ability to forewarn students and to utilize these problems to teach is a matter of language.

Breaking down the problem and assessing it are critical in the office hour. Having the linguistic ability to do so is a challenge. One ITA queried a student directly, "What is your problem? You mean you have problem in all of these?" Students are often unable to state explicitly what their problem is because they lack not an answer but a methodology, a strategy, an assumption, or an understanding of a relationship. The TA in the office hour has the advantage of time and focus to probe, give advice, warn, remind, and encourage students.

The Classroom

The Socratic style of the office hour is in sharp contrast to the characteristic lecture style of the classroom. The constraints of the classroom TA to finish with the materials, get students ready for the test, give quizzes, and cover a great deal of material in short periods of time precludes the question-and-response style of the office hour. Typically the classroom TA adopts a lecturing and modeling approach. Classroom TAs are expected to give examples, analogies, and metaphors to facilitate learning. Restating, paraphrasing, summarizing, and giving clear introductions are characterized as effective teaching discourse. Again, interaction in the classroom, as in the lab, is related to discipline-specific goals and philosophy. For example, an economics ITA uses an interactive style in the following excerpt:

[6] **TA:** But uh if you open another restaurant, will it still . . . what happens to Angelo's Restaurant?
    S: It'll still be packed.
    TA: It'll still be packed.

A biology TA uses a narrative to engage students:

[7] **TA:** an' he mentioned before about the monarch butterflies . . . and they get protection by some of them tasting bad an' hanging out in big groups. You know, if one of 'em gets eaten then the birds that eat 'em learn real quickly that they taste awful and they make you feel bad.

The goal of the classroom ITA is often to transmit as much information as possible. The topic covered is determined by the teacher, the emphasis is the teacher's, and the students are expected to be prepared to learn, ready to integrate the new with old. The classroom language is frequently more direct, content weighted, and less negotiable than the office hour.

- You get a series, a complicated series of nuclear reactions of thermonuclear reactions. . . .
- You expect that animals will learn . . . what's good to eat an' what's not good to eat at a young age. A lot of other animals depend on that, um, like the centipedes or millipedes. . . .
- Let's look at part B. It's slightly more complicated. You have an integral from 0 to x squared not just x, of f of. . . . And the question is the same, find f of 4.

Inquiries such as *Well, what should we do?* and *Do you have any ideas how to go about it?* are, however, interspersed throughout an effective classroom lecture. The language of the office hour is, unlike that of the classroom, characteristically probing. The student and teacher often negotiate the topic of the interaction in the process of problem solving. Interestingly, an analysis of effective office-hour TAs revealed one ITA who used a lecture-style approach in the office hour. Excerpt 8 contains a rather lengthy narrative:

[8] **TA:** Ok, this should be a function such that when you take the derivative of this new function you get this old one. When you have to differentiate, you start with this and you just differentiate . . . like in x. Take the derivative of x and you get . . . . When you want to find though the antiderivative, you have to look for this so you can see this as the derivative of something and try to look at where it comes from, so if your question is not what is the antiderivative . . . just by looking at . . . and in this case I don't have rules for getting antiderivative. I have methods, but I don't have a rule, so I cannot say well this it it. So I have to do something with this to work it out. . . .

    S: . . . to work that out . . . integration of parts?

    TA: So in this case the appropriate method is integration by parts.

This TA consistently used a direct style, appearing confident and competent. The student, however, had little opportunity to negotiate the solution and little time to test out her hypotheses. It is not obvious that this student learned any less than the student in the interactive physics office hour, referred to above, but if problem solving and critical thinking skills are to be developed in the office hour, an ITA needs to take a more responsive approach toward the heuristics of learning. This issue is again one of philosophy, that is, of determining the role of the TA within each department across contexts and of understanding the function of language in these contexts.

At the beginning of this chapter, recognizing that the pedagogical context of ITAs is more often an interactional context, we stated that the research in ITA training needed to focus on a better understanding of the interactive language of these contexts. Understanding and analyzing the language of effective teaching has, of course, implications for the practical aspects of training, such as materials development and syllabus and curriculum decisions. The analysis shows that similarities do exist across contexts; for example, TAs in all three contexts link the old to the new, reassure, congratulate, give advice, warn, and remind. The differences, however, suggest a clear need to focus attention on differentiating the language and function according to instructional context.

The proper direction for trainers is to develop a fluid and dynamic syllabus of moves and categories to guide materials development. The more tantalizing issue is how to present materials with an objectivity that will provide ITAs with alternatives that do not preclude their ability to use whatever language and teaching abilities they may have. In our view, tapes and transcripts such as those that form the raw materials for our analysis of the moves and categories of ITA discourse can play an important part in training materials. They are particularly effective tools for presenting alternatives to ITAs, who can then choose strategies that build on and enhance their existing language and teaching skills. Our experience with such materials supports the claim quoted at the beginning of this chapter—that "discourse analysis itself can be useful for language learners as a tool for speaking and listening instruction" (Riggenbach, 1990, p. 152).

Materials for ITA Training

As we have observed elsewhere (Axelson & Madden, 1990), a short video sequence of actual teacher-student interaction, coupled with a transcript of what is said, is a powerful trigger for student discussion and analysis. The transcript helps students focus on microlevel issues of language as well as macrolevel issues in the interaction. In small groups, students can evaluate the pros and cons of the teacher's behavior, regarding it as an option that stimulates thinking about alternatives. Such consideration of a teacher's performance allows the student to identify positive features of teaching and language that seem compatible with his or her own style and proclivities. The trainer can then couple this experience with opportunities to experiment with options in activities that simulate teaching contexts. Further, students can be brought to reflect on the effectiveness of their own performance. A sequence of activities would follow this pattern:

1. consideration of a video and/or transcript of a teacher's behavior from which ITAs cull features of teaching and language and brainstorm other options
2. opportunities for ITAs to havé their own experience in a similar situation, either simulated or real
3. feedback on and evaluation of the ITAs' performance.

The two sets of materials below bring the ITA through this series of activities. The first set, in Task 1, is drawn from office hours and centers on a video and transcript of an interaction referred to at the beginning of this chapter as potentially challenging for an ITA. In contrast to more tidy, single-issue role plays and trigger tapes, the student presents a multifaceted problem. Her concerns are many and intertwined, so the ITA must sort out and identify the issues in order to respond. Furthermore, the problems she raises are core ones in the relationship between students and TAs. She cites lack of attendance, failure to turn in homework (although she claims that she does it), frustration and lack of understanding of the material, loss of motivation, concern about the TA's opinion of her, fear that she will not pass the course, and the question of needing a tutor, which may be construed more broadly as a request for advice and assistance in dealing with her situation. Beyond these issues, the student poses problems of style and language for the ITA. She speaks fast, hops from issue to issue, and uses expressions the ITA may not know. Her manner is a bit "hyper"; some viewers see this as a sincere expression of her anxiety, but others interpret it as discomfort with being observed in the insincere act of flattering the TA to get a passing grade. Therefore, her behavior raises not only the question of whether she deserves the TA's serious attention and help but the issue of differing perceptions of other people's behavior and the extent to which TAs can or should rely on such feelings in their interactions with students.

Task 1: A student seeks end-of-term advice in office hours for an elementary statistics course

Watch the videotape and follow along with the transcript.

S: Hi.
TA: Hi. Good morning.
S: [Comment about taping?]

TA: Yeah, this is my office hours.

S: Oh no!

TA: Oh! No, that's fine. [laughs] Come on in. Have a seat please.

S: All right. I came to talk about

TA: Yeah

S: not so much for the last homework but myself in class.

TA: Mmhmm

S: Um [pause] I don't know if you've noticed that I mean I've I don't come to [pause] lab

TA: Right.

S: as often as I should.

TA: Right right.

S: And I haven't been turning my homeworks in as often as I should. I do them but I don't always turn them in.

TA: Mmhmm

S: It's just that I don't come to lab because I get frustrated, and like I don't

TA: About about the

S: the material.

TA: Unhunh

S: And because like I don't, I'm not, *I don't think I'm grasping it very quickly.*

TA: Mmhmm

S: So if I don't understand it, then *I'll be like, Aw forget it,* I don't need to go.

TA: Mmhmm

S: And and it c- you know I don't realize that it's gonna be explained to me in lecture—because I have lecture right after lab

TA: Mmhmm

S: But um and *I didn't want you to think that I was just blowing off the class,* and just—I mean like I know I need to do a lot of work.

TA: Mmhmm

S: But I know that if I, you know, work hard I can't—I can pass the class at least.

TA: Mmhmm

S: I just, I don't know, I mean c-, I need [pause] I don't know if I should get a tutor, I was thinking about it

TA:	Mmhmm
S:	I try to come to office hours
TA:	Mmhmm

S: to have—for help with my homework sometimes [pause] I can't think of uh . . . uh . . . what else it was I wanted to talk to you about . . . um

TA: OK.

In considering this office-hour situation, we first call on our students to be active listeners, to try to interpret and understand the student's behavior. The ITAs, in small groups of four or five, are given the transcript and asked to watch the video, which we stop at the point where the transcript ends. They are then given time to discuss the video. The following questions serve as guidelines for the discussion.

Task 2: Discussion questions

In your group, discuss these questions. Have someone take notes on the opinions and ideas of your group. Be prepared to share your ideas with the rest of the class.

1. Look at the three underlined passages in the transcript. What do you think these expressions of the student mean?
   a. "I don't think I'm grasping it very quickly"
   b. "then I'll be like, Aw forget it"
   c. "I didn't want you to think that I was just blowing off the class"
2. What do you think this student wants from her TA? What do you think she is asking for?
3. If you were her TA, how could you respond? What more would you want to know from her? What advice could you give her?

Now, watch the videotape again to see how this TA responded to the student.

4. What do you think he does well?
5. What would you change to improve his performance?

The first question focuses on the student's language and is an opportunity to clarify what she has said. It may introduce students to new expressions and invites comments on her style of speech. The second question focuses on what the student has come for. This question involves a look at her motives: Is she sincere? The ITAs' reactions can stimulate discussion of if and how such feelings about the motives of students should determine the nature of the TA's response. The third question goes beyond the transcript, inviting brainstorming on how to respond to this student. The question is intentionally broad, allowing students to raise a wide range of elements in the interaction with this student. This discussion brings to the fore evaluative criteria that are then used to assess what the TA on the tape actually did. We play a portion of the tape beyond the transcript. At this point the ITAs in training are very well equipped to see both positive and negative aspects of the actual ITA's response to the student.

Such discussion and analysis, though both lively and fun (everyone loves to be an armchair critic!), may not in itself teach language. Beyond it, students need opportunities to face similar situations themselves and try out their ideas about how to respond. Therefore, we follow this viewing-discussion activity with role plays and videotaped student questions to which ITAs are asked to respond as though they were in a real interaction with the undergraduate on the video. These activities may be structured to move from less complex to more complex situations, for example, from single-issue encounters to multiple-issue ones, or, as Tyler (this volume) has suggested, from encounters with less inherent conflict to those with more. Through their efforts to perform in these activities, their critiques of their own performances, and feedback from their fellow students and instructors, ITAs can develop a repertoire of appropriate responses with which they are comfortable.

The second set of materials centers on the lab and results from our perception that ITAs need strategies to enable them to participate in the informal, question-dominated discourse of the lab. First, using two transcripts and class handouts shared by Myers (Myers, Axelson, & Madden, 1991), we discuss strategies to clarify and negotiate meaning in lab interactions. In particular, we focus on the *echo question* as an effective strategy, showing one transcript in which an ITA uses this strategy and another in which an ITA does not use it. Students are asked in the first case to identify what problem the ITA has in the conversation and how he or she solves it. In discussion, the echo question is identified as an effective technique for clarification, allowing one to maintain the conversational tone as well as negotiate meaning. The meaning of the student's laughter is also discussed in evaluating the outcomes of the ITA's experimentation with *squish*.

Task 3: Solving a communication problem in the lab

A student in a Chemistry lab is trying to insert a large piece of filter paper into a small crucible.

S1: Is this not right yet?
TA: Let me think—ah—ah stop—let's modify our setup—crumble—crumble—crumble? right? crumble—crumble your paper to

S1: . . . squish / it down?
TA: / to skiss it down
S2: do you want the paper above?
S1: like that?
TA: like that—like like this—crumble—
     / oh crumble your sample
S1: / squish it?
S2: / all the paper in there?
TA: skish? squiss?
S1:   squish [laughs]
TA: squish—squish yeah squish—squish it
S1: [laughs]
TA: squish it into the into the crucible
S1: squish is good.

Having discussed this example, we then look at an unsuccessful interaction between a lab ITA and a student and ask the students to think of ways to make the ITA's participation in the conversation more effective. If they do not generate possible echo questions spontaneously, we prompt them to do so. Discussion focuses on the relative merits of various responses, such as whether *Pardon me?* is a more effective response than *What?* The benefits of using what one does understand in an interaction to find out about what one does not understand can be extolled.

Task 4: A communication problem in the lab

How can the ITA's part in this conversation be improved?

S: When we shut it off, we have to take the hose off here first—no wait—how is that again? Take the hose off this here first
*TA: What?
S: When we shut it off—in order for it not—you know—we have to take the hose off here first—don't we?
TA: Water goes through here—is correct?
S: Yeah—water goes in through there . . . .
TA: . . . uh . . .
S: . . . but when it's all done—should we take this off of here before we shut the water off?
TA: . . . uh . . . .
S: Oh no—we take this off first . . .
TA: Ok—after shut off water then remove this.

*Think of an echo question the ITA could ask instead of "What?"

Discussion of these two transcripts could be followed up with role plays and other classroom activities to allow students to use echo questions for clarification. Another option is to allow students to reflect on their own language in an environment in which similar conversational breakdowns are likely to occur. For example, at the University of Michigan, some international graduate students in chemistry who are not regarded as ready for an ITA lab assignment are employed as equipment room assistants. There, undergraduates bring them the products of experiments for testing on various equipment. Similarly, not-quite-ready-for-prime-time international graduate students in other fields may be assigned to positions as graders with office hours. These students are interacting with undergraduates and can learn from their own experiences. Furthermore, they are likely to be taking our course on interacting skills for ITAs. As a part of this course, we assign them to audiotape themselves during their office hours or on the job in the equipment room. Alternatively, we may videotape them in that setting. They are then asked to complete a worksheet, which they discuss either in a meeting with the instructor or in a class meeting. As a part of this assignment, students are asked to transcribe a portion of their tape in which some kind of breakdown occurred. Task 5 shows a transcription assignment given after the echo question activities in class and the response of a prospective ITA in the course.

Task 5: Transcription assignment with student responses

B. Choose one encounter with a student in which the student did not understand you or you did not understand the student. Transcribe that encounter. Look closely at the transcript. What did you and the student do to solve the problem? Did you give or seek clarification? If so, how did you do so? What changes would you make to improve an encounter of this type in the future?

Student's response to the assignment:

1. **TA:** To loose the screw, you need spanner.
   S: Panner
   TA: No. Spanner.
   S: Sanner. Spanner. Oh spanner. OK I see. Where can I get?
   TA: Go to chem. stand. They will help you.

2. **TA:** Do you like sports?
   S: I like water polo.
   TA: Water—what?
   S: Water polo.
   TA: Water—

S: polo.
TA: OK water polo. Could you explain water polo?

The student's response provides a starting point for discussion and feedback in class. One might ask, for example, whether the undergraduate actually understood the term *spanner* and what happened when he or she went to the chemistry stand and asked for one. Others in the class can see the benefits of the echo question in the context of small talk with a student. Most importantly, the ITA's summary comment on the assignment and the use of echo questions—"I think echo question is powerful to draw the right word and phrase. They always give me a repeated word or correct word. That is better than straightforward question or formal kind question"—indicates that he knows he now has a tool in his repertoire that will work well for him in clarifying and negotiating meaning while maintaining a comfortable interaction and atmosphere.

Conclusion

We began this chapter by analyzing the overarching pedagogical objectives, discourse categories, and language moves of the lab, office hours, and the classroom in an attempt to differentiate the three major contexts in which ITAs teach. Our perspective was that of the analyst and trainer, looking for tools to organize the acts of TAs into some form that would enable us to choose what to teach in ITA training. We found that the settings in which ITAs teach make different demands on teaching and language behaviors, necessitating a close look at the teaching assignments of ITAs as a part of designing training for them. Furthermore, we saw the fluidity and multifunctionality of various discourse categories and moves, a fact that requires trainers to avoid a prescriptive approach. Rather than simplifying the act of teaching into something "teachable," trainers must find ways to present it in all its complexity, while fostering the growth of each trainee's repertoire of moves and awareness of categories and objectives. Within this expanded "discourse space," each ITA can then choose appropriate language and other acts that enhance his or her skills and style as a teacher. Finally, we have tried to take the fruit of our analysis into the classroom, with materials based on transcripts and tapes of actual teacher performances, presented in a way that encourages ITAs to analyze them and consider them as options within a wider array of possibilities, as tools with which they can experiment rather than as prescriptions for success.

Notes

1. We are aware that the variability across contexts is highlighted even further by categorizing, for example, *transitions* as a pedagogical objective in the office hour and as a discourse category in the classroom. This represents our attempt to show that the same function may in fact be a more salient objective in one instructional context than in another or that, in certain situations, a function may be one of many categories that fulfill a particular objective. These interpretations are open to modification, as mentioned, and are meant to serve as guidelines in assessing the discourse needs of ITAs within a flexible and mutable framework.

2. Facilitating learning refers to the three major pedagogical categories of (a) facilitating student performance and problem solving, (b) facilitating problem solving, and (c) facilitating student understanding of material in the lab, office hour, and classroom, respectively.

III

.

Interaction and Performance

10

ITAs, Interaction, and Communicative Effectiveness

George Yule
Louisiana State University

■

Many training courses for international teaching assistants (ITAs) continue to focus primarily on the lecture-style presentation of instructional material. Nevertheless, interest is growing in the performance of ITAs in the types of interactive situations that arise outside the lecture hall, such as during office-hour consultations, laboratory work, tutorial sessions, or in any one of the many discipline-specific one-on-one meetings that ITAs are expected to cope with. Because it is within the face-to-face interactive setting that ITAs are most likely to receive immediate feedback on the effectiveness (or the lack thereof) of their communication, a sound pedagogical motivation seems to exist for creating activities within ITA programs that provide experience in coping with the communicative demands of face-to-face interaction in English.

The Benefits of Interaction

One disadvantage of devoting a lot of attention to ITAs' oral presentation of lecture material is that, if successful, it will develop ability in only the transactional function of spoken language use—the one-way transfer of information in which most attention is devoted to the message (cf. Brown & Yule, 1983). It will not necessarily foster the interactional function— the two-way exchange of information in which attention is devoted in greater measure to the listener. If the ITAs' L2 spoken performance contains nontargetlike features that create difficulties for the listener, the lecture-style format will simply provide those ITAs with an opportunity to practise those features. Even when the performances are videotaped and reviewed individually, the ITAs will receive feedback on their performance flaws at a substantial remove from the point of their production.

Moreover, because the lecture format is designed to have the ITAs concentrate on *their* performance, message, and delivery, it tends to devote very little attention to the needs of the listener(s). It effectively reinforces a belief that many ITAs appear to share: If the teacher knows his or her material really well and gives a good performance (in his or her own eyes), then the students will learn. If, however, the ITA as teacher performs in accordance with that belief yet does not take the specific needs of a particular group of students into account, then he or she can end up talking over the heads of the students, using unfamiliar vocabulary or even familiar vocabulary in an unfamiliar way. The most obvious "unfamiliar way" is caused by nontargetlike pronunciation. The ITA who was heard to announce, "In my country all people same—here every one is eunuch," during a lecture was met with confused looks among his audience, but they did not ask for clarification and he did not react to their apparent confusion. (Some did report guessing that the mispronounced word was probably *unique*.) This type of outcome has to be viewed as a major disadvantage of letting ITAs practise their spoken English in primarily lecture-style presentations.

Although it has less of the face validity associated with lecture presentations, the benefits for ITAs of practising one-on-one interaction can still be related to the demands of the spoken language associated with their teaching role, as demonstrated by Davies, Tyler, and Koran (1989). More generally, the interactive setting has been shown to be the best site for promoting both comprehensible input and comprehensible output in studies of second language learning. Summaries of the arguments and the evidence for this theoretical position are found in Long and Porter (1985), Pica (1987), and Varonis and Gass (1985).

In the reported research, conditions that lead to language learning in the classroom result from two-way tasks with a required exchange of information, in which pairs of learners who do not share an L1 or the same proficiency level in the L2 have to resolve a problem. Under these conditions learners produce substantial negotiation of meaning, of the type that forces the learners to give clear messages and to ask for clarification when messages are not clear during the interaction. In contrast to the silence that greeted the earlier *eunuch* example during a lecture presentation, the initial communication problem is resolved during the following interaction:

[1] **ITA 1:** they fuck us on the meaning
ITA 2: they what?
ITA 1: they fock us on the meaning
ITA 2: oh focus?
ITA 1: yeah they focus on the meaning always

Instead of sitting in quiet bewilderment (or even shock), the listener here has the opportunity to draw attention to a difficulty in communication and eventually reach a solution.

Even more interesting are the results reported by Gass and Varonis (1989), which provide some evidence that, as a result of modifications of speech during interaction, the learners involved make longer-term changes in their English language performance. What is particularly important about these results is that, instead of being tied to something relatively amorphous like *acquisition*, the beneficial effects of interactive language experiences are witnessed in the second language *performance* of the learners. It is the spoken language performance of ITAs, not their inherent acquisition state, that is at issue during their training programs, and the fact that beneficial changes in L2 performance have been shown to emerge from interactive language use creates a powerful incentive to build specifically interactive tasks into training programs.

An Interactive Task

Having argued in principle that a certain type of activity will benefit ITAs' performance, I report on a series of studies that used a particular task design to explore how ITAs coped with communication difficulties in face-to-face interaction. The task was designed to create specific communication difficulties for the interactants by providing them with worlds of reference that were in conflict at certain points. Brown, Anderson, Shillcock, and Yule (1984) reported on an early use of this type of task with British teenagers, and more recently a handbook for language teachers (Anderson & Lynch, 1988) presented examples of this task type.

In the version reported here, the ITAs were organized into pairs, and the members of each pair received similar maps showing a grid of city streets with buildings marked *Church, School, Bookstore*, and so on. One ITA, whose map showed a delivery route to 10 locations, had to describe the route to the other ITA, who then drew the route on his map.[1] The ITAs were also told that one of the maps was older than the other and that, because of changes, they would encounter some differences between their two maps. The task was successfully completed when the "sender" (who knows the route) had communicated the delivery route to the "receiver."

Some typical referential problems were built into the task design. One building in the sender's map displayed the sign *Hats* whereas the same building in the receiver's map was marked *Bicycles*. Similarly, the sender's map showed a single office building whereas the receiver's map contained that office building plus two others. (An illustration of the problem is presented in the Appendix.) I discuss other specific differences in connection with illustrative extracts presented later. One demanding feature of this kind of task is that the participants necessarily encounter mismatches in their referential worlds and are forced to arrive at a mutually acceptable means of resolving the differences. The resolution of these problems inevitably involves the ITAs in attempts to negotiate meaning, to listen carefully and speak clearly, to take another's perspective into account, and to make communicative intent sensitive to the constraints of another's knowledge rather than simply an expression of one's own knowledge. As it turned out, only certain pairings of ITAs resulted in fully negotiated solutions to referential problems, and I begin with some examples of what happens when senders and receivers do not cooperate.

"You Listen to Me"

The results of one small-scale investigation lend some important insights into how difficult some ITAs find viewing the world of reference from a perspective other than their own. In this investigation, 12 ITAs from the People's Republic of China, all self-reported Mandarin L1 speakers, were divided into pairs with roughly similar TOEFL scores to perform a version of the task described earlier, with four differences distinguishing their two versions of the map. In each pair, the ITA assigned the role of sender (S) had the older map, and the other, with the newer map, was designated the receiver (R). The tape-recorded data from these interactions include examples of clarification requests (Excerpts 2, 3) and comprehension checks (Excerpts 4, 5) that, as indicators of the negotiation of meaning, are taken to be important elements in the development of ability in a second language (cf. Hatch, 1978; Long, 1981).

[2] **S:** you turn right—at the first join of the road
    R: eh what—of the road?
    S: turn to the right—that means turn to the north

[3] **S:** start from the bottom
    R: what's bottom?
    S: from the left—on the left corner—bottom left

[4] **S:** go in the rest direction
    R: west?
    S: yeah west

[5] **S:** when you see the first T-junction turn left
    R: T-junk?

S: the first T-junction
R: oh T-junction?

These negotiations of the interlocutor's meaning are matched by attempts at the negotiation of interlocutor's referent, as illustrated in Excerpts 6 and 7.

[6] **R:** you don't have Bicycles?
    S: no /okay
    R: /the Bicycle—/eh
    S: /okay you listen to me—there is a block under the School
    R: under the—yeah
    S: okay there's building in that block
    R: eh—yeah
    S: okay the building's name's Hats—H -A - T -S
    R: H - ?
    S: A - T - S
    R: A - T - S Hats
    S: okay?
    R: yes
    S: draw that building—okay enter the building

[7] **S:** okay turn right
    R: I turn right is go back—go up
    S: no no no no no—Dentist is in your back
    R: wait—where is your Dentist?
    S: okay—you don't listen to me
    R: I listen to you
    S: TURN RIGHT—the right-hand side

Excerpts 6 and 7 contain examples of features that created the most dominant impression to emerge from this study. Although the receiver and sender appear to use a form of negotiation toward the resolution of referential conflicts throughout the data, that negotiation is characterized by what seems like competition and confrontation rather than cooperation. Moreover, in the vast majority of cases, whether the referential conflict is discussed at length or only briefly, it is resolved by the sender's mandating an end to the discussion. That mandate inevitably denies the relevance of the receiver's referential world and in most cases imposes the sender's version on the receiver. At the end of Excerpt 6, the receiver has to draw a new building to make his world fit the sender's world, and the sender ignores the existence of the alternative referent (*Bicycles*), mentioned by the receiver as being in that location. Accompanying this type of mandate are frequent expressions of who should be in control, such as *You listen to me* near the beginning of Excerpt 6 and the reprimand *You don't listen to me* in Excerpt 7. Other markers include frequent interruptions, with increased amplitude, by the sender and a tendency to repeat instructions verbatim, without elaboration, in response to comprehension difficulties indicated by the receiver. The receiver sometimes tries these tactics but is eventually overruled, as in Excerpt 8, and when things go wrong, inevitably the receiver is blamed for the misunderstanding, as illustrated in Excerpt 9.

[8] **S:** it's not a turn
     R: it's REALLY A TURN
     S: no no no—okay it—
     R: if we call it a turn /we can—
     S: /okay okay if you—WILL YOU LISTEN
           TO ME PLEASE? okay listen to me—now

[9] **R:** I go to the direction—is go to the Bank direction—is right?
     S: Bank?
     R: Bank first
     S: oh no no no no no no no—you—you got it wrong

Perhaps because they consistently see the receiver as causing problems or failing to listen correctly, many senders fall back on strategies that involve only a personal account of the task and disregard the receiver, as illustrated by the "I enter Hats . . . I turn back" forms in Excerpt 10, or simply abandon parts of the task, as shown in the last line of Excerpt 11.

[10] **S:** there's a building—do you see it building?
      R: yes
      S: yes—is Hats—Hats
      R: no—it's a Bicycles
      S: Bicycle?
      R: Hats—Hats nothing
      S: oh I—but I don't Bicycles—it's Hats
      R: well—
      S: okay I enter Hats and then left the Hats to the east east direction—I turn back

[11] **S:** there is no Hats on your map—is that so?
      R: yeah no Hats
      S: okay then we just—eh—eh—give it up

It is tempting to see in some of those strategies indications of the types of problems some ITAs have when they encounter communication difficulties in the wider second language environment of the U.S. college. Such a view would involve attributing the strategies to the ITAs as if they were inherently characteristic of their communicative behavior. However, I think a more basic explanation has to do with the ITAs' perceptions of the task and the interlocutor. Generally, ITAs in the sender role appear to be asserting their authority in the task and to interpret their interlocutors' contradictory statements as challenges to that authority. As senders, they want to assume the kind of "dominant" role that Woken and Swales (1989) and Zuengler (1989b) have described for learners even in interactions between native and nonnative speakers in which the nonnative speaker has recognized expertise. The problem in this study appears to be partly attributable to the fact that, with same L1 and similar L2 proficiencies, neither participant is recognized *by the other* at the outset as having greater expertise and, as the interaction progresses, that expertise or authority has to be imposed rather than assumed. The net effect is that one can observe those negotiations of meaning that are beneficial in terms of language learning but not the successful negotiations of referents that are required if communication is to be effective. Ignoring the listener's perspective and simply abandoning referential goals are not effective ways of communicating. An attempt was made to remedy this effect in the next two studies reported.

Resolving Referential Conflicts

To take into account the potential effect of perceived authority and interactive role, in later studies I allocated roles in the task to ITAs quite differently using the same basic task materials. Pairs consisted of ITAs with different L1s and different levels of English language ability. In one study (cf. Yule, 1990), 10 ITAs from India (with greater fluency and more experience with spoken English) were paired with 10 ITAs from China or Korea (with lower fluency and limited experience in speaking English). In five of the pairs, the Indian ITA was given the sender role and, in the other five, the receiver role. In a related study (Yule & Macdonald, 1990), 20 ITAs from a wide range of L1 backgrounds, who had all demonstrated very high English language proficiency (mean TOEFL score of 625), were paired with 20 ITAs, also from a wide range of L1 backgrounds, who had substantially lower TOEFL proficiency scores (mean of 562). In 10 pairs the speaker with higher proficiency was given the sender role and, in the other 10 pairs, the receiver role.

The results from the studies were broadly similar. When the ITA with greater fluency and proficiency took the sender's role, the receiver's role appeared to diminish greatly. Either because the lower-proficiency ITA became very passive in the receiver role, simply acknowledging directions with *okay* and *uh huh*, or because the higher-proficiency sender placed very little importance on the receiver's contributions, the general effect was that of a one-way performance by the higher-proficiency sender. The pairs negotiated referential conflicts relatively rarely, with the higher-proficiency sender tending to mandate (often inappropriate) solutions, as illustrated in Excerpt 12, or to abandon referential goals, as in Excerpt 13.

[12] **S:** we go to Office—which is below Records
    R: Office below?
    S: Records
    R: Records—oh there is a four please
    S: there's a ?
    R: there is a four Office
    S: okay the very first Office

In Excerpt 12, only one of the receiver's Office locations is identical to the sender's single Office, and deciding that it must be the first one encountered is not only arbitrary but fairly irresponsible in terms of communicative effectiveness. Also communicatively ineffective, given the demands of the task, is the strategy of simply abandoning a referential goal, as shown in Excerpt 13.

[13] **S:** go to Hats
    R: Hats? Hats?
    S: Hats H - A - T - S
    R: I haven't got a Hats on my map
    S: you haven't got Hats?
    R: yeah
    S: okay—if you don't have Hats then please go to Office

In these cases, the linguistic authority and the information authority of the role seemed to combine to create a fairly egocentric perspective on the sender's part. The sender concentrated on his role, often used introductory expressions like *let me tell you* and *okay I will explain you*, and frequently made *in MY map* the only relevant point of reference. It is as if the receiver had extremely limited competence and, if the authoritative sender perceived the message required by the task as too complex, he had to change the message to make it easier. The general result was that the pairs consisting of a sender with high L2 ability and a receiver with low L2 ability completed the task fairly rapidly, yet the delivery routes drawn by the receivers rarely matched those of the senders, simply because the senders had not given directions that were appropriate to the receivers' world of reference. The rather obvious analogy, in terms of classroom teaching, is with teachers who teach what they know without trying to make the information fit appropriately into what the students already know or need to know.

When the roles were reversed and the lower-fluency or lower-proficiency ITA took the sender's role, the outcome was generally quite different. Most noticeable was that the participants contributed more equally to the interaction and shared substantially more information from both worlds of reference. In contrast to earlier excerpts, when the referential problem involved the Hats store, in Excerpt 14 both the lower-proficiency sender and the higher-proficiency receiver tried to make their separate referential worlds compatible.

[14] **S:** below the School
    R: you know but—
    S: H - A - T - S
    R: but there's nothing called H - A - T - S you know below the School—there is one Bicycles
    S: okay
    R: is there any Bicycles?
    S: Bicycles? no—do you—can you find the Church?
    R: yeah yeah
    S: not the first one Church we passed—we passed that one—is not that one—the other one Church
    R: okay I eh—I see one Church
    S: and eh—Hats is above the Church and below the School
    R: okay that place is called as Bicycles here
    S: okay then you enter the Bicycles

In the final line of Excerpt 14, the sender adopted the referential label of the receiver to give him directions for his delivery route. This line is a particularly salient example of the concept of *seeing the other's perspective* that is generally assumed to be helpful in resolving communication difficulties.

The authority of the sender's role enabled the lower-proficiency ITA to take a more active communicative part, but the authority that resides with the receiver because of his greater linguistic proficiency seems to have resulted in more active responses to the directions received. Instead of the typical backchannel responses (*okay, uh-huh*) of lower-proficiency receivers, the higher-proficiency ITA as receiver was more likely to produce confirmation responses, as in the second turn in Excerpt 15, and confirmation checks, as in the fourth turn.

[15] **S:** then you go to the Bookstore I think that's the first to the left
　　R: yeah—first to the left
　　S: and then you continue on the road—coming out of the Bookstore
　　R: coming out—okay I go first left at the Bookstore?

This active, checking type of response can prevent the acceptance of poorly specified and arbitrary directions, exemplified in Excerpt 12 earlier, by presenting relevant information from the receiver's world that allows the sender to be more specific and hence more communicatively effective, as illustrated in Excerpt 16.

[16] **S:** you go—you stop by the Office
　　R: now there are many Offices
　　S: the first Office
　　R: ah the first Office—I mean which Office—the one Office is to the north—one to the south one to the east
　　S: east—east side is the Office

By sharing the two forms of authority, the lower-to-higher pairs displayed substantially fewer (wrongly) mandated or abandoned referential assignments and more negotiated resolutions, with the result that they communicated the required information more successfully.

Conclusion

The type of exercise I have described is designed not only to foster general interactive skills but to create specific opportunities for learning how to recognize and resolve communication difficulties. Such an exercise should make it possible to sensitize ITAs to different types of resolutions for communication difficulties and to have them realize which ones lead to outcomes that are communicatively successful and which do not.

Generally, the best way to promote more effective communication skills in interactive tasks seems to be to organize the pairs (if possible) as follows:

■ The participants do not share the same L1.
■ The participants do not have the same L2 proficiency level.
■ The lower-proficiency participant takes the role of the dominant speaker.

One of the key findings of the series of studies reported here is that interactive communication was most successful when the proficient ITA was placed in a role in which he was forced to *listen* to his interlocutor and to make sense of his interlocutor's perspective rather than being given (yet another) opportunity to speak and emphasize his own perspective. ITAs' communicative skills may benefit if they have more opportunities to listen, particularly in interactive tasks containing some mismatch in the perspectives of the participants. Trainers have tended to emphasize presentation skills in ITA programs, providing repeated opportunities for ITAs to take the authoritative role and to concentrate on themselves, their delivery, and their display of expertise, perhaps to the neglect of their L2 interactive skills, most notably their ability—and hence perhaps also their willingness—to listen to those without that expertise, their students. If trainers can give ITAs the ability to listen more effectively to those without expertise, then ITAs may learn to recognize the needs of nonexperts and address those needs more effectively when they speak.

Acknowledgments

For support and advice in connection with the research reported in this paper, I thank Elin Epperson, Wayne Gregory, Regina Hoffman, Doris Macdonald, Maggie Powers, and Winnie Trufant. I also thank the Council on Research, Louisiana State University, for generous support.

Note

1. These studies were all conducted with the ITA population at Louisiana State University, where the ratio of male to female ITAs is consistently around 7 to 1. One result is that the participants in the reported research are overwhelmingly males, a phenomenon reflected here in the use of male gender pronouns as the unmarked case. It would not be surprising if the results reported here did not, in fact, characterize the interactive behavior of a group of female ITAs, but the research on that question remains to be done.

Appendix

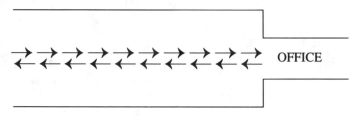

Sender's Version

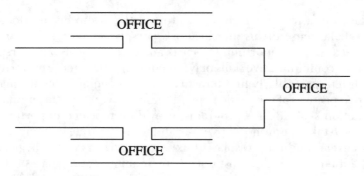

Receiver's Version

■ 11 ■

Demystifying Cross-Cultural (Mis)communication: Improving Performance Through Balanced Feedback in a Situated Context

Catherine E. Davies
University of Alabama

Andrea E. Tyler
University of Florida

■

In this chapter we present a teaching-research methodology based on straightforward techniques of eliciting pragmatic feedback in a situated context. The techniques lead to collaborative analysis of interpretive cues in ongoing interaction. Originally inspired by Gumperz and Roberts (1980) and Jupp, Roberts, and Cook-Gumperz (1982), the methodology simultaneously discovers sources of miscommunication between international teaching assistants (ITAs) and U.S. undergraduates and develops pedagogical techniques that make these sources explicit to participants and thus open to modification. The methodology also highlights successful communication and makes explicit how it is accomplished. We believe that ITA trainers can easily adopt this teaching methodology because it does not require a potentially intimidating expertise in formal pragmatics and discourse analysis; trainers act primarily as facilitators, directing learners' attention so that their consciousness operates in the language development process in ways researchers are just beginning to understand (cf. Schmidt, 1990, for extensive discussion). A further pedagogical benefit of the methodology is that it encourages native English-speaking undergraduates to be involved productively with ITAs; see Davies, Tyler, and Koran (1989) for an elaboration of the logistics of such involvement.

The theoretical context for the teaching-research methodology is a central controversy within language acquisition theory: the role of so-called *negative evidence*, defined as "indications given to learners that certain strings are not grammatical" (Birdsong, 1989, p. 127). Typically provided in the form of error correction and as part of explicit grammar teaching, negative evidence contrasts with *positive evidence*, which consists of the corpus of utterances the learner is exposed to and takes notice of, revealing what is linguistically possible (White, 1989).

The controversy over negative evidence revolves around two related questions. The first is whether negative evidence is in fact necessary or even useful for language acquisition; the second, contingent on an affirmative answer to the first, is how explicit and consistent negative feedback must be in order to be effective. The most extreme Chomskyan position, privileging innate processes, is that negative evidence is neither necessary nor useful (Schwartz, 1987). A version of this position has been maintained for second language acquisition by Krashen (1981), who suggested that explicit negative evidence in the form of corrections actually hinders language acquisition, activating the so-called *affective filter* within his theoretical framework. A contrasting position, taken by Birdsong (1989), is that the role and value of negative evidence in second language acquisition depend on a range of learner and situational variables. The notion of negative evidence was initially applied in relation to syntactic phenomena in first language acquisition (Gold, 1967; Chomsky, 1981); over the past 25 years the scope of the inquiry into the role of negative evidence has expanded to include phonology and morphology in both first and second language acquisition but has remained restricted to considerations of linguistic form (Birdsong, 1989).

We argue two related points, one theoretical and the other methodological, on the basis of findings about the nature of the sources of cross-cultural miscommunication and the fact that L1 and L2 speakers are generally unaware of these sources (e.g., Gumperz, 1982a; Tannen, 1985). The first point expands the scope of the theoretical construct of negative evidence in second language development to include pragmatic and discourse phenomena. The second point is the importance of a teaching methodology that facilitates intake in relation to all relevant aspects of language by focusing learners' attention through balanced feedback in a situated context. Here we draw on Schmidt's (1990) definition of intake as "what learners consciously notice" (p. 149).

Central to our approach is the extension to second language development of Bruner's (1981b) claim for first language acquisition that "pragmatics provides the most general support system for mastery of the formal aspects of language" (p. 32). This perspective suggests that, when strategically given, explicit negative evidence oriented to pragmatics not only facilitates language development but may in fact be crucial to it. For example, familiarizing an ITA with typical cultural expectations for ending an advising session with a student (Bardovi-Harlig & Hartford, 1990) will allow the ITA to pay more attention to particular formal structures that typically occur in such an interaction. We characterize "strategically given feedback" in four ways: It is situated, balanced, non-threatening, and demystifying.

Gumperz' (1982a) theory of conversational inference provides a further rationale for the importance of explicit situated feedback. According to his theory, listeners interpret language in context according to a complex constellation of cues from different levels of linguistic organization that operate relationally rather than with identifiable meanings that can be abstracted out. His work on communication in interethnic communication situations highlights the covert nature of the ways contextualization cues trigger culturally specific interpretations of speaker intent. Thus we attempt to make learners aware of contextualization cues commonly used by English speakers in channeling interpretive processes and to build an awareness of where the nonnative speakers' use of English differs from native speakers' expectations.

Video allows us both to give explicit situated feedback and to focus learners' attention on implicit negative evidence offered by native speakers through interaction (Chaudron, 1977; Schachter, 1986). Because feedback should be balanced, we include not only negative but also positive evidence. Clearly, learners need to be taught how to identify and use negative evidence; we argue further for a recognition of the value of explicit positive evidence. Learners should always receive balanced feedback that draws their attention both to successes (explicit positive evidence) and to areas in need of modification (negative evidence). Finally, strategically given feedback should be both nonthreatening (i.e., not activating the affective filter, in Krashen's terms) and demystifying (i.e., serving to empower the learner by revealing, for example, an unrecognized pattern).

The Teaching-Research Process

The Teaching Methodology

This chapter grows out of our work with the ITA training programs and the English Language Institutes at the University of Florida and the University of Alabama. The methodology relies heavily on placing ITAs in relatively natural communicative situations, such as tutoring sessions with undergraduates, small-group discussions, or role plays with undergraduates based on typical problematic situations (cf. Tyler, this volume), that are videotaped and subsequently reviewed. The review sessions vary depending on the nature of the interaction being videotaped and the communication problems involved. For instance, the sessions may involve just an ESL instructor and the individual ITA some time after the interaction has occurred, or the native English-speaking participants immediately after the exchange. Similarly, the type of feedback varies. Sometimes, as in the first example below, the feedback focuses on particular, recurring grammatical or pronunciation problems. In other instances, as in the second example below, the feedback is solely in terms of pragmatics and the English-speaking interlocutor's responses. Such feedback includes attending to the English speaker's recasts, requests for clarification, facial expressions, and interruptions as well as to what the ITA said to evoke the particular response. Thus our text is natural or naturalistic discourse jointly produced between learners and native English speakers, and the language instruction the ITAs receive is selected, balanced, and directed within a situated context.

One aspect of the negative-evidence issue discussed above is that little explicit negative evidence seems typically to be available in everyday conversation. Some researchers have noted that contributions such as recasts (another term for paraphrase), expansions, and confirmation checks offer important if less explicit forms of negative evidence (Schachter, 1986; Moerk, 1991; cf. Birdsong, 1989, for general discussion); however, such implicit evidence may often be unsystematic and ambiguous and thus again of questionable use to the language learner (Pinker, 1984; Schumann, 1975). Finally, there is the question of individual variation in attending to negative evidence during a communicative exchange (cf. Bialystok & Ryan, 1985). It is not clear that all language learners are able to attend to implicit negative evidence during the course of a conversation. Anecdotal evidence suggests that learners are too busy thinking about what to say next and figuring out their interlocutor's message to attend to the feedback on grammatical form offered in recasts. Our approach addresses this potential confusion by making the interlocutor's implicit negative evidence appropriately explicit. In addition, we take care to point out where the exchange has gone well and where the appropriate signals have been given. The approach also supports anxious ITAs who are unable to attend to recasts during the actual exchange by allowing them to review the videotaped version under less stress-inducing circumstances.

Because contextualization cues are typically constellations of elements from different levels of linguistic organization (e.g., syntax, prosody, morphological encoding of tense or aspect, lexical discourse markers), the feedback session ideally addresses, in nontechnical terms, any relevant aspects of the communication (cf. Gumperz & Tannen, 1979). The questions that we start with, and that form the basis for the pragmatic feedback, are as follows:

■ What were you trying to communicate?
■ Is that the message you got?

This pair of questions, addressed to both the ITA and the native-speaking student in turn at the start of the session, seeks to elicit global communicative goals for the interaction and the degree of success achieved. The same questions may also be used to establish local communicative intent and degree of uptake for any individual utterances. In the case of clear mismatches between communicative intent and interpretation, which should be probed to discover the reason(s) for the mismatch, a follow-up question for the native English speaker should be

■ Now that you know what [your interlocutor] was trying to communicate, how could he or she have said it in a way that would have been clear to you?

In response to this question, native speakers provide situated modeling of appropriate conversational contributions.

Another basic question, which should be addressed to both the ITA and the native-speaking student, points toward key segments of the interaction that can be probed to yield sources of cross-linguistic or cross-cultural misunderstanding:

■ Were there any moments when you felt uncomfortable or confused?

Depending on the degree of trust established in the teaching setting and the emotional quality of the interaction being examined, participants will be more or less willing to admit to having felt "uncomfortable"; they will usually be more likely to admit to feeling "confused." This admission can be followed up with a question like the following:

■ Can you say what it was about what [your interlocutor] said that led to your confusion?

The next question, which should be addressed first to the native-speaking student, is designed to elicit information for the ITA concerning native-speaker schemas in the situation:

■ Was there anything you expected or wanted to hear from the other person that you did not?

For the sake of appropriate balance in self-disclosure, the question should also be asked of the ITA.

Finally, the following open-ended question is designed to provide an opportunity for participants to volunteer anything else they judge to be important:

■ What other feedback would you like to give each other?

We find this question form, which presupposes a substantive response, more productive than a question form that does not, e.g., *Is there some/any other feedback.* . . . Often politeness constraints yield either some specific positive evidence or a global affirmation for the ITA from the native English speaker.

As the questions above show, our approach assumes a shift in the conceptualization of language *acquisition* to language *socialization* as represented in the work of Cook-Gumperz, Corsaro, and Streeck (1986) and Schieffelin and Ochs (1986). Watson-Gegeo (1988) has pointed out the implications of this shift: that language learned through social interaction focuses attention on all dimensions of context. Language learning necessarily involves learning such things as "social and cultural norms, procedures for interpretation, and forms of reasoning" (p. 582). The reorientation to language socialization allows us to draw on schema theory both at its foundations in Bartlett's (1932) original conceptualization of active, developing patterns of expectations (cf. Tannen, 1979, for a discussion of the application of this notion in different disciplines) and in its conjunction with prototype theory (Holland & Quinn, 1987):

> The prototypical scenarios unfolded in the simplified worlds of cultural models, the nestedness of these presupposed models one within another, and the applicability of certain of these models to multiple domains all go far to explain how individuals can learn culture and communicate it to others, so that many come to share the same understandings. (p. 35)

Communicative competence entails sharing schemas, discourse strategies, contextualization cues, and interpretive conventions; it also involves dealing with constrained but variable expectations. We believe that the methodology outlined here creates appropriate circumstances for such language socialization. As it directs learners' attention to various dimensions of their own interactional discourse, the teaching process trains learners to operate at the level of metacommunicative awareness and analysis. This awareness subsumes both the metalinguistic and the metapragmatic.

The Method in Action

We turn now to four transcripts of video excerpts of the teaching-research process that illustrate our claims. The transcripts represent two pre- and postfeedback pairs that involve different kinds of feedback.

Our transcription format is designed to be easy to follow and to highlight aspects of the interaction that we emphasize in our analyses. The transcription represents the flow of the interaction in real time, with each line having a place for each participant's utterances so that pauses and overlaps are obvious. It also includes iconic representations of intonation contours in Example 2: in 2A, to give a feeling for the prosodic style of both participants and to illustrate our analysis; in 2B, to provide the prosodic basis for our analysis of the ITA's discourse. Because nonverbal dimensions of the interaction did not emerge as salient except in 2B, we have marked eye contact only at that key point.

Example 1

Excerpts 1A and 1B come from the central portion of any tutoring interaction: the teaching activity. The ITA was a native speaker of Chinese who had been in the United States for 3 years. During that time he had taught a physics lab course for five semesters. The student was from Jamaica, operating in standard Jamaican English.

[1A]
1 T: So so VC *equals to* this *equals to* MC VC yeah so M VC bar
 S:
2 T: *equals to* MB VB p- yeah VVP and divided by MC
 S: Shouldn't
3 T: OK it divided by   yeah
 S: it be divided by this   Oh oh yes I see what
4 T: yeah   yeah   But this is one
 S: you're saying now MC is equal to that
5 T: [story] OK uh actually VVP *equals to* MC VVP *equals to* MC
 S: OK
6 T: VC bar divided by MP
 S:

Two main points emerge from Excerpt 1A: a fossilized error and the ITA's discourse strategy. The fossilized error that occurred repeatedly for speaker T is *equals to*; the ITA apparently combined *equals* and *is equal to*. The student probably had no difficulty understanding what the ITA was communicating, especially because the verbal channel was continuously paralleled by the written as the ITA referred to the figures on the paper in front of them—unless occasions arise in which the preposition *to* and the number *two* could be confused. A reason for trying to change this construction, which the ITA uses frequently as part of his academic discourse, is the potential loss of credibility for the ITA if undergraduates are likely to equate mistakes in English with lack of intelligence or competence. We are unaware of documentation other than anecdotal of such attitudes by undergraduates toward ITAs, but such attributions are commonly directed toward speakers of nonstandard varieties (cf. Ryan & Giles, 1982). We have also chosen this excerpt because it includes an example of naturally occurring negative evidence that the nonnative speaker apparently does not notice. In line 4 the student used the appropriate form of the ITA's fossilized construction *is equal to*, and the ITA carried on with his fossilized constructions (line 5).

The other main aspect to note in the prefeedback tutoring session (a very small part of which is included in Excerpt 1A) is teaching style. The ITA followed a typical U.S. math teaching strategy of verbalizing all of the operations and calculations (Rounds, 1987a). The ITA also exercised extreme control, doing all of the work himself and even focusing the interaction within his own space, far away from the student; symbolic of the control that the ITA exerted was his appropriation and management of the student's calculator throughout the interaction.

The feedback for this ITA involved watching the video and discussing it with the instructor. Recurring grammatical and pronunciation errors were pointed out, including *equals to* and some more pragmatically oriented aspects, such as framing a problem and involving the student more in the interaction. The ITA was asked to look at the video by himself and keep track of how many times he said *equals to* and to form a general impression of the relative amounts of time the two participants spoke.

Excerpt 1B is taken from a tutoring session that took place 4 weeks later between the same ITA and student. Before the next session the ITA also had become more sensitized to the use of discourse markers for signaling rhetorical organization and the use of modals in English for conveying politeness.

[1B]
 1 T: Ahm I think the main point here is the Boyle's Law is ah
   S:
 2 T: P the pressure times volume *equals*   ah *equals*
   S:
 3 T: constant   So ahm the experiment is in this way that
   S: umhm
 4 T: ah Y 1 there Y 1 Y 2 and air B *equals to* this Y 0 Y 1 Y 2
   S:
 5 T: This is the mercury here so air B is Y 1 minus Y0 absolute
   S:
 6 T: value [ ]   and air at G *equals to* air Y 2 minus Y 1 OK
   S: OK   OK [ ]

7 T: this is centimeter   Uhm yeah and H equals to   H is
  S: yeah

8 T: the height   of the mercury   air at G times cosine theta
  S: uh huh

9 T: and PB *equals* P atmospheric plus H and then VB *equals to* LD
  S:

10 T: and then calculate VB PB times VB OK and ah there's
  S: OK

11 T: two graphs   one is
  S: Yeah two graphs one log and one Cartesian

12 T: log P V because ah PV *equals to* NRT so log P plus log V
  S:

13 T: *equals* log NRT   So log P equals minus log V plus log NRT
  S: Right

14 T: so there is a component here   is minus 1   so
  S: uh huh   um hm

15 T: this slope *equals* minus 1   would
  S: slope   OK

16 T: you like ah to finish it   heheh OK   because ah
  S: OK ah

17 T: that's the same thing
  S:

In Excerpt 1B the ITA produced more correct *equals* constructions (from 0 in the first excerpt to a slightly more than 50% occurrence in the second excerpt [*equals to* = 5; *equals* = 6]). In terms of discourse strategy, the ITA began with, "I think the main point here is . . ." in line 1, framing what was to come for the student; the ITA had not previously done this sort of overt discourse structuring. More collaborative interaction with the student is evident, and the ITA shifted control to the student, using a verbal construction to convey politeness ("Would you like to finish it?") in lines 15 and 16.

Our playback methodology, in this case used with each participant separately to probe his assumptions, motivations, and interpretations of the interaction, revealed a caveat concerning the hasty application of culturally based explanations on the basis of observation alone. The temptation might be to explain the authoritarian teaching style in the interaction represented by Excerpt 1A in terms of cultural patterning; in fact, in this case the Chinese ITA was acting on attitudes that he believed he had picked up in the context of U.S. society—that an African-American student would need more help—and thus he took over without giving the student a chance to demonstrate his degree of competence. By the time of Excerpt 1B—4 weeks after the Excerpt 1A—he had had a chance to let the student demonstrate his competence and was therefore willing to share control. ITA educators need to be aware of the complex interplay of cultural patterning with many other dimensions of context (cf. Tyler & Davies, 1990a).

An important issue within the negative-evidence controversy is the lack of clear evidence that negative feedback, even though it may have the effect of on-the-spot error correction, has a long-term effect on language production (cf. Day, 1986; Cathcart & Winn-Bell Olsen, 1976; Chaudron, 1983). The widespread assumption seems to be that speakers have single rules for each construction and that, once they have the rule, they should produce the form correctly; language teachers know that the situation is more complicated. Krashen has offered an explanation in terms of two separate competences—one learned and one acquired. We argue instead (along with variationists like Ellis [1986] and Tarone [1983, 1985]) for a more complex understanding of the learner's grammar in which two competing structures or rules exist simultaneously. Access to a construction depends largely on automaticity and cognitive load. A learner will produce the "old" incorrect construction right alongside the new one, especially in situations of anxiety or heavy processing. Gradually, over time, as the new construction gains in automaticity, it competes with the old construction and eventually gains ascendancy. Our evidence appears to support a model along the lines of the gradual diffusion model suggested by Gatbonton-Siegalowitz (1978) for phonology. Thus the kind of feedback process in which we give balanced feedback, including explicit negative evidence in relation to grammar and pragmatics, and then shift responsibility to the student can positively if gradually affect the acquisition of the linguistic code significantly.

Example 2

The second pair of pre- and postfeedback excerpts are from a role play involving the same ITA and an overwrought undergraduate who needed not only to set up a tutoring arrangement but, more important, to be reassured. In this case, the teacher-researcher, without replaying the video, asked for immediate feedback from the participants and from other native English speakers who had observed the role play.

[2A]

```
1
T: Hi      my name is Sen S E N                          Frances
S:    hi                        Sen um I'm I'm Frances
2
T:
S: Yes umm I'm awfully worried cause I just don't know where
3
T:
S: to start with physics and   I have to take it  and I'm
```

```
4
T:                              oh yeah
S:   failing    miserably          I don't know where to start
5
T:
S:   with it at all  and  and  I spoke to the  teacher about it and
6
T:                                        oh ah  I think it's a
S:   and he said I should come and see   you
7
T:   not  very  serious  problem              because ah
S:                                OH hahahahaha it feels very serious
8
T:  because  mostly ah most problem  I think is ah is ah homework
S:                                                              yes
9
T:   y— you can do every homework very clearly  and  I think
S:
10
T:   there's  no  problem  for  the  examination of  final  course
S:                                                           so I
11
T:           sooo             aaya  what's a convenient time and
S:   just need to do extra work
12
T:  we can arrange the time and ah ahm to do work for your every
S:
13
T:  homework          because ah
S:            mhmm I see        So when I get something in class I
14
T:                            yeah yeah  we can discuss this
S:  can come 'n' bring it to you 'n'       look at it
15
T:   this homework problem
S:  ok                       oh that would be great hahaha thank you
```

In the review session, which took place immediately after the role play with both participants present, the ITA, Sen, said that he had been attempting to reassure the student with his first response (lines 6 and 7: "I think it's a not very serious problem"). The feedback he received from the student, Frances, was that the utterance invalidated her feelings and the seriousness of her concern because he hadn't yet heard about her difficulties. The ITA was given positive evidence in the form of an affirmation that his communicative intent to provide reassurance was appropriate even though the verbal realization was not successful. The ITA's attention was also directed to the point at which the student provided implicit negative evidence in her response that contradicted the ITA (line 7: "OH [laughter] it feels very serious"). The student also indicated generally what she had wanted to hear from him. There was no spontaneous feedback on whether the participants had ended the negotiation with the same interpretation of the nature of the tutoring arrangement.

Immediately after receiving this purely pragmatic feedback the ITA and student replayed the role play:

[2B]

```
 1
T: hi  my  name  is  Sen
S:                          um I'm  Frances  I'm  having  an  an  awful
 2
T:
S: lot  of  problems  with  with  physics    and  it's  very  important
 3
T:
S:  that I   that I  get  the  the  course   but   and  I   I  got a D  on
 4
T:
S:  my  last  paper  an um   I couldn't figure out  why it was  so bad
 5
T:
S:  and I thought I'd understood it and and I hadn't nn   so I'm
 6                                    Eye contact
T:
S:  not really quite sure what to do  *  umm   I  asked    a  ahm   the
 7                                                         ooa  ah
T:
S:  teacher and he said   I should try  and  see you
 8
T: don't worry too much    I'm sure I can help you    unn
S:                                              hahahahaha
 9
T: hehehe          unn                            hahahahaha
S: hahaha   I hope so      heheheh I seem to be beyond help hahah
10
T: aa ya  ya I think we can    arrange a time andah    I think
S:
11
T: most  problem  of  student  is  ah   about  their  homework  because
S:
12
T: is  very  difficult  transfer  the   the  problem  to  the
S:
13
T:  mathematical  formula   so--  I think ah  if we can  umm
S:
14
T:  discuss the homework together   an ah  do  every  homework
```

```
S:
15
T:                    ya ya               yes
S:   that would help      if I could talk to someone      because
16
T:
S:   I seem to think I understand in class    and then when I get
17
T:          ya       I s-        ya and ah  and I think there's no
S:   home      I can't remember
18
T:   problem for your        final examination
S:                                            hahaha
```

The student was much happier with this interaction, feeling reassured and sensing that her feelings had been acknowledged, although she pointed out that at one clear moment (in line 6) the ITA was not able to pick up on her eye contact cue that she wanted him to take the floor. Ironically, his delay in taking the floor was an overcompensation in response to her feedback—that she had wanted to be given the opportunity to explain her difficulties before he tried to offer reassurance. In general, however, both participants and all the observers felt that this interaction had gone more smoothly.

The Research Methodology

In this section we sketch the results of our research methodology, which builds on the results of the teaching methodology and then uses close linguistic analysis of the video data to clarify the sources of the participants' feelings and interpretations. We attempt to understand the process of conversational inference, in Gumperz's terms, in order to demystify cross-cultural communication and miscommunication. Our basic question is: What underlies the feelings of the ITA and the student that the second interaction was better than the first? We focus on two broad categories: conversation management and discourse-structuring cues.

Conversation Management

With regard to conversation management, in particular in relation to timing or synchrony (Erickson & Shultz, 1982), quite a bit of overlap is evident in Excerpt 2A (defined simply as one person apparently beginning a turn-at-talk while another is still speaking), a good example of which is at line 14. Excerpt 2B, on the other hand, contains one instance of overlap, at line 17. Excerpt 2A contains two instances from the ITA of what might be considered listenership backchannels (vocalizations indicating not the initiation of a turn-at-talk but simply participation as a listener; for English speakers classically *mmhmm*) at lines 4 and 14, but the backchannels in Excerpt 2B at lines 15 and 17 are much more smoothly timed in relation to the student's utterances.

A striking difference (not as obvious in this transcript format) is that between the length of the ITA's uninterrupted turns-at-talk in the two versions. The student allowed the ITA to produce a longer turn in Excerpt 2B, apparently because she felt less need to break in for clarification, than at lines 10 and 13 in Excerpt 2A, where she tried paraphrases prefaced by *so* ("so I just need to do extra work," and "so when I get something in class I can come and bring it to you")—which in each case was not exactly what the ITA meant.

The two exchanges differ in terms of apparent responsiveness, by which we mean the degree to which the participants appeared to be listening to each other and responding appropriately—internal evidence being incidence of nonsequiturs and very ambiguous sentences. In Excerpt 2A the feeling of nonresponsiveness is probably most clear at line 11, in the sequence of the student's paraphrase and the ITA's question concerning time. The student's attempt at paraphrase, "so I just need to do extra work," was intended to elicit confirmation or clarification. The ITA's vocalization in his next turn, "aaya," is not clearly interpretable as confirmation or rejection, and his next question, "what's a convenient time?" is thus interpretable as not directly responsive to the student's utterance.

In light of the ITA's contributions to the exchange in terms of role-congruent behavior, in Excerpt 2A his attempts to reassure ironically undermined another dimension of his role, the establishment of authority and credibility. His attempt at reassurance in Excerpt 2A ("I think it's a not very serious problem") actually undercut his credibility with the student because he offered the reassurance when he did not yet know the nature of her problem. Moreover, his use of *I think* sounds like the conventional hedge. The student may have interpreted this phrase as a lack of confidence or knowledge on the tutor's part. In fact, the ITA probably meant it in its nonhedge use. In contrast, in Excerpt 2B he used *I'm sure* ("I'm sure I can help you") at line 8, for which no hedge interpretation is possible.

In general, Excerpt 2B exhibits a smoothness at the micro level that is lacking in Excerpt 2A. The ITA changed his initial response to the reassuring, "Don't worry too much; I'm sure that I can help you," inspiring confidence in the student. The student responded at lines 8 and 9 with a self-deprecating but relieved, "I thought I was beyond help." The ITA followed up with another confidence-inspiring utterance, which indicated that he knew about the typical sources of students' problems and what to do about them. There is no question here of the misinterpretation that the student must do "extra" work but simply a clear indication that the ITA will help with homework. The student responded first at line 15 with a direct statement linking cohesively to the ITA's previous utterance, "that would help," and then by further elaborating the problem and disclosing her study approach to the ITA. Next, at line 17, the ITA used a variation of a previously unsuccessful utterance from his initial role play (Excerpt 2A): "I think there's no problem for your final examination." In this case it worked as intended because it came *after* an interaction in which the student had been reassured that the ITA knew what he was doing; it is also specific—in relation to the future final examination.

Discourse-Structuring Cues

Turning now to the second category, discourse-structuring cues, previous research in the discourse produced by Chinese speakers in a lecture situation (Tyler, Jefferies, & Davies, 1988; Tyler, 1992) revealed problems with discourse-structuring cues in terms of appropriate use of lexical discourse markers (e.g., *so, anyway*), syntactic incorporation (linking and embedding of clauses), and specificity (establishing relationships among words in terms of reference). The same types of errors occurred in this tutor's speech in the dialogue situation. Consider again the transcript of the prefeedback role play in Excerpt 2A, starting at line 6:

> I think it's a not very serious problem/(interrupted)/ because ah mostly because ah most problem I think is ah is ah homework/ (interrupted)/ You can do every homework very clearly and I think there's no problem for the examination of final course

The lack of clarity stems from the interaction of several discourse-structuring miscues. The Chinese speaker's use of prosodics (i.e., "tone of voice," including stress, intonation contours, and pause patterns), lexical discourse markers, tense and aspect marking, and specificity cues all worked to obscure the relationships among the ideas. First, conflicting signals made it difficult to know how to integrate the clause "because most problem I think is homework" into the surrounding discourse. The lexical discourse marker *because*, in lines 7 and 8, indicate that the clause is syntactically dependent and thus must be syntactically connected to either the preceding or the following clause. However, the prosodic cues (i.e., the relatively long pauses before and after the clause and rising/ falling intonation contours on *serious problem* and *homework*) indicate that it should not be integrated into either the preceding or following clause. Notice that the English speaker broke in after each of these prosodic contours, suggesting that she had interpreted them as sentence finality markers.

The next clause, "You can do every homework very clearly," is particularly difficult to interpret. As pointed out, it is unclear whether the clause should be integrated into the preceding clause, yielding, *Because most problem I think is homework, you can do every problem very clearly*, or be interpreted as independent, yielding, *Because most problem I think is homework. You can do every problem very clearly*. The modal *can* creates additional ambiguity. It is obviously not the appropriate choice as it stands, so the listener must find an alternative to construct a coherent meaning. The pronunciation of *can* may mask a negative marker, which would be reasonable *if* the clause is interpreted as independent *and* the speaker is expressing sympathy toward or understanding of the student's problem; this would yield *Because most problem I think is homework. You can't do every problem very clearly*. Alternatively, the speaker may have been substituting *can* for *need to*, or even be signaling a conditional structure (as in *If you can do all your homework*). The problem is that no clear way exists to choose among these competing interpretations. Moreover, any of these interpretations requires the listener to repair the discourse through a series of inferences. The student's tentative attempt at a paraphrase ("So if I just do extra homework?") indicates her confusion. Note also that more local problems with word order in the phrases "a not very serious problem" and "examination of your final course" add to the confusion.

Now consider the transcript of the postfeedback role play (Excerpt 2B), starting at line 10:

> I think most problem of student is ah about their homework because is very difficult transfer the problem to the mathematical formula. So I think ah if we can discuss the homework together and ah do every homework . . .

Notice that the basic ideas and the order in which they are presented are very similar to those in the Excerpt 2A. Unlike that excerpt, however, this discourse offers little difficulty in interpretation. The lexical discourse markers *because* and *so* appear to be used in appropriate ways, offering unambiguous signals about the relationships among the clauses. There are no conflicting signals between morphosyntactic cues and prosody, so questions about how to integrate a particular clause into the discourse do not arise. The speaker has used an *if*-clause, which allows straightforward interpretation of his suggestion on how to correct the problem. In addition, the speaker has added important details that clarify his remarks (e.g., "problem *of student*") and an explanation as to why homework is the problem, "is very difficult transfer the problem to the mathematical formula").

The Chinese speaker articulated the same number of words in each exchange (66). However, the saliency of his words differed significantly from exchange to exchange. In the first exchange he produced a greater number of false starts and hesitation markers; in the second he expanded his ideas and added meaningful information.

What we find particularly interesting is that the speaker received no feedback concerning any of the problems of interpretation caused by the linguistic code. He was able to adjust his syntactic structuring (with the *if*-clause), use of lexical discourse markers, prosody, and lexicalization (i.e., being more explicit by encoding more of his message in words rather than relying on his listener's ability to infer and fill in his meaning) after receiving feedback of a solely pragmatic nature. For some experimental follow-up yielding support for the findings documented in this paper, see Tyler and Davies (1990b).

Discussion

In trying to explain the modifications documented here that occurred after ITAs received feedback in the form of various kinds of negative and positive evidence, we find Schmidt's (1990) treatment of the role of consciousness in second language learning most compelling. Schmidt's position that conscious awareness at the level of "noticing" (p. 129) is necessary for language learning finds support in the instance documented here of the improvement of a fossilized error. The high frequency of occurrences of the correct form in input in the ITA's academic milieu underscores the point that simple exposure is not always enough and that the ITA's attention may have to be directed appropriately to the error. In a clear example of error correction oriented to grammatical form (the *equals to* construction), that is, the classical negative evidence, improvement was documented at an interval of 4 weeks under natural tutoring conditions. The ITA's attention had been drawn to the error and the correct construction had been provided and explained; in addition, the act of documenting his own errors on videotape focused the ITA's attention on the error.

The relation between pragmatic feedback and the documented modifications produced is less easily explained. The second set of role plays offers a dramatic example of how feedback oriented purely to pragmatics apparently yielded a range of performance improvements in different dimensions of language (i.e., syntactic structuring, use of lexical discourse markers, prosody, and lexicalization). We do not believe that the ITA improved because he suddenly *learned* these aspects of the linguistic code. Rather, we suggest, the pragmatically oriented teaching methodology described here created circumstances that allowed him to *perform* better.

In the case discussed here, the pragmatic feedback involved validating communicative intent while giving explicit feedback about a native speaker's interpretation of a problematic utterance and directing the ITA's attention to the implicit negative evidence offered by the interlocutor's response. The ITA also received some general clues about the native speaker's schema for the situation. This process appears to be a form of Oller's (1983) "pragmatic mapping," which he defines as "the inferential linking of utterances to contexts of experience" (p. 3). The apparent effects of the pragmatic feedback might be understood in terms of Bruner's (1981b, 1986) ideas concerning first language acquisition: that pragmatic framing provides a kind of scaffolding that supports the development of grammar in that it allows the learner to focus on form. We suggest that the methodology presented here creates circumstances that allow the second language learner to receive feedback that fulfills the same function as that the adult gives the child in first language acquisition.

Also consistent with the shift to the notion of "socialization" in relation to language learning and a cognitive focus on interpretive processes (cf. Gumperz's theory of conversational inference, 1982a) is a perspective that takes into account both the speaker (production) and the listener (interpretation). Pragmatic feedback oriented toward socializing the ITA into the schema may have some far-reaching effects related to the reduction of "anxiety," a term used here very loosely. The first effect is to allow the ITA to relax and be relatively comfortable in the situation, which in itself often seems to have a salutary effect on accuracy of production (Guiora, Hallahmi, Brannon, Dull, & Scovel, 1972). More accurate performance may be related to the freeing up of cognitive processing capacity from the demands both of the condition called anxiety and also of any bottom-up attempts to calculate the current culturally different schema. Anxiety reduction is also related to demystification of the problems for ITAs, along with the development of confidence in their ability to cope with any future miscommunications by using the resource of native speakers to discover cues. In effect ITAs are learning how to learn about these processes, thus becoming empowered to pursue their own language socialization. Anecdotal evidence shows that ITAs' confidence in their ability to negotiate and thus in their willingness to engage in interaction with native speakers does increase. In fact, toward the end of the semester the ITA discussed here came to class one day and proudly told us about finally feeling free to talk to his professors during a physics reception: "Before I always kept my lips closed tight if any of my professors are nearby. I didn't want my poor English ability make them think I was stupid."

Taking into account *the native-speaking student listener*—for whom multiple, complex potential sources of miscues exist at many levels of linguistic organization in the nonnative speaker's production (Tyler, Jefferies, & Davies, 1988; Tyler & Davies, 1990a)—the socialization of *the nonnative-speaking ITA* into the schema by means of pragmatic feedback can have the following important effects: The relative comfort and ease of the ITA can help to establish rapport and put the student more at ease; reduction in anxiety can free the student to pay better attention to the whole context of the interaction in interpreting what is going on; and the ITA's adherence to the cultural schema allows the student to in effect "fill in" and compensate unconsciously for ITA performance errors in much the same way as for fellow native speakers. Thus the ITA speaker enlists the interpretive capabilities of the student listener to screen performance errors (cf. McGregor, 1986, for discussion of related issues of "language for hearers").

Both participants become better listeners and more effective partners in conversation. A mutually enhancing effect can be set in motion that again contributes to the conditions for further successful interactions, not only in the possible continuation of a relationship between any two interactants but in the confidence and the favorable attitude each participant develops toward future interaction with members of the other category. A not-insignificant aspect of this favorable effect on both sides of a cross-cultural encounter is that the participants become less likely to attribute interactional difficulties to either personal characteristics of the individual or negative stereotypes of the group in question (cf. Gumperz & Tannen, 1979; Jones & Nisbett, 1972).

The ITA can gather negative evidence of the sort that we are concerned with only under certain conditions—when trust has developed and when there is a native speaker or analyst capable of perceiving the problems and offering useful, balanced feedback. Certainly access to video technology is helpful, in light of the out-of-awareness quality of much in the process of communication. Some cross-cultural expertise is also needed, as research in cross-cultural communication indicates that sources of miscommunication are largely inaccessible to participants (Gumperz, 1982a; Erickson & Shultz, 1982). In fairly unusual circumstances, second language learners might be able to establish relationships with native speakers in which this kind of feedback takes place (cf. Davies, 1988; 1991a). Given the rarity of such circumstances for most language learners (White, 1989, p. 40), it is not surprising that ESL professionals frequently encounter international students like the ITA discussed here, who, despite having lived in the United States for several years, have not developed effective English communication skills. Such ITAs report that they rarely use English except in the most basic exchanges and that they often experience communication breakdowns without knowing why the breakdowns occur (Davies et al., 1989). The challenge to language teachers is to find ways to facilitate the process of language socialization, in effect helping ITAs learn how to operate at the level of metacommunicative awareness and analysis. Our framework offers a way of approaching the process by which interactants build common ground by establishing and maintaining conversational involvement, which, as Gumperz has so aptly pointed out, is the essential basis of communicative competence.

Acknowledgment

Davies gratefully acknowledges support in this research from the University of Alabama in the form of 1991 Faculty Summer Research Grant 1590.

▪ 12 ▪

Native and Nonnative Teaching Assistants: A Case Study of Discourse Domains and Genres

Dan Douglas
Iowa State University

Larry Selinker
University of Michigan

▪

For a number of years we have been exploring the question of variation in language use among international teaching assistants (ITAs). In this chapter we report on a case study comparing the use of English in two domains and two genres by a U.S. teaching assistant (TA) and a Sri Lankan TA at Iowa State University. We first discuss the discourse domains concept as the theoretical underpinning of the study, then summarize our work up to the present as background. Finally, we present an analysis of data from the two TAs to illustrate variation in relation to discourse domain and an overlapping concept, genre. We conclude by suggesting that ITA researchers and trainers need to take the notions of both discourse domains and genre into account in investigating the interlanguage (IL) of ITAs and in producing ITA training materials.

Discourse Domains and Genres

In this section we outline two perspectives on language acquisition and use, that of discourse domain and that of genre. The notion of discourse domain, developed in our own work since 1985, is the primary focus here. However, we find the notion of genre, developed most thoroughly by Swales (1990), to be enlightening and useful in analyzing variation in language use in the present study.

A discourse domain is a cognitive construct created by a language learner as a context for IL development. Researchers have described such a construct, which, in Widdowson's words, "organizes language in preparation for use" (1983, p. 37), with a range of terms: schema

(Rumelhart, 1980), script (Shank & Abelson, 1977), superstructure (van Dijk & Kintsch, 1983), and frame (Goffman, 1974). These concepts have been used to discuss models of both first and second language production and comprehension. We do not wish to join the debate on how they are different and related (see Widdowson, 1983, for an interesting discussion), but we feel the need for a distinct term, discourse domain, to distinguish clearly the idea of external features of context from the learner's internal interpretation of them.

Learners construct discourse domains in connection with life experiences that have importance for them such that they talk, read, and write about them frequently and exercise content control over them. Zuengler (1989a) has suggested that discourse domains may be a part of a speaker's identity (coequivalent with such identifiers as social class, peer group, ethnicity, gender, and age) with respect to whether or not speakers consider themselves "knowers" or relative "experts" at performing some task. A domain is a dynamic, changeable construct that may nevertheless become a permanent part of the learner's cognitive system. Learners may also create a domain temporarily for an important purpose, such as writing a doctoral dissertation, seeking employment, or taking a vacation abroad. As an internal context for IL development, a domain is associated with the second language acquisition processes of transfer, fossilization, and backsliding, which, we hypothesize, do not occur globally across ILs but differentially within domains. The discourse domain concept may thus be seen as a vehicle for uniting IL, second language acquisition, and language for specific purposes (LSP) studies (cf. Selinker & Douglas, 1987). We see discourse domains as *mediators* between external contextual features and internal features of communicative competence. They first establish for the learner what the external context *counts as* and then they marshal the components of competence required to deal with it (see Douglas, 1992, for a more detailed discussion).

Studies of IL use in context, such as those involving ITAs, need to take into account which features of external context, including genre, *count* for the learner, and what they count *as*, as they proceed with the tasks of analysis and synthesis in the processes of acquisition and production. Recently we have been exploring the possibility of manipulating contextual features in oral proficiency tests to bring about differential domain engagement among ITAs (Douglas & Selinker, 1993; in press; 1991). We have constructed field-specific mathematics and chemistry versions of the Educational Testing Service's Speaking Proficiency in English Assessment Kit (SPEAK) oral proficiency test to see whether they tests would yield better measures of prospective TAs' spoken English proficiency than the more general SPEAK. This work has led us to reconsider Hymes' original "communicative competence" formulation (Hymes, 1972b) that involves judgments about what is systemically possible, psycholinguistically feasible, and socioculturally appropriate and about what the accomplishment of a particular linguistic event entails. As a result of these studies we have arrived at a much-expanded notion of the nature of "context" as it relates to the construction of discourse domains by language learners, including ITAs.

Our work has focused on how IL competence may develop differentially with respect to different discourse domains. A learner, we have found, may demonstrate certain IL features (e.g., sentence embedding) in one domain but not in others. In attempting to account for that variation in ITAs, our concern is to explain variation in IL performance, particularly connected with subject matter discourse as well as with ordinary conversation. To do so we need to introduce into our conceptualization the notion of *genre*. In LSP studies, genre has been defined as a class of communicative events the members of which share a set of communicative purposes that shape discourse structure and constrain choice of content and style (cf. Swales, 1990, p. 58). An instructive example of a genre for LSP is that of the "research article introduction" (Swales, 1990), where such content and style conventions as "establishing a territory," "establishing a niche" within that territory, and "occupying the niche" (Swales, 1990, pp. 140–142) help to define the genre. Importantly from our perspective, these genre conventions appear to be used across a wide variety of fields, and Swales (1990) has argued strongly that, for example, article introductions in engineering, physics, linguistics, and medicine follow the generic conventions. An important point, however, is that although a single genre may appear across a number of fields, within a single field a number of genres may be used. Thus within, say, linguistics are found not only research articles but also abstracts, lectures, theses, grant proposals, and other genres. For the purposes of the present analysis, then, we propose two independent levels of analysis, one by discourse domain and the other by genre. We need to consider the possibility that domain and genre interact in a complex way to influence language acquisition and production.

Previous Work on ITAs and Discourse Domains

Since the publication of our discourse domains hypothesis (Selinker & Douglas, 1985), we have been wrestling with a methodology for identifying differences associated with domains, which we had originally defined as "personally and internally constructed 'slices' of an L2 learner's life" (p. 190). Our intention has been to take a true IL perspective in studying IL forms and attendant rhetoric, semantics, pragmatics, and discourse without focusing on "error" per se but linking variation in forms to learner-constructed domains of language use. We claim that learners construct ILs within discourse domains so that they might possess a number of different domains with a somewhat different IL associated with each. In language use situations, we have hypothesized, learners engage a discourse domain and the IL associated with it. Although it is not directly concerned with ITAs and discourse domains, we begin with discussion of a study by Briggs (1987) that illustrates well some of the ideas we wish to explore.

In her study of differences between English native and nonnative speakers in a graduate architecture class, Briggs (1987) described differences between talk in different genres in the same domain: work talk in a studio and work talk in a juried formal presentation. In the studio, the nonnative speakers (NNSs) could use context to compensate for a lack of precision in their English IL whereas in the presentation they could not. Briggs speculated that the LSP context may contribute to differential fossilization of learners' strategic competence. In one situation, the studio, strategies other than talk were available for getting the message across; for example, the student could pick up a pen and draw, perhaps encouraging fossilization at the point of the achievement of communicative needs. However, in a different genre, the formal presentation of completed work, the students could not resort to drawing and had to provide a more precise version of the IL, a situation encouraging further IL development. This study suggests that, in addition to variation by domain, variation by genre warrants further investigation. In fact, the effect of the interaction between domain and genre seems to be an area worth exploring.

In 1986 we studied the IL of an ITA in chemistry at Iowa State University (Douglas & Selinker, 1986). We collected videotaped data on the subject presenting a minilecture during a performance test required for ITA certification, responding to questions from the audience after the lecture, and being interviewed about a problem in chemistry and about aspects of his personal life by one of the researchers. Each of these data types was collected on two occasions about 3 months apart. We thus had performance data from this subject in two domains—talk about work and talk about personal life—in three genres—lecturing, answering questions from an audience, and conversing in a one-on-one interview—in two time periods. Our analysis focused on whether changes observed over time in the subject's performance in, say, lecturing about chemistry carried over into his performance in a different genre in the same domain, say, responding to questions about chemistry or, alternatively, whether such changes carried over into a different domain, say, that of personal life story. Our data suggested that IL variation seemed to be associated with domain. For example, in the work-talk domain the subject used the modals *can* and *could* in a target-language–like fashion to indicate factual or hypothetical possibility. However, in the life-story domain the TA used modals quite differently: He switched between *could* and *can* to distinguish concrete, specific topics from abstract, general ones. In other words, he was using modals, and other features, differently in the two domains.

We hypothesized that ILs change longitudinally within domains but that such changes may not carry over across domains. The notion of genre may be useful in thinking about transfer here: Swales (1990) has suggested that, if domain boundaries are indeed relatively impermeable to the effects of transfer, then his approach to genre analysis (namely, that genres do cross domain boundaries) appears to be undermined. However, domains and genres are independent and not hierarchical (i.e., a single domain may employ a number of genres, and a single genre may be employed across several domains). For example, the domain *work talk* may employ the genres of a lecture to undergraduate chemistry students, a research presentation to professors, and a question-answer sequence in the lab. Similarly, the genre of the office-hour consultation may include both informal chat about personal matters or the weather as well as talk in the domain of problem solving. This view of the independence of domain and genre clarifies an earlier view that appeared to equate the two notions (cf. Selinker & Douglas, 1989b).

The Current Study

In the study reported here, we investigated the differential engagement of domain in a U.S. TA and an international TA to explore further variability in relation to genre and especially the question of the transfer of rhetorical and grammatical features from one domain to another.

Method

Subjects. We collected data from two TAs in the statistics department at Iowa State University. Both were experienced teachers and had been recommended to us by their supervisor as "good" TAs. Each was teaching an introductory statistics course for business majors. One subject was a woman from Baltimore, in the final year of her MA studies in statistics; the other was a man from Sri Lanka, in his third year of doctoral studies. His first language is Sinhalese, and English is a second language for him, learned in the classroom and used only for reading before coming to the United States. He had been in the United States for 5 years at the time of the study, having earned his MA at the University of Illinois at Urbana-Champaign.

Procedure. The subjects were videotaped in three contexts: presenting a lecture in their statistics classes, being interviewed by a U.S. freshman about material from the lecture, and being interviewed by the same freshman about their leisure activities and interests. The classroom videos were recorded as part of another project, collecting a series of tapes from 10 TAs to be used as exemplary material in a remedial course for NNS TAs. An entire 50-minute class was recorded early in the fall 1986 semester. Each class was a "normal" one, that is, not set up especially for the taping, though of course each TA was somewhat nervous at the outset and had tried to prepare a "good" class.

The interviews were conducted in the office of one of the researchers and were set up to simulate as much as possible a typical office visit. The interviewer was a first-year student in engineering who had been selected from a freshman composition class by his instructor as being interested, personable, and intelligent. The undergraduate first watched each video-taped lecture and took notes on it. Next, each TA, together with the student, reviewed his or her own taped lecture, and the student asked a number of questions based on his notes. The interview with the NNS TA lasted for a little less than 15 minutes, and that with the U.S. TA lasted for just under 20.

Immediately following the interviews about the lectures, the student asked the TAs about their leisure activities and interests, having been instructed by the researcher not to "get too personal." The topics raised included, in the case of the U.S. TA, sports (she is an avid baseball fan) and plans for the future, and in the case of the NNS TA, sports, music, and his home country. These interviews lasted only about 4 1/2 minutes with the NNS TA and about 3 minutes with the U.S. TA.

In addition to the primary video data, we obtained two types of secondary data: retrospective commentary by the two subjects on their own performances as they watched the videotapes, and commentary by specialist informants as they watched the tapes. Our principal specialist informant was a professor from the statistics department who commented on the lectures, but numerous colleagues and students have also viewed the tapes and provided comments reflecting their various points of view and areas of expertise. The purpose of the secondary data is to help guide the subsequent analysis of the primary data.

Analysis

The area in the data that has been most productive for us from the point of view of theory building is that of discourse markers. Discourse markers have been studied quite extensively by various scholars; we refer the reader to Schiffrin (1987) for a full discussion. We use the term here to refer to the feature of discourse discussed by Chaudron and Richards

(1986) that they have called "micro-markers" and "macro-markers." Chaudron and Richards are interested in investigating the role of signals of organization in NNS comprehension of information in lectures. They consider the influence of discourse signals related to "top-down" processing and those related to "bottom-up" processing (Adams & Collins, 1979) and distinguish between organization and the saliency of the organization (Meyer, Brandt, & Bluth, 1980) to investigate the effect of micro-markers (signals of lower-level information in the text) and macro-markers (signals of higher-level information) on comprehension of lectures. Micro-markers, they suggest, serve as filled pauses, "giving listeners more time to process individual segments of a piece of discourse" (p. 116)— "bottom-up" processing. Examples are markers of temporality (*then, now,* or *after this*), causation (*because*), contrast (*but*), emphasis (*in fact*), and segmentation (*well, OK,* or *all right*). Macro-markers, on the other hand, are related to background knowledge and serve as confirmation and support for listeners' expectations and predictions about the lecture. Examples are *What I'm going to talk about today is . . . , You probably know something about already . . .* , or *What we have come to by now is that . . .* .Chaudron and Richards were interested in the role of such signals in comprehension; however, it struck us that discourse markers would be a useful avenue of investigation in our study of the relationship between differential ITA interlanguage use and discourse domain and genre.

We began by counting and classifying instances of discourse markers in the data from our two TAs. Examples of both types of marker in our data are given below.

Micro-markers	*Macro-markers*
OK, so, but, because, now	Why don't we start with . . .
Naturally,	What can you tell me about . . .
The next thing	OK, the idea of R-squared adjusted is . . .
	A favorite example is . . .
	Ok, the next topic is . . .

The identification of micro- and macro-markers in our data presented an analytical difficulty: It was not always clear which tokens belonged to the category macro-marker and which to micro-marker. Meyer et al.'s (1980) distinction between organization and saliency of organization was helpful: "The structure of text specifies the logical connection among ideas in text as well as the subordination of some ideas to others" (p. 74). In terms of data analysis, what one must first do is identify the macro, rhetorical, and content structures of the text, without reference to discourse markers and then classify the markers according to their function in the text, either as markers of superordination (macro-markers) or of lower-level relationships among ideas (micro-markers).

Results

Table 1 shows the results of our quantification. In their lectures the two TAs used both types of markers fairly equally. That is, if the NS TA's performance is the norm, the NNS TA matches it. However, the interview data tells a different story. The NS TA used far fewer macro-markers in both the work-talk interview and the life-story interview than in the lecture, but the NNS TA used about as many macro-markers in the work-talk interview as he did in the lecture. His use of macro-markers in the life-story interview, however, paralleled that of the NS TA.

Discussion

First we comment on the primary, or videotaped, data, which were derived from the secondary data, commentary from a subject specialist informant. Our informant, a statistics professor who viewed our lecture tapes, confirmed for us that both TAs were doing an adequate job of presenting their material and that their performances contained nothing unusual or particularly problematic. His main concern, voiced a number of times as he watched the tapes, was that each TA was a bit weak in "motivating" certain points. For example, he said that the NNS TA "motivated his topic" in terms of mathematical identities, whereas he could have made the point about "R-squared adjusted" by considering what happens as one adds more variables. Our informant made the same sort of point about the NS TA: "OK, what's motivating 17—why would you pick 17?" We see this "motivation" point as related to teaching maturity, and it may signal a difference between professors and TAs.

In the analysis of the language data, the NS TA used a roughly equal number of macro- and micro-markers in the lecture but a far greater proportion of micro-markers in the two interviews, one in the domain of work talk and the other in that of talk about personal life. The NNS TA used both marker types in the lecture to a degree similar to that of the NS baseline; however, in the interviews he matched the NS norm only in the life-story domain. Significantly, in the interview about work, our subject did not match the NS performance; instead, he used macro-markers to a degree similar to that in the lecture.

The NS TA and the NNS TA thus showed differential interaction between domain and genre in their performances: When engaged in

Table 1 ▪ Use of Discourse Markers by NS and NNS TAs, by Domain and Genre

| TA and domain | Genre and marker | | | |
| | Lecture | | Interview | |
	Micro	Macro	Micro	Macro
NS TA				
Work talk	26	33	50	7
	(44%)	(56%)	(88%)	(12%)
Life story	—	—	8	1
			(89%)	(11%)
NNS TA				
Work talk	24	25	25	18
	(49%)	(51%)	(58%)	(42%)
Life story	—	—	17	2
			(89%)	(11%)

the work-talk domain, the NS TA distinguished between the lecture and the interview genres; within the interview genre, she did not distinguish between discourse domains. The ITA, on the other hand, did not distinguish between genres when engaged in the work-talk domain but showed domain-related differences within the interview genre. Is there perhaps a developmental sequence in domain-related IL development? The ITA apparently overgeneralized rhetorical and grammatical features within a domain without taking account of genre. That is, the ITA may have transferred the feature of lecture presentation to an interview situation within the same domain of work talk. This phenomenon is related to the notion of *domain transfer*, discussed elsewhere (Selinker & Douglas, 1991), and may give a clue about how to investigate the vexing question of the direction of domain transfer: A more careful, more extensive look at the interaction between domain and genre is necessary to determine if that interaction is related somehow to differential transfer of IL features.

Conclusion

Recent decades of work in IL and second language acquisition studies have shown how greatly IL performance can vary with context. Numerous studies in recent years (see Tarone, 1988, for a discussion) have shown phonological, morphological, lexical, syntactic, and pragmatic variation with regard to task, linguistic context, processing factors, social norms, and changes in interlocutor, topic, and function. We suggest that all these types of factors are subsets of variation with *context*, as we define it, following Hymes (1972b; see Douglas, 1992, for discussion). We feel (and have since 1985) that, until researchers come to grips with the notion of context in a workable research framework, work on IL development and use will be incomplete and perhaps wrong. This concept has significant implications for ITA research and training, as the area is IL in context *par excellence*.

Incorporating the notion of genre into our analytical framework has helped us understand more deeply the concept of discourse domain and how it affects second language acquisition and use. Our findings here reinforce and, indeed, strengthen the assertion in our research methodology paper (Selinker & Douglas, 1989b) that without careful IL genre analysis, second language acquisition research results can be misinterpreted. This is a fruitful area for future research.

Although, as is usually the case, many more studies of ITA interlanguage development and use are necessary, this study reveals the possibility that stages of ITA interlanguage development may involve transfer of IL rhetorical and grammatical features within a single domain but across genres. More advanced ITAs, and NS TAs, may possess greater facility to take account not only of domain but also of genre.

These considerations have implications for ITA training: They suggest that trainers must help ITAs learn to differentiate between genres within a single domain of work talk, for example. In terms of this study, specific rhetorical and grammatical features appropriate in a lecture will not necessarily be appropriate in the recitation class or the office-hour consultation. In an ITA course, a trainer might be able to make trainees aware that structures appropriate in a lecture genre may be inappropriately transferred to the office-hour genre. Only through careful studies of TA and ITA discourse can trainers learn precisely what those structures may be and under what circumstances they may and may not transfer appropriately.

References

■

Abraham, R., Anderson-Hsieh, J., Douglas, D., Myers, C., & Plakans, B. (1988). *Evaluation and instructional program for international teaching assistants.* Paper presented at the 22nd Annual TESOL Convention, Chicago, IL.

Abraham, R., & Plakans, B. (1988). Evaluating a screening/training program for NNS teaching assistants. *TESOL Quarterly, 22,* 505–508.

Adams, M. J., & Collins, A. (1979). A schema-theoretic view of reading. In R. O. Freedle (Ed.), *New directions in discourse processing* (pp. 1–22). Norwood, NJ: Ablex.

Anderson, A., & Lynch, T. (1988). *Listening.* Oxford: Oxford University Press.

Anderson-Hsieh, J. (1990). Teaching suprasegmentals to international teaching assistants using field-specific materials. *English for Specific Purposes, 9,* 195–214.

Andrews, J. (1980). The verbal structure of teacher questions: Its impact on class discussion. *POD Quarterly, 2,* 129–163.

Ard, J. (1987). The foreign TA problem from an acquisition-theoretic point of view. *English for Specific Purposes, 6,* 133–144.

Ard, J. (1989). Grounding an ITA curriculum: Theoretical and practical concerns. *English for Specific Purposes, 8,* 125–138.

Axelson E., & Madden, C. (1990). Videotaped materials for communicative ITA training. *IDEAL, 5,* 1–11.

Bachman, L. (1990). *Fundamental considerations in language testing.* New York: Oxford University Press.

Bailey, K. M. (1982). *Teaching in a second language: The communicative competence of non-native speaking teaching assistants.* Unpublished doctoral dissertation, University of California, Los Angeles. (University Microfilms No. 83-06, 009)

Bailey, K. M. (1983). Foreign teaching assistants in U.S. universities: Problems in interaction and communication. *TESOL Quarterly, 17,* 308-310.

Bailey, K. M. (1984). A typology of teaching assistants. In Bailey, Pialorsi, & Zukowski/Faust (1984), pp. 110–130.

Bailey, K. M. (1985). If I had known then what I know now: Performance testing of foreign teaching assistants. In P. Hauptman, R. Leblanc, & M. Wesche (Eds.), *Second language performance testing* (pp. 153–180). Ottawa: University of Ottawa Press.

Bailey, K. M., Pialorski, F., & Zukowski/Faust, J. (Eds.). (1984). *Foreign teaching assistants in U.S. universities.* Washington, DC: NAFSA.

Bardovi-Harlig, K., & Hartford, B. S. (1990). Congruence in native and nonnative conversation: Status balance in the academic advising session. *Language Learning, 40,* 467–501.

Barnes, G., Finger, A., Hoekje, B., & Ruffin, P. (1989). *Towards standards: A survey of ITA programs*. Paper presented at the 23rd Annual TESOL Convention, San Antonio, TX.

Barnes, G., & van Naerssen, M. (1991). *Issues of health, safety and security for ITAs*. Paper presented at the National Association of Foreign Student Affairs Convention, Boston, MA.

Bartlett, F. C. (1932). *Remembering*. Oxford: Oxford University Press.

Berns, M. (1989). *An ITA profile and its implications for course design*. Paper presented at the Preconference Symposium on ITA Training, 23rd Annual TESOL Convention, San Antonio, TX.

Bialystok, E., & Ryan, E. B. (1985). Toward a definition of metalinguistic skill. *Merrill-Palmer Quarterly, 31*, 229–259.

Biber, D. (1988). *Variation across speech and writing*. Cambridge: Cambridge University Press.

Birdsong, D. (1989). *Metalinguistic performance and interlinguistic competence*. Berlin: Springer-Verlag.

Bloom, B. S. (1956). *Taxonomy of educational objectives*. New York: Longmans Green.

Boyd, F. (1989a). Developing presentation skills: A perspective derived from professional education. *English for Specific Purposes, 8*, 195–203.

Boyd, F. (1989b). *Effective programs for small institutions*. Paper presented at the Preconference Symposium on ITA Training, 23rd Annual TESOL Convention, San Antonio, TX.

Briggs, S. (1987). When course success varies from discourse success. Research note in L. Selinker & D. Douglas (Eds.), *ESP Journal, 6* [Special issue], 153–156.

Briggs, S., & Hofer, B. (1991). Undergraduate perceptions of ITA effectiveness. In Nyquist, Abbott, Wulff, & Sprague (1991), pp. 435–445.

Brown, G., Anderson, A., Shillcock, N., & Yule, G. (1984). *Teaching talk: Strategies for production and assessment*. Cambridge: Cambridge University Press.

Brown, J., & Yule, G. (1983). *Teaching the spoken language*. Cambridge: Cambridge University Press.

Brown, K. (1988). *Effects of perceived country of origin, educational status, and native speakerness on American college student attitudes toward non-native instructors*. Unpublished doctoral dissertation, University of Minnesota, Minneapolis. (University Microfilms No. 88-15, 268)

Brown, K., Fishman, P., & Jones, N. (1989). *Legal and policy issues in the language proficiency assessment of international teaching assistants* (Monograph 90-1). Houston: University of Houston Law Center, Institute for Higher Education Law and Governance.

Bruner, J. S. (1981a). Interaction and language acquisition. In W. Deutsche (Ed.), *The child's construction of language*. New York: Academic Press.

Bruner, J. S. (1981b). The social context of language acquisition. *Language and Communication, 1*, 155–178.

Bruner, J. S. (1985). Vygotsky: A historical and conceptual perspective. In J.

Wertsch (Ed.), *Culture, communication, and cognition: Vygotskian perspectives* (pp. 21–35). Cambridge: Cambridge University Press.

Bruner, J. S. (1986). *Actual minds, possible worlds.* Cambridge, MA: Harvard University Press.

Byrd, P. (1987). Being seduced by face validity: Linguistic and administrative issues in videotaped teaching simulation testing. In Chism & Warner (1987), pp. 355–357.

Byrd, P., & Constantinides, J. C. (1988). FTA training programs: Searching for appropriate teaching styles. *English for Specific Purposes, 7,* 123–129.

Byrd, P., & Constantinides, J. C. (1992). The language of teaching mathematics: Implications for training ITAs. *TESOL Quarterly, 26,* 163–167.

Byrd, P., Constantinides, J., & Pennington, M. (1989). *The foreign teaching assistant's manual.* New York: Collier Macmillan.

Canale, M. (1983). From communicative competence to language pedagogy. In J. Richards & R. Schmidt (Eds.), *Language and communication* (pp. 2–28). London: Longman.

Canale, M., & Swain, M. (1980). Theoretical bases for communicative approaches to second language teaching and testing. *Applied Linguistics, 1,* 1–47.

Carlson, L. (1983). *Dialogue games: An approach to discourse analysis.* Dordrecht, Netherlands: Reidel.

Carrell, P., Sarwark, S., & Plakans, B. (1987). Innovative ITA screening techniques. In Chism & Warner (1987), pp. 351–354.

Cathcart, R. L., & Winn-Bell Olsen, J. E. (1976). Teachers' and students' preferences for correction of classroom conversation errors. In F. Fanselow & R. H. Crymes (Eds.), *On TESOL '76* (pp. 41–53). Washington, DC: TESOL.

Chaudron, C. (1977). A descriptive model of discourse in the corrective treatment of learners' errors. *Language Learning, 27,* 29–46.

Chaudron, C. (1983). Research on metalinguistic judgments: A review of theory, methods, and results. *Language Learning, 33,* 343–377.

Chaudron, C. (1988). *Second language classrooms: Research on teaching and learning.* Cambridge: Cambridge University Press.

Chaudron, C., & Richards, J. (1986). The effect of discourse markers on the comprehension of lectures. *Applied Linguistics, 7,* 113–127.

Chesler, M., & Fox, R. (1966). *Roleplaying methods in the classroom.* Chicago: Science Research Associates.

Chism, N. V. N., & Warner, S. B. (Eds.). (1987). *Institutional responsibilities and responses in the employment and education of teaching assistants: Readings from a national conference.* Columbus, OH: The Ohio State University, Center for Teaching Excellence.

Chomsky, N. (1981). *Lectures on government and binding.* Dordrecht: Foris.

Clark, H. (1980). *Language teaching techniques.* Brattleboro, VT: Prolingua.

Clark, J., & Swinton, C. (1980). *The Test of Spoken English as a measure of communicative ability in English-medium instructional settings* (TOEFL Research Report 7). Princeton, NJ: Educational Testing Service.

Collis, M., & Dalton, J., (1990). *Becoming responsible leaders*. Portsmouth, NH: Heinemann.

Connor, U., & Kaplan, R. B. (Eds.). (1987). *Writing across languages: Analysis of L2 text*. Reading, MA: Addison-Wesley.

Conrad, S. (1987). *Kinesic behavior of business lectures: A description and implications for EAP*. Unpublished master's thesis, Monterey Institute of International Studies, TESOL Program, Monterey, CA.

Constantinides, J. (1989). ITA training programs. In J. Nyquist, D. Abbott, & D. Wulff (Eds.), *Teaching assistant training in the 1990's* (New Directions in Teaching and Learning No. 39). San Francisco: Jossey-Bass.

Constantino, M. (1987). Intercultural communication for international teaching assistants: Observations on theory, pedagogy, and research. In Chism & Warner (1987), pp. 290–300.

Cook-Gumperz, J., Corsaro, W., & Streeck, J. (Eds.). (1986). *Children's worlds and children's language*. The Hague: Mouton.

Coulthard, M. (1977). *An introduction to discourse analysis*. London: Longman.

Courchene, R., & de Bagheera, J. (1985). A theoretical framework for development of performance tests. In P. Hauptman, R. LeBlanc, & M. Wesche (Eds.), *Second language performance testing* (pp. 45–58). Ottawa: University of Ottawa Press.

Damico, J. (1985). Clinical discourse analysis: A functional approach to language assessment. In C. Simon (Ed.), *Communication skills and classroom success* (pp. 165–203). San Diego: College Hill Press.

Danielewicz, J. (1984). The interaction between text and context: A study of how adults and children use spoken and written language in four contexts. In A. Pellegrini & T. Yawkey (Eds.), *The development of oral and written language in social contexts* (pp. 243–260). Norwood, NJ: Ablex.

Davies, C. E. (1988). *Illuminating crosscultural interaction: Feedback on pragmatic and discourse competence in a peer conversation group program*. Paper presented at the Southeastern Regional TESOL Conference, Orlando, FL.

Davies, C. E. (1991a). *Learning the discourse of friendship*. Paper presented at the National Association of Foreign Student Affairs Regional Conference, Biloxi, MS.

Davies, C. E. (1991b). *Pragmatic feedback in ITA training*. Paper presented at the Preconference Symposium on ITA Training, 25th Annual TESOL Convention, New York, NY.

Davies, C. E., & Tyler, A. (1989). *Positive results from negative evidence*. Paper presented at the 23rd Annual TESOL Convention, San Antonio, TX.

Davies, C. E., Tyler, A., & Koran, J. J. (1989). Face-to-face with English speakers: An advanced training class for international teaching assistants. *English for Specific Purposes, 8*, 139–153.

Davis, B. (1984). *A study of the effectiveness of training for foreign teaching assistants*. Unpublished doctoral dissertation, The Ohio University, Columbus.

Davis, M. (1973). How to sidestep the good questions. *Learning, 1*, 79–81.

Day, R. R. (Ed.) (1986). *Talking to learn: Conversation in second language acquisition*. Rowley, MA: Newbury House.

Di Pietro, R. (1987). *Strategic interactions*. Cambridge: Cambridge University Press.

van Dijk, T., & Kintsch, W. (1983). *Strategies of discourse comprehension*. New York: Academic Press.

Dillon, J. T. (1986a). Student questions and individual learning. *Educational Theory, 36,* 333–341.

Dillon, J. T. (1986b). Questioning. In O. Hargie (Ed.), *A handbook of communication skills* (pp. 95–127). New York: New York University Press.

Doughty, C., & Pica, T. (1986). Information gap tasks: Do they facilitate second language acquisition? *TESOL Quarterly, 20,* 305–325.

Douglas, D. (1992). *Testing methods in context-based second language research*. Paper presented at the American Association of Applied Linguistics Conference, Seattle, WA.

Douglas, D., & Myers, C. (1989). TAs on TV: Demonstrating communication strategies for international teaching assistants. *English for Specific Purposes, 8,* 169–179.

Douglas, D., & Myers, C. (1990). *Teaching assistant communication strategies* [Videotape and instructor's manual]. Ames, IA: Iowa State University Media Production Unit.

Douglas, D., & Selinker, L. (1986). *The interlanguage of a teaching assistant: Two discourse domains*. Paper presented at the 20th Annual TESOL Convention, Anaheim, CA.

Douglas, D., & Selinker, L. (1991). *SPEAK and CHEMSPEAK: Measuring the English speaking ability of international teaching assistants in chemistry*. Paper presented at the Language Testing Research Colloquium, Princeton, NJ.

Douglas, D., & Selinker, L. (1993). Performance on a general versus a field-specific test of speaking proficiency by international teaching assistants. In D. Douglas & C. Chapelle (Eds.), *A new decade of language testing research* (pp. 235–256). Alexandria, VA: TESOL.

Douglas, D., & Selinker, L. (in press). Analyzing oral proficiency test performance in general and specific purpose contexts. *System*.

Eisenstein, M., & Starbuck, R. (1989). The effect of emotional investment in L2 production. In S. Gass, C. Madden, D. Preston, & L. Selinker (Eds.), *Variation in second language acquisition: Psycholinguistic issues* (pp. 125–140). Clevedon, Avon: Multilingual Matters.

Ellis, R. (1986). *Understanding second language acquisition*. London: Oxford University Press.

Erickson, F., & Schultz, J. (1982). *The counselor as gatekeeper: Social interaction in interviews*. New York: Academic Press.

Erickson, R. (1982). Classroom discourse as improvisation: Relationships between academic task structure and social participation structure in lessons. In L. C. Wilkinson (Ed.), *Communicating in the classroom* (pp. 153–181). New York: Academic Press.

Faerch, C., Haastrup, K., & Phillipson, R. (1984). *Learner language and language learning*. Clevedon, Avon: Multilingual Matters.

Faerch, C., & Kasper, G. (1983). Plans and strategies in foreign language communication. In C. Faerch & G. Kasper (Eds.), *Strategies in interlanguage communication*. London: Longman.

Fisher, M. (1985). Rethinking the foreign TA problem. In J. Andrews (Ed.), *Strengthening the teaching assistant faculty* (New Directions for Teaching and Learning No. 22) (pp. 63–73). San Francisco: Jossey-Bass.

Gallego, J.-C., Goodwin, J., & Turner, J. (1991). ITA oral assessment: The examinee's perspective. In Nyquist, Abbott, Wulff, & Sprague (1991), pp. 404–412.

Gass, S., & Varonis, E. (1984). The effect of familiarity on comprehensibility of non-native speech. *Language Learning, 34*, 65–90.

Gass, S., & Varonis, E. (1985). Variation in native speaker speech modification to non-native speakers. *Studies in Second Language Acquisition, 7*, 37–58.

Gass, S. M., & Varonis, E. M. (1989). Incorporated repairs in nonnative discourse. In M. Eisenstein (Ed.), *The dynamic interlanguage* (pp. 71–86). New York: Plenum Press.

Gatbonton-Siegalowitz, E. (1978). Patterned phonetic variability in second-language speech: A gradual diffusion model. *Canadian Modern Language Review, 34*, 335–347.

Gillespie, J. (1988). *Foreign and U.S. teaching assistants: An analysis of verbal and nonverbal classroom interaction.* Unpublished doctoral dissertation, University of Illinois at Urbana-Champaign. (University Microfilms No. 88-23, 135)

Gillette, S. (1982). Lecture discourse of a foreign TA: A preliminary needs analysis. In K. Winkler (Ed.), *ESL working papers* (pp. 18–39). Minneapolis: University of Minnesota.

Goffman, E. (1974). *Frame analysis.* New York: Harper & Row.

Gold, E. M. (1967). Language identification in the limit. *Information and Control, 10*, 447–474.

Goody, E. N. (1978). Towards a theory of questions. In E. N. Goody (Ed.), *Questions and politeness* (pp. 17–43). Cambridge: Cambridge University Press.

Grabe, W. (1990). Foreword. *Annual Review of Applied Linguistics, 11*, vii–xi.

Gray, P., & Buerkel-Rothfuss, N. (1991). Teaching assistant training: The view from the trenches. In Nyquist, Abbott, Wulff, & Sprague (1991), pp. 40–51.

Green, G. (1989). *Pragmatics and natural language understanding.* New York: Lawrence Erlbaum Associates.

Grice, H. P. (1975). Logic and conversation. In P. Cole & J. Morgan (Eds.), *Syntax and semantics 3: Speech acts* (pp. 41–58). New York: Academic Press.

Guiora, A., Hallahmi, B., Brannon, R., Dull, C., & Scovel, T. (1972). The effects of experimentally induced changes in ego status on pronunciation ability in a second language: An exploratory study. *Comprehensive Psychiatry, 13*, 421–428.

Gumperz, J. J. (1982a). *Discourse strategies.* Cambridge: Cambridge University Press.

Gumperz, J. J. (Ed.). (1982b). *Language and social identity.* Cambridge: Cambridge University Press.

Gumperz, J. J., Jupp, T. C., & Roberts, C. (1979). *Crosstalk: A study of cross-cultural communication.* Southall, England: The National Centre for Industrial Training in association with the BBC.

Gumperz, J. J., & Roberts, C. (1980). *Developing awareness skills for inter-ethnic communication* (Occasional Paper No. 12). Singapore: SEAMEO Regional Language Centre.

Gumperz, J. J., & Tannen, D. (1979). Individual and social differences in language use. In W. Wang & C. Fillmore (Eds.), *Individual differences in language ability and language behavior* (pp. 305–325). New York: Academic Press.

Hatch, E. (1978). Discourse analysis and second language acquisition. In E. Hatch (Ed.), *Second language acquisition: A book of readings* (pp. 402–435). Rowley, MA: Newbury House.

Hendel, D., Dunham, T., Smith, J., Solberg, J., Tzenis, C., Carrier, C., & Smith, K. (1993). Implications of student evaluations of teaching for ITA development. In Lewis (1993).

Hinds, M. (1973). *Skits in English as a second language.* New York: Regents.

Hinofotis, F. B., & Bailey, K. (1981). American undergraduates' reactions to the communication skills of foreign teaching assistants. In J. Fisher, M. Clarke, & J. Schacter (Eds.), *On TESOL '80, Building bridges: Research and practice in teaching English as a second language* (pp. 120–136). Washington, DC: TESOL.

Hinofotis, F. B., Bailey, K., & Stern, S. (1981). Assessing the oral proficiency of prospective teaching assistants: Instrument development. In A. S. Palmer, P. J. M. Groot, & G. A. Trosper (Eds.), *The construct validation of tests of communicative competence* (pp. 106–126). Washington, DC: TESOL.

Hoekje, B., & Linnell, K. (1991). *Language evaluation and performance testing for international teaching assistants.* Paper presented at the Third National Conference on the Employment and Training of Graduate Teaching Assistants, Austin, TX.

Hoekje, B., & Tanner, M. (1987). *Establishing authority in the classroom.* Paper presented at the 21st Annual TESOL Convention, Miami, FL.

Hoekje, B., & Williams, J. (1992). Communicative competence and the dilemma of international teaching assistant education. *TESOL Quarterly, 26,* 242–269.

Holland, D. C., & Quinn, N. (1987). *Cultural models in language and thought.* Cambridge: Cambridge University Press.

Hyman, R. (1982). *Questioning in the college classroom* (IDEA Paper 8). Manhattan, KS: Center for Faculty Evaluation and Development.

Hymes, D. (1972a). *Foundations in sociolinguistics.* Philadelphia: University of Pennsylvania Press.

Hymes, D. (1972b). On communicative competence. In J. B. Pride & J. Holmes (Eds.), *Sociolinguistics* (pp. 269–293). Harmondsworth, UK: Penguin.

Jacobson, W. (1986). An assessment of the communicative needs of non-native speakers of English in an undergraduate physics lab. *English for Specific Purposes, 5,* 173–187.

Johncock, P. (1991). FTA tests and university FTA testing policies at U.S. universities. *College and University* (Spring), 130–137.

Johns, A., & Dudley-Evans, T. (1991). English for specific purposes: International in scope, specific in purpose. *TESOL Quarterly, 25,* 297–314.

Jones, E. E., & Nisbett, E. N. (1972). The actor and observer: Divergent perceptions of the causes of behavior. In E. E. Jones et al. (Eds.), *Attribution: Perceiving the causes of behavior* (pp. 79–94). Morristown, NJ: General Learning Press.

Jupp, T., Roberts, C., & Cook-Gumperz, J. (1982). Language and social disadvantage: The hidden process. In Gumperz (1982), pp. 232–256.

Kaplan, R. B. (1989). The life and times of ITA programs. *English for Specific Purposes, 8,* 109–125.

Katchen, J. (1990). The other side of classroom discourse: What happens when the students are native speakers and the teacher uses L2. In A. Labarca & L. Bailey (Eds.), *Issues in L2: theory as practice/practice as theory* (pp. 217–232). Norwood, NJ: Ablex.

Kearsley, G. P. (1976). Questions and question-asking in verbal discourse: A cross-disciplinary review. *Journal of Psycholinguistic Research, 5,* 355–375.

Klein, W. (1986). *Second language acquisition.* Cambridge: Cambridge University Press.

Krashen, S. (1981). *Second language acquisition and second language learning.* New York: Pergamon.

Kress, G. (1990). Critical discourse analysis. *Annual Review of Applied Linguistics, 11,* 84–100.

Kulik, J., Kulik, C.-L., Cole, M., & Briggs, S. (1985). *Student evaluations of foreign teaching assistants* (CRLT Report). Ann Arbor: The University of Michigan.

Kurfiss, J. (1988). *Critical thinking* (Ashe-ERIC Higher Education Report No. 2). Washington, DC: The George Washington University.

Landa, M. (1988). Training international students as teaching assistants. In J. Mestenhauser, G. Marty, & I. Steglitz (Eds.), *Culture, learning and the disciplines: Theory and practice in cross-cultural orientation* (pp. 50–57). Washington, DC: NAFSA.

Landa, M., & Perry, W. (1984). An evaluation of a training course for foreign teaching assistants. In Bailey, Pialorsi, & Zukowski/Faust (1984), pp. 89–100.

Lane, L. (1989). *ITA pronunciation strategies.* Paper presented at the Preconference Symposium on ITA Training, 23rd Annual TESOL Convention, San Antonio, TX.

Langham, C. (1989). *Discourse strategies and classroom learning: American and foreign teaching assistants.* Unpublished doctoral dissertation, University of California, San Diego. (University Microfilms No. 90-03, 775)

Lewis, K. G. (Ed.). (1993). *The TA experience: Preparing for multiple roles (Selected readings from a national conference).* Stillwater, OK: New Forums Press.

Long, M. H. (1981). Input, interaction and second language acquisition. In H. Winitz (Ed.), *Native language and foreign language acquisition* (pp. 259–278). New York: Annals of the New York Academy of Sciences 379.

Long, M. H. (1983). Inside the "black box": Methodological issues in classroom research on language learning. In H. W. Seliger & M. H. Long (Eds.),

Classroom oriented research in second language acquisition (pp. 3–35). Rowley, MA: Newbury House.

Long, M. H., & Porter, P. A. (1985). Group work, interlanguage talk and second language acquisition. *TESOL Quarterly, 19, 207–228.*

Long, M. H., & Sato, C. J. (1983). Classroom foreigner talk discourse: Forms and functions of teachers' questions. In H. W. Seliger & M. H. Long (Eds.), *Classroom oriented research in second language acquisition* (pp. 268–286). New York: Newbury House.

Mackay, R., & Bosquet, M. (1982). LSP curriculum development—from policy to practice. In R. Mackay & J. D. Palmer (Eds.), *Languages for specific purposes: Program design and evaluation.* Rowley, MA: Newbury House.

Madden, C., & Axelson, E. (1990). *Language training objectives for international teaching assistants.* Paper presented at the 24th Annual TESOL Convention, San Francisco, CA.

Maley, A., & Duff, A. (1978). The use of dramatic techniques in foreign language learning. *Recherches et Echanges, 3.*

McGregor, G. (Ed.). (1986). *Language for hearers.* New York: Pergamon.

McKeachie, W. J. (1978). *Teaching tips.* Lexington, MA: D. C. Heath.

McKenna, E. (1987). Preparing foreign students to enter discourse communities in the United States. *English for Specific Purposes, 6, 187–202.*

Mehan, H. (1979a). *Learning lessons.* Cambridge, MA: Harvard University Press.

Mehan, H. (1979b). "What time is it, Denise?": Asking known information questions in classroom discourse. *Theory into Practice, 18, 285–294.*

Meyer, B., Brandt, D., & Bluth, G. (1980). Use of top-level structure in text: Key for reading comprehension in ninth-grade students. *Reading Research Quarterly, 16, 72–103.*

A Michigan Education. (1990). Ann Arbor: University of Michigan.

Moerk, E. L. (1991). Positive evidence for negative evidence. *First Language, 11,* 219–251.

Moffett, J. (1967). *Drama: What is happening.* Champaign, IL: National Council of Teachers of English.

Montgomery, M. (1976). *The structure of lectures.* Unpublished master's thesis, University of Birmingham.

Morley, J. (1992). *EAP oral communication curriculum: Discourse structure, communicability, and intelligibility considerations.* Paper presented at the National Association of Foreign Student Advisors–Association of International Educators Conference, Chicago, IL.

Munby, J. (1978). *Communicative syllabus design.* Cambridge: Cambridge University Press.

Murray, H. (1985). Classroom teaching behaviors related to teaching effectiveness. In J. Donald & M. Sullivan (Eds.), *Using research to improve teaching* (pp. 21–34). San Francisco: Jossey-Bass.

Myers, C. (1991). *ITA discourse and training for lab assistants.* Paper presented at the Preconference Symposium on ITA Training, 25th Annual TESOL Convention, New York, NY.

Myers, C., Axelson, E., & Madden, C. (1991). *Discourse for the ITA: Multiple roles.* Paper presented at the Third National Conference on the Employment and Training of Graduate Teaching Assistants, Austin, TX.

Myers, C., & Douglas, D. (1991). *The ITA as lab assistant: Strategies for success.* Paper presented at the National Association of Foreign Student Advisors Convention, Boston, MA.

Myers, C., & Plakans, B. (1990). *The discourse community of the university scientific laboratory.* Paper presented at the 24th Annual TESOL Convention, San Francisco, CA.

Myers, C., & Plakans, B. (1991). Under controlled conditions: The ITA as laboratory assistant. In Nyquist, Abbott, Wulff, & Sprague (1991), pp. 368–374.

Nelson, G. (1990). *International teaching assistants: A review of research.* Paper presented at the 24th Annual TESOL Convention, San Francisco, CA.

Nyquist, J. D., Abbott, R. D., Wulff, D. H., & Sprague, J. (Eds.). (1991). *Preparing the professoriate of tomorrow to teach: Selected readings on TA training.* Dubuque, IA: Kendall/Hunt.

Oller, J. W., Jr. (1983). Some working ideas for language teaching. In Oller & Richard-Amato (1983), pp. 3–19.

Oller, J. W., Jr., & Richard-Amato, P. A. (1983). *Ideas that work: A smorgasbord of ideas for language teachers.* Rowley, MA: Newbury House.

Orth, J. (1982). *University undergraduate evaluational reactions to the speech of foreign teaching assistants.* Unpublished doctoral dissertation, University of Texas, Austin.

Peterson, F. (1989). *Tips for physics lab instructors.* Unpublished manuscript, Iowa State University, Physics Department.

Pialorsi, F. (1984) Toward an anthropology of the classroom: An essay on foreign teaching assistants and U.S. students. In Bailey, Pialorsi, & Zukowski/Faust (1984), pp. 16–21.

Pica, T. (1987). Second language acquisition, social interaction and the classroom. *Applied Linguistics, 8,* 3–21.

Pica, T. (1989). Classroom interaction, negotiation and comprehension: Redefining relationships. *Papers in Applied Linguistics, 1,* 7–35.

Pica, T., Barnes, G., & Finger, A. (1990). *Teaching matters: Skills and strategies for international teaching assistants.* New York: Newbury House.

Pica, T., Young, R., & Doughty, C. (1987). The impact of interaction on comprehension. *TESOL Quarterly, 21,* 737–58.

Pinker, S. (1984). *Language learnability and language development.* Cambridge, MA: Harvard University Press.

Plakans, B. (1987). *Comprehension problems of teaching assistants who are nonnative speakers of English: How U.S. students ask them questions and why they may have difficulty answering.* Unpublished master's thesis, Iowa State University, Ames.

Plakans, B., & Abraham, R. (1990). The testing and evaluation of international teaching assistants. In D. Douglas (Ed.), *English language testing in U.S. colleges and universities* (pp. 68–81). Washington, DC: NAFSA.

Reddy, M. (1979). The conduit metaphor—A case of frame conflict in our language about language. In A. Ortony (Ed.), *Metaphor and thought* (pp. 284–324). Cambridge: Cambridge University Press.

Rice, D. (1984). A one-semester program for orienting the new foreign teaching assistant. In Bailey, Pialorsi, & Zukowski/Faust (1984), pp. 69–75.

Riggenbach, H. (1990). Discourse analysis and spoken language instruction. *Annual Review of Applied Linguistics, 2*, 152–163.

Robinson, A. (1993). Information units and cohesive devices in teaching assistant responses to student questions. *Journal of Graduate Teaching Assistant Development, 1*, 5–15.

Rodriguez, R., & White, R. (1983). From role play to the real world. In Oller & Richard-Amato (1983), pp. 246–258.

Rounds, P. L. (1986). Talking the mathematics through: Disciplinary transaction and socio-educational interaction (Doctoral dissertation, University of Michigan, 1985). *Dissertation Abstracts International, 46*, 3338A.

Rounds, P. L. (1987a). Characterizing successful classroom discourse for NNS teaching assistant training. *TESOL Quarterly, 21*, 643–671.

Rounds, P. L. (1987b). Multifunctional pronoun use in an educational setting. *English for Specific Purposes, 6*, 13–29.

Rounds, P. L. (1990). *Student questions: What do we know about them?* Paper presented at the Preconference Symposium on ITA Training, 24th Annual TESOL Convention, San Francisco, CA.

Rowe, M. B. (1973). *Teaching science as continuous theory.* New York: McGraw-Hill.

Rowe, M. B. (1974). Wait-time and rewards as instructional variables. Their influence on language, logic and fate control: Part 1: Wait time. *Journal of Research in Science Teaching, 9*, 81–84.

Rumelhart, D. (1980). Schemata: The building blocks of cognition. In R. J. Spiro, B. C. Bruce, & W. E. Brewer (Eds.), *Theoretical issues in reading comprehension* (pp. 33–58). Hillsdale, NJ: Lawrence Erlbaum Associates.

Rutherford, W. (1987). *Second language grammar: Learning and teaching.* New York: Longman.

Rutherford, W. (1988). Aspects of pedagogical grammar. In W. Rutherford & M. Sharwood Smith (Eds.), *Grammar and second language teaching* (pp. 171–185). New York: Newbury House.

Ryan, E. B., & Giles, H. (1982). *Attitudes toward language variation: Social and applied contexts.* London: Edward Arnold.

vom Saal, D. R. (1987). The undergraduate experience and international teaching assistants. In Chism & Warner (1987), pp. 267–274.

Sacks, H., Schegloff, E., & Jefferson, G. (1974). A simplest systematics for the organization of turn-taking in conversation. *Language, 50*, 696–735.

Sarwark, S. (1991). *Is it working? Evaluations of ITA screening and training.* Paper presented at the Preconference Symposium on ITA Training, 25th Annual TESOL Convention, New York, NY.

Savignon, S. (1983). *Communicative competence: Theory and classroom practice.* Reading, MA: Addison-Wesley.

Scarcella, R. (1983). Sociodrama for social interaction. In Oller & Richard-Amato (1983), pp. 239–245.

Schachter, J. (1986). Three approaches to the study of input. *Language Learning*, *36*, 211–225.

Schegloff, E. (1981). Discourse as an interactional achievement: Some uses of "uh-huh" and other things that come between sentences. In D. Tannen (Ed.), *Analyzing discourse: Text and talk* (Georgetown University Round Table on Languages and Linguistics). Washington, DC: Georgetown University Press.

Schieffelin, B. B., & Ochs, E. (1986). *Language socialization across cultures.* Cambridge: Cambridge University Press.

Schiffrin, D. (1987). *Discourse markers.* Cambridge: Cambridge University Press.

Schmidt, R. W. (1990). The role of consciousness in second language learning. *Applied Linguistics, 11*, 129–158.

Schneider, K., & Stevens, S. (1987). Curriculum considerations for a campus-wide international teaching associate training program. In Chism & Warner (1987), pp. 284–289.

Schneider, K., & Stevens, S. (1991). American undergraduate students as trainers in an international teaching assistant training program. In J. Nyquist, R. Abbott, D. Wulff, & J. Sprague (Eds.), *Preparing the professoriate of tomorrow to teach: Selected readings on TA training* (pp. 361–367). Dubuque, IA: Kendall/Hunt.

Schumann, J. (1975). Transcripts of "Jorge." In C. Cazden et al. (Eds.), *Second language acquisition sequences in children, adolescents and adults* (Final Report, Program No. 730744). Washington, DC: U.S. Department of Health, Education and Welfare.

Schwartz, B. D. (1987). *Ruling out negative evidence in second language acquisition.* Unpublished manuscript, University of Southern California, Department of Linguistics.

Scollon, R., & Scollon, S. (1981). *Narrative, literacy, and face in interethnic communication.* Norwood, NJ: Ablex.

Selinker, L., & Douglas, D. (1985). Wrestling with "context" in interlanguage theory. *Applied Linguistics, 6*, 190–204.

Selinker, L., & Douglas, D. (1987). LSP and interlanguage: Some empirical studies. In L. Selinker & D. Douglas (Eds.), *ESP Journal, 6* [Special issue], 75–86.

Selinker, L., & Douglas, D. (1989a). Markedness in discourse domains: Native and non-native teaching assistants. *Papers in Applied Linguistics, 1*, 69–81.

Selinker, L., & Douglas, D. (1989b). Research methodology in contextually-based second language research. *Second Language Research, 5*, 93–126.

Selinker, L., & Douglas, D. (1991). *Research methodology in contextually-based second language research II.* Paper presented at a conference on theory construction and methodology in second language research, Michigan State University, East Lansing.

Shaftel, F., & Shaftel, G. (1967). *Role-playing for social values.* Englewood Cliffs, NJ: Prentice-Hall.

Shank, R. C., & Abelson, R. P. (1977). *Scripts, plans, goals and understanding.* Hillsdale, NJ: Lawrence Erlbaum Associates.

Shaw, P. A. (1983). *The language of engineering professors: A discourse and registral analysis of a speech event.* Unpublished doctoral dissertation, University of Southern California, Los Angeles.

Shaw, P. A. (1985). The language of engineering professors: A discourse and registral analysis of a speech event (Doctoral dissertation, University of Southern California, 1983). *Dissertation Abstracts International, 45,* 2085.

Shaw, P. A., & Bailey, K. (1990). Cultural differences in academic settings. In R. C. Scarcella, E. S. Andersen, & S. D. Krashen (Eds.), *Developing communicative competence in a second language* (pp. 317–328). New York: Newbury House.

Shaw, P. A., & Garate, E. M. (1984). Linguistic competence, communicative needs, and university pedagogy: Toward a framework for TA training. In Bailey, Pialorsi, & Zukowski/Faust (1984), pp. 22–40.

Simon, C., & Holway, C. (1985). Presentation of communication evaluation information. In C. Simon (Ed.), Communication skills and classroom success. San Diego: College Hill Press.

Simon, T. (1991). *Evaluating the oral proficiency of TAs.* Paper presented at the Third National Conference on the Employment and Training of Graduate Teaching Assistants, Austin, TX.

Sinclair, J. (1987). Classroom discourse: Progress and prospects. *RELC Journal, 18,* 1–14.

Sinclair, J., & Coulthard, R. M. (1975). *Towards an analysis of discourse: The English used by teachers and pupils.* London: Oxford University Press.

Smith, J. (1989a). *Curriculum development for ITA programs: Planning for the diverse training needs of university departments.* Paper presented at the Second National Conference on the Training and Employment of Graduate Teaching Assistants, Seattle, WA.

Smith, J. (1989b). Topic and variation in ITA oral proficiency: SPEAK and field-specific tests. *English for Specific Purposes, 8,* 155–167.

Smith, J. (1992). *Topic and variation in the oral proficiency of international teaching assistants.* Unpublished doctoral dissertation, University of Minnesota, Minneapolis.

Smith, J., Meyers, C., & Burkhalter, A. (1992). *Communicate: Strategies for international teaching assistants.* Englewood Cliffs, NJ: Prentice-Hall/Regents.

Smith, R. M. (1987). Training international TAs at Texas Tech: An overview. In Chism & Warner (1987), pp. 318–320.

Smith, R. M., Byrd, P., Constantinides, J., & Barrett, R. P. (1991). Instructional development programs for international TAs: A systems analysis approach. *POD Network, 10,* 151–168.

Smith, R. M., Byrd, P., Nelson, G., Barrett, R. P., & Constantinides, J. (Eds.). (1993). *Crossing pedagogical oceans: International teachings assistants in U.S. undergraduate education* (ASHE-ERIC Higher Education Report).

Sperber, D., & Wilson, D. (1986). *Relevance: Communication and cognition.* Cambridge, MA: Harvard University Press.

Stenson, N., Smith, J., & Perry, W. (1983). Facilitating teacher growth: An approach to training and evaluation. *MinneTESOL Journal, 3,* 42–55.

Stern, S. (1983). Why drama works: A psycholinguistic perspective. In Oller & Richard-Amato (1983), pp. 207–225.

Stevens, S. (1988). *Improving the international teaching assistant experience: An evaluative study of a training program.* Unpublished doctoral dissertation, University of Delaware, Newark.

Stevens, S. (1989). A "dramatic" approach to improving the intelligibility of ITAs. *English for Specific Purposes, 8,* 181–194.

Strodt-Lopez, B. (1987). Personal anecdotes in university classes. *Anthropological Linguistics, 29,* 194–258.

Strodt-Lopez, B. (1991). Tying it all in: Asides in university lectures. *Applied Linguistics, 12,* 117–140.

Stubbs, M. (1983). *Discourse analysis: The sociolinguistic analysis of natural language.* Chicago: University of Chicago Press.

Swales, J. (1990). *Genre analysis: English in academic and research settings.* Cambridge: Cambridge University Press.

Tannen, D. (1979). What's in a frame? Surface evidence for underlying expectations. In R. O. Freedle (Ed.), *New directions in discourse processing* (pp. 137–181). Norwood, NJ: Ablex.

Tannen, D. (1982). Oral and literate strategies in speech and written narrative. *Language, 58,* 1–21.

Tannen, D. (1985). Cross-cultural communication. In T. van Dijk (Ed.), *Handbook of discourse analysis 4. Discourse analysis in society* (pp. 203–215). London: Academic Press.

Tanner, M. (1991a). Incorporating research on question-asking into ITA training. In Nyquist, Abbott, Wulff, & Sprague (1991), pp. 375–381.

Tanner, M. (1991b). *NNSTA-student interaction: An analysis of TAs' questions and student responses in a laboratory setting.* Unpublished doctoral dissertation, University of Pennsylvania, Philadelphia.

Tarone, E. (1983). On the variability of interlanguage systems. *Applied Linguistics, 4,* 142–163.

Tarone, E. (1985). Variability in interlanguage use: A study of style-shifting in morphology and syntax. *Language Learning, 35,* 373–403.

Tarone, E. (1988). *Variation in interlanguage.* London: Edward Arnold.

Turitz, N. (1984). A survey of teaching programs for foreign teaching assistants in American universities. In Bailey, Pialorsi, & Zukowski/Faust (1984), pp. 43–50.

Tyler, A. (1988). *Discourse structure and coherence in international TAs' spoken discourse.* Paper presented at the 22nd Annual TESOL Convention, Chicago, IL.

Tyler, A. (1990). *Examining cross-linguistic miscommunication.* Paper presented at the Preconference Symposium on ITA Training, 24th Annual TESOL Convention, San Francisco, CA.

Tyler, A. (1991). *Discourse structure and comprehensibility: A comparative analysis.* Paper presented at the 25th Annual TESOL Convention, New York, NY.

Tyler, A. (1992). Discourse structure and the perception of coherence in international teaching assistants' spoken discourse. *TESOL Quarterly, 26,* 713-729.

Tyler, A., & Davies, C. E. (1990a). Cross-linguistic communication missteps. *Text, 10,* 385–411.

Tyler, A., & Davies, C. E. (1990b). *Effects of pragmatic feedback on second language acquisition.* Paper presented at the 24th Annual TESOL Convention, San Francisco, CA.

Tyler, A., Jefferies, A., & Davies, C. E. (1988). The effect of discourse structuring devices on listener perceptions of coherence in non-native university teachers' spoken discourse. *World Englishes, 7,* 101–110.

Varonis, E., & Gass, S. (1985). Non-native/non-native conversations: A model for negotiation of meaning. *Applied Linguistics, 6,* 71–90.

Vygotsky, J. (1978). *Mind and society: The development of higher psychological processes.* Cambridge: Cambridge University Press.

Vygotsky, J. (1987). *Thought and language.* Cambridge, MA: MIT Press.

Watson-Gegeo, K. A. (1988). Ethnography in ESL: Defining the essentials. *TESOL Quarterly, 22,* 575–592.

Wennerstrom, A. (1991a). *ITA training: Analysis of natural discourse.* Paper presented at the Preconference Symposium on ITA Training, 25th Annual TESOL Convention, New York, NY.

Wennerstrom, A. (1991b). *Techniques for teachers: A Guide for nonnative speakers of English* [Workbook and videotape]. Ann Arbor: The University of Michigan Press.

Wesche, M. (1985). Introduction. In P. Hauptman, R. LeBlanc, & M. Wesche (Eds.), *Second language performance testing.* Ottawa: University of Ottawa Press.

Wesche, M. (1987). Second language performance testing: The Ontario test of ESL as an example. *Language Testing, 4,* 28–47.

White, L. (1989). *Universal grammar and second language acquisition.* Amsterdam: John Benjamins.

Widdowson, H. (1978). *Teaching language as communication.* Oxford: Oxford University Press.

Widdowson, H. (1983). *Learning purpose and language use.* Oxford: Oxford University Press.

Wilkins, D. A. (1977). *Notional syllabi.* Oxford: Oxford University Press.

Williams, J. (1989). *The elaboration of discourse marking and intelligibility.* Paper presented at Annual American Association of Applied Linguistics Conference, Washington, DC.

Williams, J., Barnes, G., & Finger, A. (1987). *FTAs: Report on a needs analysis.* Paper presented at the 21st Annual TESOL Convention, Miami, FL.

Winter, E. O. (1977). A clause-relational approach to English texts: A study of some predictive lexical items in written discourse. *Instructional Science, 6*(1), 1–92.

Woken, M., & Swales, J. (1989). Expertise and authority in native–non-native conversations: The need for a variable account. In S. Gass, C. Madden, D. Preston, & L. Selinker (Eds.), *Variation in second language acquisition. Vol. 1: Discourse and pragmatics* (pp. 211–227). Philadelphia: Multilingual Matters.

Young, R. (1989a). *Curriculum renewal in training programs for international teaching assistants.* Paper presented at the National Association of Foreign Student Advisors conference, Minneapolis, MN.

Young, R. (Ed.) (1989b). *English for Specific Purposes, 8*(2) [Special issue].

Young, R. (1989c). Introduction: The training of international teaching assistants. *English for Specific Purposes, 8,* 101–107.

Young, R. (1990). Curriculum renewal in training programs for international teaching assistants. *Journal of Intensive English Studies, 4,* 59–77.

Yule, G. (1990). Interactive conflict resolution in English. *World Englishes, 9,* 53–62.

Yule, G., & Gregory, W. (1989). The advantages of interaction. *Papers in Applied Linguistics, 1,* 37–44.

Yule, G., & Macdonald, D. (1990). Resolving referential conflicts in L2 interaction: The effect of proficiency and interactive role. *Language Learning, 40,* 539–556.

Zuengler, J. (1989a). Identity and IL development and use. *Applied Linguistics, 10,* 80–96.

Zuengler, J. (1989b). Performance variation in NS-NNS interactions: Ethnolinguistic difference or discourse domain? In S. Gass, C. Madden, D. Preston, & L. Selinker (Eds.), *Variation in second language acquisition. Vol. 1: Discourse and pragmatics* (pp. 228–244). Philadelphia: Multilingual Matters.

Also available from TESOL

All Things to All People:
A Primer for K–12 ESL Teachers in Small Programs
Donald C. Flemming, Lucie C. Germer, and Christiane Kelley

A World of Books:
An Annotated Reading List for ESL/EFL Students
Dorothy S. Brown

Coherence in Writing:
Resesearch and Pedagogical Perspectives
Ulla Connor and Ann Johns, Editors

Common Threads of Practice:
Teaching English to Children Around the World
Katharine Davies Samway and Denise McKeon, Editors

Dialogue Journal Writing with Nonnative English Speakers:
A Handbook for Teachers
Joy Kreeft Peyton and Leslee Reed

Dialogue Journal Writing with Nonnative English Speakers:
An Instructional Packet for Teachers and Workshop Leaders
Joy Kreeft Peyton and Jana Staton

Directory of Professional Preparation Programs
in TESOL in the United States, 1992–1994

Diversity as Resource:
Redefining Cultural Literacy
Denise E. Murray, Editor

A New Decade of Language Testing Research:
Selected Papers From
the 1990 Language Testing Research Colloquium
Dan Douglas and Carol Chapelle, Editors

New Ways in Teacher Education
Donald Freeman with Steve Cornwell, Editors

New Ways in Teaching Reading
Richard R. Day, Editor

For more information, contact
Teachers of English to Speakers of Other Languages, Inc.
1600 Cameron Street, Suite 300
Alexandria, Virginia 22314 USA
Tel 703-836-0774 • Fax 703-836-7864